Mental Health and Emerging Adulthood among Homeless Young People

Mental Health and Emerging Adulthood among Homeless Young People

Les B. Whitbeck

University of Nebraska, Lincoln

with The Midwest Longitudinal Study
of Homeless Adolescents Team

Psychology Press
Taylor & Francis Group

New York   Hove

Psychology Press
Taylor & Francis Group
270 Madison Avenue
New York, NY 10016

Psychology Press
Taylor & Francis Group
27 Church Road
Hove, East Sussex BN3 2FA

© 2009 by Taylor & Francis Group, LLC
Psychology Press is an imprint of Taylor & Francis Group, an Informa business

Printed in the United States of America on acid-free paper
10 9 8 7 6 5 4 3 2 1

International Standard Book Number-13: 978-1-84169-751-2 (Hardcover) 978-1-84169-752-9 (0)

Library of Congress Cataloging-in-Publication Data

Whitbeck, Leslie B.
    Mental health and emerging adulthood among homeless young people / Leslie B. Whitbeck.
      p. ; cm.
    Includes bibliographical references.
    ISBN 978-1-84169-751-2 (hardback : alk. paper) -- ISBN 978-1-84169-752-9 (pbk. : alk. paper)
    1. Adolescent psychiatry. 2. Homeless teenagers--Mental health. I. Title.
    [DNLM: 1. Adolescent Psychology. 2. Homeless Youth. 3. Adolescent Behavior--psychology. 4. Adolescent Health Services. 5. Cohort Studies. WS 462 W579m 2009]
    RJ503.W395 2009
    616.8900835--dc22

          2008042346

Visit the Taylor & Francis Web site at
http://www.taylorandfrancis.com

and the Psychology Press Web site at
http://www.psypress.com

Contents

Section 3: Unintentional and intentional injuries from adolescent to early adulthood

Chapter 8   Victimization and revictimization among homeless and runaway adolescents 121
   With Devan M. Crawford

Chapter 9   Self-mutilating behaviors from adolescence to young adulthood.. 145
   With Katherine A. Johnson

Section 4: Adult roles: social networks, intimate relationships, economic adjustment, and emerging adulthood

Preface

As far as we know this is the first study to follow homeless and runaway adolescents into early adulthood. It also is the first study to screen for psychiatric diagnoses at late adolescence and early adulthood. This makes it an important first step in addressing the numerous questions about what happens to these young people. For example, how does running away affect later life chances and mental health? Will the developmental effects be long-lasting? What are the important risk and protective factors that affect successful transition to adulthood?

Homeless youth at one time attracted a good deal of media attention, but they since have slipped off the national radar. We hope this book will remind the nation that these youth are still out there on the streets, that the risks they face are grave, and that they are leaving homes for reasons other than wanderlust and adventure. The most conservative estimates suggest that more than 1 million young people between the ages of 15 and 17 run away each year. If an outbreak of a disease affecting adolescents reached these levels, it would attract national attention. Yet, though running away represents harm prior to leaving home and life-threatening risk while the adolescents are on their own, there is little national outcry, and not enough is being done.

Very little is known regarding the prevalence and course or mental illness and substance use disorders in special populations such as this one. Accordingly, this book is directed toward policy makers, psychologists, sociologists, health professionals, social services workers, and students. It will augment undergraduate and graduate courses in homelessness, adolescent psychology, social deviance, human development in the social environment, and policy courses found in a variety of departments including psychology, sociology, social work, public health, political science, policy administration, and urban studies.

The book focuses on the highest-risk population of adolescents in the country. Part 1 sets the stage by defining and enumerating homeless adolescents and *homeless young adults*. It also reviews what we know about homeless young people and presents theoretical perspectives that guide the work of researchers such as Jeffrey Arnett (2000) on emerging adulthood and the work of Terrie Moffitt (1997) and others on the origins and persistence of maladaptive behaviors. Chapter 2 gives a detailed overview of the study, the sample, attrition rates across time, measurement, and procedures. The focus of Part 2 is the mental health of the adolescents. We review findings regarding each of the psychiatric diagnoses screened in the study including conduct disorder, major depressive episode, posttraumatic stress disorder, and the substance use disorders at two time points: late adolescence and early adulthood. In these chapters we address the emergence and persistence of the disorders across time.

Part 3 is the core of the book. It details the risk factors associated with homelessness including victimization, revictimization, and self-injury. We believe that these experiences will shape the psychology and worldviews of the adolescents into their adult years. In Part 4, we focus on preparation for and adjustment to emerging adulthood by discussing protective factors such as social network support, establishment of intimate relationships, education, and employment. This section also includes a discussion of adaptation and participation in the street economy. The final section of the book, Part 5, reconsiders the usefulness of psychiatric diagnosis in the context of street life and addresses the question of overdiagnosing the adolescents. We conclude with a chapter summarizing where the young people were in their transition to adulthood at the end of the study.

Each chapter begins with a thorough literature review that brings the reader up to date on the topic area as it applies to homeless and runaway youth, followed by the presentation of the study findings interspersed with excerpts of the subjects' experiences in their own words. This research is meant to be translated into policy. Each chapter concludes with separate sections discussing the theoretical and policy implications of the findings that provide real-world insights and applications of the research findings.

As this project progressed, it truly became a labor of love for the researchers and interviewers. As we learned the stories of these young people and what was happening to them, all of us came to care about them.

Acknowledgments

Our front line was a team of courageous and dedicated interviewers who worked nights and weekends in perilous neighborhoods for too little pay. Elizabeth Crowely, Christine Johnson, Drew Haught, Karen Roswurm, Shane Stewart, and Theresa Tumbleson are extraordinary people who were able to establish trust and enduring relationships with a difficult population. Because of the challenges of the job and low pay, we expected considerable interviewer turnover. All of these interviewers stayed with us to the end. They truly care about these kids.

Youth outreach agencies in Cedar Rapids, Des Moines, Iowa City, Kansas City, Lincoln, Omaha, and Wichita provided homes for our interviewers. Their experience, knowledge of their city's street cultures, and helpful advice throughout the data collection process made this research possible. These community resources are underappreciated and underfunded, yet they somehow manage to survive year to year to carry on this important work. Without them it is hard to imagine what these young people would do.

Although I have attempted to acknowledge the multiple contributions of the investigative team and graduate research assistants by chapter, this does not begin to account for the all the work Dr. Kurt Johnson, the project director, put into this study. Kurt handled the day-to-day management of the project, developed the tracking manual, supervised the interviewers, and managed a complicated 13-wave data set. Also, thanks to longtime friend, colleague, and coinvestigator Dr. Dan Hoyt, who consulted and contributed to every phase of the project.

It took a long time and many, many weekly analytic meetings to complete all the analyses that have gone into this book. Thanks to Devan Crawford, Katie Johnson, Trina Rose, Michael Black, Edan Jorgensen, and all of the graduate research assistants who attended and contributed to these meetings as this volume grew chapter by chapter. Thanks also to our director of research, Linda Hoyt, for her work on the questionnaire, quality control, and data management. Special thanks to Devan Crawford and Emily Trotter for all the hours spent proofing and editing the text.

This project was funded by the National Institute of Mental Health (MH 57110). We appreciate the institute's willingness to take a chance on a longitudinal study of a hard-to-access population such as this one. We were lucky to have Dr. Cheryl Boyce as our project manager, and we thank her for her helpfulness and support.

We are grateful for the qualitative data shared with us by Dr. Kimberly Tyler, whose University of Nebraska Seed Grant provided funds to support 40 in-depth interviews with a subsample of the study adolescents. We also gratefully acknowledge the helpful comments of Jeffrey Arnett, Luis Vargas, and Luc Goossens, who reviewed the manuscript.

But in the end, it all comes down to the young people who opened up their lives to our interviewers and who stayed in contact as best they could over the course of the study. They wanted their stories to make a difference, and so do we.

Author royalties for this book will be donated to outreach programs for homeless and runaway young people.

section 1

Emerging adulthood among runaway and homeless youth

chapter 1

"No one knows what happens to these kids"

Interrupted adolescence and emerging adulthood

"No one knows what happens to these kids": This comment from a street worker launched this research. Although there have been numerous studies of homeless and runaway adolescents in the past three decades, we know very little about the long-term developmental consequences of running away and periods of homelessness during adolescence. Runaways who run often (three or more episodes) and stay away for long periods of time assert their independence from adult caretakers years earlier and more abruptly than their conventional counterparts. This interrupts typical developmental trajectories in myriad ways. Early independence erodes important ties to supportive adults. It increases dependence on peer groups rather than adults for social support, interrupts education, creates financial and nutritional insecurity that may result in participation in the street economy, and almost always puts them in harm's way. Experiencing early independence creates poor candidates for traditional social services interventions such as foster care or family reunification that focus on children's subordinate role in families. Most homeless adolescents cannot or do not want to return to childhood, but they are not prepared for adulthood.

In this volume we trace the development of a cohort of runaway and homeless adolescents from ages 16 to 19 years through 19 to 22 years as they move from late adolescence into early adulthood. Diagnostic interviews were conducted at Wave 1 (ages 16–19 years) using the Diagnostic Interview Schedule for Children-Revised (DISC-R) for conduct disorder and the University of Michigan-Composite International Diagnostic Interview (UM-CIDI) for major depressive disorder, posttraumatic stress disorder, and substance abuse disorders. The adolescents were reinterviewed every 3 months for 3 years with a final diagnostic evaluation at Wave 13, when they were 19–22 years old. At the Wave 13 interview, they were screened for antisocial personality disorder. Throughout the 13 waves of the study, we focused on risk and protective factors that may differentiate between those who will end up living their adult lives on society's margins and those who will make a more successful transition to adulthood.

Definitions and prevalence rates

Runaway and homeless adolescents

Estimates of the number of runaway and homeless youths have varied widely over the past several decades partially because of the difficulty in defining *homelessness*. As Wright, Rubin, and Devine (1998, p. 19) point out, "Absent an agreed-upon definition of homelessness, no count can possibly be definitive." Defining homelessness among adolescents is particularly problematic. As we show, many runaways and homeless youths have homes they can return to and relatives or friends who may take them in. All who are minors have the option of temporary shelters, foster care, group homes, or other institutional living arrangements. Most chronic runaways and homeless adolescents live a "revolving door" existence, alternating between various housed living arrangements punctuated by time directly on the streets. The amount of time unsupervised and unsheltered may vary from episodes of a single night to several months.

Although once on the streets the distinction does not make much difference, recent definitions of homelessness for adolescents have distinguished between *runaways* and *throwaways*. According the National Incidence Studies of Missing, Abducted, Runaway, and Throwaway Children (NISMART), a *runaway episode* is defined by meeting one of the following three criteria (Hammer, Finkelhor, & Sedlak, 2002, p. 2):

1. A child leaves home without permission and stays away overnight.
2. A child 14 years old or younger who is away from home chooses not to come home when expected to and stays away overnight.
3. A child 15 years old or older who is away from home chooses not to come home and stays away 2 nights.

A *throwaway episode* is defined by meeting one of the following two criteria (Hammer et al., p. 2):

1. A child is asked or told to leave home by a parent or other household adult, no adequate alternative care is arranged for the child by a household adult, and the child is out of the household overnight.
2. A child who is away from home is prevented from returning home by a parent or other household adult, no adequate alternative care is

arranged for the child by a household adult, and the child is out of the household overnight.

Our study definitions of runaway, throwaway, and homeless youth essentially follow these criteria and those of the U.S. General Accounting Office (1989). The study definition for a *runaway adolescent* was that the young person was away from home at least overnight without parental consent or knowledge. A *throwaway adolescent* was one who had been told that he or she could not return home or who had been kicked out or locked out of their parents' or caretakers' home. A *chronic runaway* refers to one who has run away three or more times (Pennbridge, Yates, David, & MacKenzie, 1990). *Homeless youth* refers to those 18 years or older who cannot return home, who have chosen to never return home, and who have no permanent residence (U.S. General Accounting Office).

Recent estimates based on data from the three components of the Second National Incidence Studies of Missing, Abducted, Runaway, and Throwaway Children (NISMART-2): The National Household Survey of Adult Caretakers, the National Household Survey of Youth, and Juvenile Facilities Study annual reporting period of 1999 indicate that 1,682,900 youth had experienced a runaway/throwaway episode. Youths aged 15–17 years accounted for two thirds (1,149,400) of the runaway/throwaway episodes. Only 4% were under 11 years (Hammer et al., 2002, p. 6). Of the episodes, 19% were less than 24 hours, 58% were 24 hours to less than 1 week, and 22% were more than 1 week (Hammer et al., p. 7).

Homelessness among young adults

Economically marginal young adults are particularly vulnerable to homelessness. Supporting oneself with a minimum wage job and no health benefits is to live one paycheck away from homelessness. For many young adults, such as chronic runaways and those aging out of the foster care system, family support may not be an alternative. For others who grew up in poverty, parents or relatives may be financially unable to provide support in times of crisis. Among adolescent runaways the proportion that remains homeless or marginally housed as they move into young adulthood is largely unknown.

Estimates of the number of young adults who experience an episode of homelessness each year range from 750,000 to 2 million, and the numbers appear to be increasing. Individuals aged 17–24 years make up 13% of the adult homeless population in the United States and 26% of homeless families (Burt, Aron, Douglas, Valente, Lee, & Iwen, 1999). Based on these estimates, the combined populations of adolescent and young adult homeless individuals probably are in excess of 3 million young people.

The social and economic impact of this subgroup is enormous. They are the most marginal youth in our society, who will require a disproportionate share of social services and health resources across time. Homelessness among adolescents and young adults not only is an immediate risk to individual health and well-being; it also has lifelong mental health and economic consequences.

Family contexts of runaway and homeless adolescents

Early independence almost always emanates from adverse circumstances within the families adolescents leave. By the time discomfort reaches the threshold where the choice to leave home seems a good one, emotional damage likely has already occurred, and the runaways carry the effects with them onto the streets. Two decades of research on runaway and homeless adolescents make it very clear that the vast majority run from or drift out of disorganized families. Several studies have documented problems in the caretaker–child relationship ranging from control group studies of bonding, attachment, and parental care (Daddis, Braddock, Cuers, Elliott, & Kelly, 1993; Schweitzer, Hier, & Terry, 1994; Votta & Manion, 2003) to caretaker and runaway child reports on parenting behaviors and mutual violence (Whitbeck, Hoyt, & Ackley, 1997b). There have been numerous studies based on adolescent self-reports that indicate high levels of caretaker physical and sexual abuse among chronic runaways and homeless youth (Farber, Kinast, McCoard, & Falkner, 1984; Janus, Archambault, Brown, & Welsh, 1995; Janus, Burgess, & McCormack, 1987; Kaufman & Widom, 1999; Kennedy, 1991; Kufeldt & Nimmo, 1987; Kurtz, Kurtz, & Jarvis, 1991; Molnar, Shade, Kral, Booth, & Watters, 1998; Mounier & Andujo, 2003; Noell, Rohde, Seeley, & Ochs, 2001; Pennbridge et al., 1990; Rotheram-Borus, Mahler, Koopman, & Langabeer, 1996; Ryan, Kilmer, Cauce, Watanabe, & Hoyt, 2000; Saltonstall, 1984; Silbert & Pines, 1981; Stiffman, 1989; Sullivan & Knutson, 2000; Tyler, Hoyt, Whitbeck, & Cauce, 2001b; Tyler, Whitbeck, Hoyt, & Cauce, 2004; Whitbeck & Hoyt, 1999; Whitbeck & Simons, 1993).

Patterson and colleagues (Patterson, Dishion, & Bank, 1984) argue that such family environments provide "basic training" for antisocial behavior. These behaviors are learned directly and indirectly through parent–child interaction. They are directly socialized by caretakers' coercive/aggressive responses to child noncompliance and whining. Often the child responds aggressively in turn, and in the majority of such confrontations the parent capitulates. The child learns that coercive/aggressive responses are rewarding. This also is learned indirectly when occasionally the parent responds aggressively and the situation escalates to the use of high-force methods for gaining compliance. The child is forced to back down. The indirect message is that the most aggressive and powerful person "wins."

When this interaction style is replicated in other social situations it often elicits a coercive/aggressive response, which further reinforces the child's view of the world. Over time, this may result in "interactional continuity" where the communication pattern gets played out in novel situations and the adolescent may drift into peer associations that tolerate or reciprocate the interaction style (Caspi & Bem, 1990). The cumulative effects of this style of interaction may include problems adjusting to supervision and regimentation at school, rejection by conventional peers, and eventually problems adjusting to supervision in the workplace. Running away, particularly chronically, is indicative of a breakdown of negotiating skills with parents, schools, and perhaps institutional living arrangements.

Detours and missed pathways to adulthood

Ideally, adolescence is a time for learning and rehearsing adult roles under the mentorship and protection of caring adults. It is a time of venturing outward independently while remaining economically and emotionally dependent on caretakers. Late adolescence is often characterized by forays into independence with retreats to home and dependency. The process of becoming independent is gradual for most adolescents, often taking several years (Goldscheider & DaVanzo, 1985; Grotevant, 1998). Eccles and colleagues (1993) delineate specific developmental tasks of adolescence that prepare young people for crucial decisions that will shape emerging adulthood. Running away and periods of homelessness interrupt or otherwise modify the timing, context, and completion of each of these fundamental developmental tasks.

Moving from dependency and subordination to parents–caretakers to independence

Chronic runaway episodes affect the parent–caretaker relationship in at least three important ways:

1. Separation from adult caretakers is earlier.
2. It is more abrupt and conflict ridden.
3. It is more pervasive and complete.

Early separation often means relinquishing adult mentoring relationships inside and outside the family that are critical to well-being in early adulthood (Roberts & Bengtson, 1996). External controls and supervision typically provided by adult caregivers and adult authority figures (e.g., teachers, coaches, group leaders) are lost during runaway episodes and may be replaced by unfamiliar, transitory, and highly structured institutional supervision by shelter and group home staff or completely lost to nonconventional peers met on the street and in shelters. Chronic runaways may also forfeit the potential for late adolescent family rapprochement when relationships between parents and offspring typically improve (Collins, 1990; Schultheiss & Blustein, 1994). We have shown elsewhere (Whitbeck & Hoyt, 1999) that once children run away, a process is put into motion where child-initiated living transitions and institutional controlled living transitions increase across time while parent–caretaker control of changes in children's living arrangements decreases. Once independence has been asserted, it is often very difficult for the adolescent to relinquish control and return to a subordinate child role. This can lead to multiple failures in traditional services contexts such as family reunification efforts, foster homes, and group homes that seek to reinstitute dependency and subordination to adult caretakers.

Exploring friendships and new sexual roles and developing intimate relationships

Peer relationships

During adolescence young people begin to separate from their caretaker's influence by expanding their social sphere to include adults and same-aged friends outside the home. For chronic runaways this process may be abrupt, abbreviated, and off-time. They have had less time to rehearse peer relationships, and, given the influence of coercive, conflicted family relationships, they often are less prepared for forming stable friendships and romantic relationships. Multiple runaway episodes almost ensure affiliation with nonconventional peers when either on the streets or in shelters (Johnson, Whitbeck, & Hoyt, 2005a; Whitbeck & Hoyt, 1999). Potential opportunities for affiliating with conventional peers are diminished by interruption of routine school and social activities. The social spheres of runaway adolescents thus become constricted and unbalanced with few, if any, conventional mentoring adults and a greater proportion of nonconventional peers.

As the runaways' ties to parents–caretakers erode, the influence of peer relationships intensifies. In an earlier study, we found that runaway and homeless adolescents were four to five times more likely to turn to friends than to parents–caretakers for emotional support and for day-to-day help or aid (Whitbeck & Hoyt, 1999). Turning to same-aged friendships for the primary emotional support typically proffered by family members increases emotional investment in peer relationships.

Romantic and intimate relationships

Chronic runaways are at once more vulnerable and less prepared to form mutually supportive romantic and intimate ties. Aside from the potential negative relationship effects of coercive/aggressive interaction styles learned in conflicted, abusive family environments, many adolescents have experienced nonconventional early sexual socialization. Depending on sample characteristics rates of caretaker sexual abuse among chronic runaway and homeless adolescents range from a high of 60% among juvenile and adult street prostitutes (Silbert & Pines, 1981) to 47% females and 19% males in a Seattle sample (MacLean, Embry, & Cauce, 1999). Sexually abused runaways are more likely to have multiple sexual partners, more likely to be subsequently victimized when on their own, and more likely to engage in survival sex than runaways who have not experienced such abuse. Although long-term consequences of sexual abuse and victimization on intimate relationships among non-runaways have been well established for some time, we still know little about the long-term effects of sexual abuse and early sexual behaviors associated with early independence on adult intimate relationships among chronic runaways.

Acquiring skills necessary for successful transition to work and parenting

The transition to work

Chronic runaways and homeless young people are remarkably resilient. They develop innovative survival strategies and social ties that allow them to make their way under very difficult situations in unpredictable environments. However, many of the skills they acquire on the streets may not be transferable to successful work and social relationships. Communication and cooperative skills necessary to succeed in the educational settings and the workplace may lose out to the "interactional continuity" of coercive/aggressive interaction styles learned in dysfunctional families of origin (Caspi & Bem, 1990; Caspi, Bem, & Elder, 1989). Such interaction styles may interfere with their ability to handle supervision, express frustration, and negotiate long-term goals necessary for successful work adjustment. Moreover, the loss of structure in school settings may erode very basic work skills such as arriving to work on time and tolerating structured activities for long periods of time.

resources, selling blood, spare changing, shoplifting, dealing drugs, theft, and survival sex. Particularly for minors, there may be few legitimate means of self-support. Early financial independence is largely forced by circumstance and is therefore opportunistic. As is the case for accepting responsibility for oneself, financial independence among chronic runaways and homeless adolescents denotes a much different set of behaviors and circumstances than it does for their conventional counterparts as they move toward adulthood. Although the goal of financial independence may be the same for homeless and housed young people, the preparation for it and the means of achieving it may be very different.

Independent decision making

Independent decision making often begins prior to leaving home and probably plays an important role in the choice to leave or in being kicked out. As noted, independent decision making in the context of asserting early independence may involve poor, sometimes risky choices. Often the independent decisions may be reactive and in opposition to authority figures and involve antisocial behaviors, school leaving, and adult-like behaviors. It is important to recognize that precocious independent decision making is difficult, if not impossible, to take away. As the runaway adolescents mature, however, the same assertive behaviors that led them away from home may result in independent decisions that will take them off the streets, back into an educational program or transitional living program.

General independence and self-sufficiency

General independence and self-sufficiency associated with early independence and making one's way on the streets require a set of skills that may be incongruent with interpretations of conventional young adult self-sufficiency. The concept of *resilience* among runaway and homeless adolescents is not straightforward. On one hand, it may mean successfully adapting to life with few or no adult caretakers to provide protection, and emotional and economic support as well as acclimating to independent living situations. On the other hand, the traditional connotation of *resilience* means maintaining competence in fundamental areas of adjustment in the face of adversity (Luthar, Cicchetti, & Becker, 2000a)—that is, the ability to succeed conventionally even given the levels of adversity they have experienced in families of origin and in their experiences associated with early independence. Although some runaway and homeless adolescents manifest this conventional resilience, *street resilience* may be antithetical to conventional conceptions of resilience. Those most innovative within the street economy and social networks may be those least resilient in terms of conventional competencies and adjustment.

Establishing an independent household

Early independence as it occurs among the young people discussed in this volume does not necessarily mean establishing an independent household. Instead, the adolescents move through "revolving doors" of being housed, doubling up, being in shelters, returning "home" to a relative's or parent's household, and being on the street again. Some become part of surrogate support systems on the streets or "street families" that share resources, protect, and provide emotional support. The pathways to independent households are very different for homeless young adults compared with their conventional counterparts. As homeless young people grow older, many struggle to set up independent households but lack the personal or financial resources to do so. Uncertain incomes, doubling up, and overcrowding often lead to evictions or moving out of shared housing. Those who have aged out of options such as foster care or group homes face few housing choices. Some may become involved in transitional living programs that remediate skills deficits for conventional independent living. For others, independent housing may be simply a matter of economics. Minimum wage jobs, no health insurance, and periods of unemployment put them one paycheck away from resuming homelessness. Some will go on to achieve conventional independent housing; others may not be able to overcome the cumulative adversities they have experienced and may remain on the margins of society.

Life chances: running away as part of an antisocial trajectory

Risk factors for young adult antisocial behaviors can be traced to early childhood (Kosterman, Graham, Hawkins, Catalano, & Herrenkohl, 2001; Loeber & Hay, 1997; Moffitt, 1997); however, pathways vary. Loeber and Hay distinguish three developmental pathways for boys: covert, overt, and authority conflict. The overt path pertains to the development of aggression and violent behaviors. The covert path has to do with concealing behaviors, and the authority conflict path denotes conflict with and avoidance of authority figures. Boys who manifested more serious problem behaviors tended to enter the overt pathway early in life; those who were "experimenters" entered problem behavior pathways later in life and were less likely to engage in problem behaviors over time.

Moffitt et al. (1996) similarly trace the roots of antisocial behaviors to early childhood and distinguish between two developmental trajectories: (1) adolescence limited and (2) life-course persistent. Adolescence-limited problem behaviors originate later in adolescence and do not continue into adulthood. Life-course persistent problem behaviors originate early and are more likely to carry into young adulthood. From this perspective, the developmental process is one of interrelated, self-perpetuating chains of events. Early, often subtle, neurological problems tend to be intergenerational (Huesmann, Eron, Lefkowitz, & Walder, 1984) or the result of low birth weight or other prenatal complications associated with very young, very poor single mothers. The most difficult children are often those whose parents are the least suited to deal with them. Early deficits are sustained and even amplified over time through ineffective parenting such as harsh, inconsistent discipline by parents and oppositional behavior and lack of conventional social behaviors on the part of the children.

We believe that the early lives of chronic runaways and homeless adolescents closely parallel Moffitt's (1997) life-course persistent trajectory. Runaway episodes and periods of homelessness amplify numerous existing risk factors that lead up to the runaway behavior (Whitbeck & Hoyt, 1999; Whitbeck, Hoyt, & Yoder, 1999). The developmental process can be stated very simply: Psychologically harmed children run away from home, and the process of running away further harms them.

The amplification of psychological risk

Recent research on the etiology of mental disorders indicates that one half of all lifetime mental disorders occur by age 14, and three fourths occur by age 24 (Kessler, Berglund, Demler, Jin, & Walters, 2005). Substance abuse disorders tend to occur later (median age = 20 years) than impulse control disorders (median age = 11 years). Prevalence rates for mental disorder are higher in the 15–24 age cohort than for any other age group (Kessler, Nelson, McGonagle, Edlund, Frank, & Leaf, 1996). Late adolescence and early adulthood are critical years for runaway and homeless youth. Two thirds of runaway episodes occur among youths aged 15–17 (Hammer et al., 2002). At the point a runaway first leaves home, he or she is already in acute distress. Experiences on the street exacerbate such stress, either amplifying existing psychological symptoms or resulting in new symptoms (Whitbeck & Hoyt, 1999; Whitbeck et al., 1999).

Goodyer (2001, p. 205) provides four subtypes of stressors that relate to life events and emotional disorders: (1) danger to self; (2) exposure to danger of others; (3) personal disappointments; and (4) loss. The experience of homelessness for adolescents encompasses all of these risk factors for mental disorder. Adolescents often leave home due to perceived danger to self

(Janus et al., 1987; Kurtz et al., 1991; Pennbridge et al., 1990; Silbert & Pines, 1981; Tyler, Hoyt, Whitbeck, & Cauce, 2001a). Many have witnessed serious violence at home and on the streets (Hagen & McCarthy, 1997; Kipke, Simon, Montgomery, Unger, & Iverson, 1997; Whitbeck & Hoyt, 1999); their lives have been fraught with personal disappointments including loss of a safe place to live, academic failure, and failures in relationships, and they have experienced loss of attachment figures through often permanent separation or failure of primary caretakers to provide for them.

In addition to these general stressors associated with risk for mental disorders, there is the unique stress of being without a safe and familiar place to live. Goodman and colleagues use trauma theory to explain the psychological stress experienced by adults who become homeless (Goodman, Saxe, & Harvey, 1991). They suggest that experiencing homelessness is traumatic for adults in three ways. First, the process of becoming homeless may produce symptoms of psychological distress. Becoming homeless means the loss of familiar routines, loss of day-to-day contacts of friends, relatives, and neighbors, and the loss of a safe and private space. Second, the condition of homelessness is incredibly stressful. A heightened sense of vulnerability, hypervigilance, anxiety, and fear may be adaptive to street life, but stress producing nonetheless. Finally, if the individual is already experiencing psychological distress when he or she becomes homeless, the experience will almost certainly exacerbate existing symptoms. If these processes are expected to produce traumatic stress for adults, the effects should be much greater for young people who need and expect adult care.

Summary and conclusions: emerging adulthood among chronic runaways and homeless youth

Although the frontier society of early America is replete with stories of adolescents making their own way or running away to make their fortunes, early independence doesn't work that way in today's society. The age of sexual maturation has decreased while the time needed for preparation for successful adulthood has increased. The result has been a prolonged adolescence and a longer "new" developmental phase of emerging adulthood. By asserting independence early, chronic runaways and homeless adolescents miss important components of both these developmental periods. However, there has been very little research addressing the effects of early independence on life chances, and important questions remain. The fundamental question comes down to: Are the effects of chronic running away so powerful that the majority of these young people will spend their lives on society's margins?

Understanding the extent of the emotional damage that has already occurred among this population or the degree to which persistent homelessness during adolescence affects the onset, persistence, and co-occurrence of mental disorders and substance abuse disorders into adulthood is fundamental to the question of life chances. Is it possible that mental disorders among some runaways are transient and adaptive? Depressive symptoms may be a natural response to experiencing homelessness. Similarly, meeting criteria for conduct disorder may be a consequence of learning survival skills necessary to cope with early independence. The manifestation of symptoms of posttraumatic stress should not be a surprising consequence of experiencing homelessness (Goodman et al., 1991). It may be that a portion of chronic runaways will not manifest life-course persistent antisocial behaviors. Various factors may function to moderate the influence of early independence such as entering into stable intimate relationships, becoming a parent, or successfully completing a transitional living program.

No single study can answer all of these questions; however, this volume is an important first step. In the following chapters we chronicle the progress of homeless and runaway adolescents across time in an attempt to evaluate the occurrence and persistence of mental and substance abuse disorders from mid- and late adolescence into early adulthood. We investigate the prevalence and correlates of symptoms of distress such as dissociative symptoms, self-mutilation, and suicidal behaviors. We conclude with potential moderators of adversity such as intimate relationships, education, and employment. The cohort of adolescents we follow into early adulthood have seen misfortune beyond their years, and the prevalence and comorbidity of psychiatric disorders are the marks they bear for it. How debilitating will these scars be as they move into early adulthood?

chapter 2

The Midwest Longitudinal Study of Homeless and Runaway Adolescents

With Kurt D. Johnson, Dan R. Hoyt, Michael Black, Trina Rose, and the Midwest Longitudinal Study of Homeless Adolescents Interviewers

This is our second major study of homeless and runaway youths in small-to medium-sized urban areas in four Midwestern states (see Whitbeck & Hoyt, 1999). We believe the Midwestern cities in which we interviewed these young people lend particular importance toward understanding the prevalence and behaviors of runaways in the United States. The cities in which we worked were not "magnet" cities for runaways such as Los Angeles, San Francisco, New Orleans, or New York, which draw more diverse and "nomadic" populations of homeless and runaway adolescents. The adolescents we interviewed represent a largely unacknowledged and unpublicized population of the country's runaway and homeless youths. If they are living in Des Moines, Omaha, or Wichita, we can assume they are also on the streets and in shelters in other similarly sized cities across the nation.

This study has several distinctive aspects aside from the setting. The most significant is the longitudinal design. Although there have been other shorter-term prospective studies in Canada (Hagen & McCarthy, 1997), the United States, and Australia (Milburn et al., 2007), the Midwest study tracked the adolescents over a period of 3 years, with interviews at 3-month intervals for a total of 13 waves of data. In this regard, it was, in part, a feasibility study to see how well homeless and runaway adolescents could be followed across time. It was also a diagnostic study in which the subjects were screened for conduct disorder (CD), major depressive episode, (MDE), posttraumatic stress disorder (PTSD), and substance abuse disorders (SUDs) at Wave 1 when aged 16–19 years, and antisocial personality disorder (APD), MDE, PTSD, and SUDs at Wave 13 when they had become young adults (19–22 years). The primary goal of the study was to track the emergence of adult mental disorders and to evaluate their effects on the transition to adulthood.

As with the first Midwest study, the project was embedded in active street agencies with outreach programs that had institutional knowledge of local street cultures and had well-established street reputations. This provided not only access but also tracking continuity. The intensive, long-term follow-up meant that we came to know our subjects very well. In fact, as time went on, our interviewers evolved into playing a case management-like role and became important in many of the adolescents' lives. There is almost certainly a "treatment" effect that emerges in this kind of intensive study that is ethically unavoidable. Our interviewers provided meals, monetary incentives, and referrals. They interacted with the adolescents in much the same way as street outreach workers.

Study sites

The study was conducted in Des Moines, Cedar Rapids, and Iowa City, Iowa; Lincoln and Omaha, Nebraska; Wichita, Kansas; and Kansas City and St. Louis, Missouri. We worked directly with street outreach programs and placed full-time interviewers in each city. St. Louis was assigned two full-time interviewers due to its size, and one interviewer was assigned to smaller shelters in Cedar Rapids and Iowa City. Although all of the sites had shelters, some had less sophisticated outreach programs than others. Several agencies had outreach vans that patrolled certain areas of the city; others sent outreach workers out on foot to areas where street kids congregate. Because the interviewers were most aware of the street environments in which recruitment and interviews took place, we asked several of them to provide a description of their study site.

Des Moines, Iowa
(interviewer Shane Stewart)

Downtown Des Moines has a constant flow of juveniles and young adults who are without homes. Most of the youths live in abandoned warehouses or buildings, under bridges, or, periodically, with friends or in shelters, group homes, or independent living programs.

Youths Emergency Shelter and Services (YESS) in Des Moines is a lockdown facility for youths 18 and under. Most of the clients at YESS are either court ordered or admitted by parents. Iowa Homeless Youths Centers (IHYC) is a transitional living center for youths from the age of

16 to 21 whose goal is to promote independent living and self-sufficiency. The problem is that IHYC has only 8 beds, with 1 emergency bed for up to 3 nights. Furthermore, they have guidelines in place that are often not appropriate for low-functioning or severely mentally ill youths. Guidelines are also a deterrent for those youths who find the street life and culture appealing. As young adults, some of these youths do not want curfews imposed, school required, and case management mandated.

There are a few shelters for men and women over the age of 18 such as the Young Men's Christian Association (YMCA), Young Women's Christian Association (YWCA), Bethel Mission, and the Door of Faith, but all require payment. There is also an overflow shelter, Churches United, which takes both men and women over the age of 18. Shelter residents at Churches United have a reputation of drug use, sexually predatory behaviors, and manipulative behaviors among street youths, so the youth tend to avoid this shelter.

There are food pantries, but they require an address and identification, and most of these youths have neither. Even when food is acquired, transportation and storage of food are a problem. Many of these youths will receive only one daily meal at the community kitchen. Since most of the youths do not have jobs, they will spend their days walking around downtown. The Walnut Street Burger King and city bus transfer station are popular hangouts. Many of the youths will visit the Youths Outreach Center to get bus tokens, hygiene items, or referrals for other services. Some hang out in the skywalks connecting downtown buildings, trying to keep warm until security guards kick them out. The "gay loop" or Riverside Drive was another popular destination until recent reports of violence such as one youth being stabbed, another being gang raped, and one being chased to a parking garage where he was beaten and thrown from the second floor led to city concern and heavy police patrolling.

New initiatives have city leaders tearing down old buildings to make way for events centers, libraries, and new businesses. This displaces the homeless population, as these buildings were where they once sought refuge. Now they are being forced to live in abandoned warehouses and boxcars on the outskirts of downtown and in shanty camps being built in nearby woods along the Des Moines and Raccoon Rivers. This only takes them farther away from available services. It also takes them away from the public eye, makes their environment more dangerous and creates less public acknowledgement of the problem.

Lincoln, Nebraska (interviewer Theresa Tumbleson)

The street climate of Lincoln, Nebraska, is somewhat different from that of other study sites in that the majority of the homeless and runaway youths grew up either in Lincoln or in the surrounding rural communities. There are homeless youths who arrive in Lincoln via trains or hitchhiking, but few stay in Lincoln for a long period of time. In addition, Lincoln lacks environments that the youths consider "homeless friendly." The Coffee House, located in downtown Lincoln, is one location that homeless youths feel safe and accepted. Those that congregate at this location are a tight-knit group, and "outsiders"—youths new to the streets or the community—may not feel welcome. Such outsiders are a hidden segment of Lincoln's homeless youths, and most reside in abandoned buildings ("squats") or efficiency apartments often with a number of other homeless and runaway young people.

Access to street youths in Lincoln is difficult due to their propensity to "disappear." However, Cedars Street Outreach workers have developed a reputation in the community as safe, nonjudgmental people who are there to help. The outreach team was instrumental in gaining participants for the study and in tracking Lincoln's street population. In addition to Cedars Street Outreach workers, the efforts of staff at Cedars Freeway Station, an emergency, short-term, crisis shelter for youths aged 13–19, also contributed significantly to recruiting and tracking study participants. The study office was located at the Freeway Station, and because it is known in the street community as a safe place, the interviewer was able to conduct initial and follow-up interviews where the study participants felt secure.

Cedars Youths Services also has two other facilities that serve homeless youths. One is Cedars Transitional Living Program (TLP), which provides apartments and teaches independent living skills to homeless youths. Transitional living workers provided information about this study to youths in the program. The Cedars Teaching and Learning with Children (TLC) program also provided contact with homeless youths they served and assisted with follow-up contact information of youths who had been discharged from their program.

As the study youths grew older and became ineligible to receive services, access to adult homeless services became important. We received help from two adult services. The first was Day Watch, which is a day shelter for homeless adults. Adults that frequent this location have access to telephones, laundry and shower facilities, food, and social services. The other facility was the Gathering Place, a soup kitchen that provides evening meals as well as referrals to social services. Although the primary population served at this location is homeless adults, the Gathering Place is known in the community for being a safe place for homeless youths as well. Staff at this location provided youths who attended the evening meals with information about the study and with contact information of this interviewer.

Omaha, Nebraska (interviewer Chris Johnson)

Homeless, runaway, and throwaway youths seem to be drawn to downtown Omaha. It is the nation's 42nd largest city, with a population of 390,007. The larger metropolitan area is made up of 5 counties, which are Douglas, Sarpy, Cass, and Washington in Nebraska and Pottawattamie County in Iowa. The main hangout for homeless youths in Omaha is the Old Market, a historical site known for its cultural diversity and the acceptance. The "Market Rats," as they call themselves, hang out on large decorative brick planters that frame the sidewalks. Their dress is very diverse and represents their identities as goths, punk, grunge, and skaters; others wear brightly colored hoodies, visors, and beads.

They also hang out at the Altar, which is the entrance from an old bank in downtown Omaha, or meet at the 420 Tables, which are located in the same park where they share drugs, particularly marijuana. There is also Glass Alley, a dark alley south of the market where drug deals take place. In bad weather they may gather under the Tenth Street Bridge. The bridge serves as refuge from the elements and a place to crash after partying or just to get away from the public. The homeless youths in Omaha stay in abandoned buildings, in cars, under bridges, on a fire escape over an alley, or even under the outside deck of a bar. They look for any space that is secluded and safe to sleep. They can be very creative and resourceful when it comes to finding a squat. Some told us that they have dodged the personnel in buildings and sleep inside businesses until morning.

The youths in the market area are served by the Youths Emergency Services (YES), Youths Street Outreach Program, a nonprofit agency that consists of two short-term shelters for 13–18 year-old adolescents. The street youths rarely stay at these shelters because they must have a guardian's consent to stay. Those old enough to be admitted without consent may not want to adhere to the structure that the group home requires. Mostly, the street youths have come to rely on the street outreach team for adult guidance, referrals, emotional support, snacks, clothes, and hygiene items. The street outreach team provides a meal and support group on Wednesday nights. The youths meet at the office for a hot meal and may stay for an educational presentation by the outreach workers or outside service agencies.

The street outreach team is based out of the YES office and near midtown Omaha. This office was the host office from which the study interviewer went out on the street with the regular outreach workers. Outreach consists of having a backpack full of snacks, juice boxes, hygiene items, bandages, and referrals to agencies. The youths also seem to appreciate the use of cell phones that outreach workers carry at all times to call home, jobs, or friends.

There are two adult homeless shelters in Omaha—the Sienna Francis House and the Open Door Mission. Both shelters are located close to downtown. The youths must be at least 19 years of age to stay at the shelters and receive a bed, shower, and meal. In addition, there are some transitional living programs in Omaha, one of which is Jacob's Place, funded by the Omaha Home for Boys. This program sets the youths up in an apartment that they share with another young person. They must maintain a job to pay rent and are encouraged to go to school. Many of the young people access the Housing Authority and try to get their names on the list for low-income housing.

Health care is a constant need for the youths, and it is very hard to access. The Charles Drew Satellite Clinic located in South Omaha serves the homeless youths, but transportation across town makes access difficult. Many of the youths use hospital emergency rooms, because they know they won't be turned away. They also use Planned Parenthood, which has several locations for exams, birth control, and treatment for sexually transmitted infections. There is also a mobile health clinic that visits North Omaha once a week that is free to the community. Dental care is particularly hard to come by but is available through Creighton Dental School for a reduced fee. Vision care is sometimes offered in conjunction with the Open Door Mission and certain eye care professionals a couple of times a year.

St. Louis, Missouri (interviewers Drew Haught and Elizabeth Crowley)

The St. Louis Metropolitan area encompasses roughly 100 square miles providing numerous neighborhoods for homeless and runaway youths to frequent. Some of these include the Delmar Loop, the Tower Grove/South Grand area of town, Washington Street, and the Central West End. There are numerous and comprehensive services available. Youths have access to low or no-cost health care, shelters, food banks, counseling and mental health services, education and job training, and legal services. A variety of agencies provide all of these services along with targeted services such as mobile outreach, transitional living programs, and substance abuse recovery programs. Many youths receive state-funded aide such as food stamps, Section 8 housing, and social security. The services in the metropolitan area are generally divided by city and county boundaries. In general, all services are provided regardless of area, though the service provider may differ.

The youths we have interviewed report that gang activity is very prevalent; however, the street interviewers were aware of only subtle outward signs of gang activity such as colors or markings of gang affiliation. As the study progressed some youths aged out of the gang and "street family" mentality. This may be due to the birth of children, obtaining employment, or becoming housed.

Wichita, Kansas (interviewer Karen Countryman-Roswurm)

The population of the metropolitan area of Wichita is somewhere around 452,000. The average Wichita resident person is not very aware of homelessness, prostitution, and drug activity in the city. Most runaways and homeless youths stay out of sight and for the most part out of mind. They are often called "couch kids." You very seldom see them staying directly on the streets. Instead, they stay at the homes of friends or acquaintances, going from place to place until their options run out. They find "instant friends" on the streets, at a teen club (certain adult clubs have teen nights), a pool hall, at the street races, or at a house party. If they are lucky they can then stay with them for awhile and continue the cycle of staying from couch to couch. Too often, this lifestyle leads to sexual exploitation.

There are several services providers for runaway and homeless youths in the Wichita area. The Wichita Children's Home has a Street Outreach Services Program (SOS) with a 24-hour crisis line. They offer food, clothing, and hygiene products as well as case management, referrals to other community resources, and health services. The Wichita Children's Home also has a Transitional Living Program (TLP) for custody and noncustody youths. This provides housing to youths who are out on the street and who are ready to learn the skills for independent living. SOS workers refer young people to other local services such as The Lord's Diner, Hunter Health Clinic, Via Christi Emergency Room, and Dressed for Success. The Lord's Diner serves dinner 365 days a year to both youths and adults. The Hunter Health Clinic provides free HIV and syphilis testing and works on a sliding scale with all other medical services. Via Christi Emergency Room has an agreement with Street Outreach to provide health services for acute conditions. Dressed for Success helps young women with appropriate clothing for job interviews and employment.

Summary

These descriptions indicate the diversity of environments in which the youths were interviewed. The interviewers essentially joined the street cultures in each city and became known and important resources to the adolescents. This "street credibility" was invaluable for recruitment and

tracking the adolescents across the 3 years of the study. Splitting an interviewer between two small cities (Iowa City and Cedar Rapids) proved
to be a mistake. This interviewer was essentially shelter-bound and was
never really available and able to integrate into the small street networks.
Lack of access to an established street outreach program was a critical
problem in Kansas City that resulted in the interviewer feeling isolated, in
staff turnover, and in poor tracking. We learned from this experience that
it is extremely difficult to establish effective outreach independently.

Subject recruitment

Sampling design

Research with homeless populations presents some important challenges
for sample design. While some probability sampling methods have been
implemented in studies of homeless populations (Burnam & Koegel, 1988;
Koegel, Burnam, & Morton, 1996; Robertson, Westerfelt, & Irving, 1991;
Sumner, Andersen, Wenzel, & Gelberg, 2001; Witkin, Milburn, Rotheram-
Borus, Batterham, May, & Brooks, 2005), there is no method for developing
a sampling frame that has been verified to be unbiased. Many studies have
clearly documented the difficulty associated with any attempt to enu-
merate homeless populations (Burt & Taeuber, 1991; Dennis, 1991; Rossi,
Wright, Fisher, & Willis, 1987). For example, the Shelter and Street Night
experiments conducted by the U.S. Census demonstrated the substantial difficulties associated with locating homeless populations (Wright &
Devine, 1992). In even the "best-case" scenario in New Orleans, where the
enumeration was conducted in a geographically limited area, only 66%
of the decoys that had been deployed were located by the enumeration
teams (Devine & Wright, 1992).

There are important time dimensions to sampling homeless populations related to seasonal changes, to changes in service system eligibility, and to the duration of the sampling period (Iachan & Dennis, 1991).
Methods that include systematic sampling of site locations at different
times of the day, different days of the week, and across seasons will provide an optimal sampling frame for homeless populations because they
take into account the various rhythms of movement of transient life
(Dennis, Iachan, Thornberry, & Bray, 1991; Iachan, 1989). We designed a
sampling strategy for the current study that incorporated sampling units
of fixed (e.g., shelters) and natural (e.g., street hangouts) sites similar to the
design used by Kipke in her Los Angeles study of homeless youths (Kipke,
Montgomery, Simon, Unger, & Johnson, 1997) with a year-long window of
sampling to capture the time dimensions.

Our sample of homeless and runaway youths, aged 16 to 19 years, was recruited by repeatedly checking locations where homeless adolescents were likely to be found in each of the study cities. Locations included shelters and outreach programs serving homeless youths, drop-in centers, and various "street" locations where homeless young people were most likely to congregate. Research has demonstrated that using sampling designs involving multiple points of entry to homeless populations are most effective in generating a diverse sample (Burt, 1996; Koegel et al., 1996). The outreach interviewers all had prior experience in their respective cities as youth outreach workers and brought considerable knowledge regarding optimal areas of the city for locating youths on their own. The sampling protocol included going to these locations in the cities at varying times of the day on both weekdays and weekends. This sampling protocol was conducted repeatedly over the course of 12 months.

Since episodes of homelessness among young people vary widely in duration, the 1-year time frame provided an increased probability of capturing youths who have short-term exposure to homelessness. Short-duration sampling schemes are likely to result in samples that overrepresent the long-term, chronic, homeless population (Phelan & Link, 1999). On the other hand, sampling strategies that have inadequate inclusion of street intercepts in the sampling frame might produce underestimates of chronic populations. An analysis of the history of homelessness among the initial sample demonstrated a good variability for amount of time that the adolescents had been on their own. Based on the life history interviews, only 7.8% of the adolescents in our sample had spent 7 days or less living in shelters, on the street, or in unsupervised situations prior to being recruited for the study. Approximately 9.0% had been on their own more than a week but less than a month and another 11.6% from between 1 and 3 months. Thus, only a little more than one fourth of the sample (28.4%) had histories of being on their own for less than 3 months. At the other end of the distribution, more than one third of the sample (36.2%) had been on their own for more than a year. In sum, the procedures used produced a sample of homeless adolescents that has greater variability in chronicity of homelessness than might be anticipated in short-term point-prevalence studies.

Recruitment procedures

As noted, seven full-time street interviewers were employed by the project, one in each city except St. Louis, where two were assigned due to the size of the metropolitan area we needed to cover. All but one of the street interviewers were experienced street workers who had been employed by street outreach agencies; several had experienced periods of homelessness themselves. Those who had no direct street experience had bachelor's degrees in social services or the equivalent.

To be eligible to participate in the study, young persons had to be between the ages of 16 and 19 years and homeless. Our definition of *homeless* was that the adolescents must be residing in a shelter, on the street, or living independently (e.g., friends, transitional living) because they had run away, been pushed out, or drifted out of their family of origin. All of the adolescents were interviewed either in shelters, on the streets, or in independent living situations (e.g., transitional living, apartments, squats with friends). The interviewers were instructed to go to these locations are various times of the day on weekdays and weekends. They were to approach shelter residents and to locate eligible respondents in various locations throughout the cities. In shelters and drop-in centers, only adolescents who met criteria as runaways were interviewed. On the streets, adolescents who were known to be homeless were approached as were those who appeared to be homeless. The interviewers were to continue recruiting during the first year of the study until their caseload reached 60 adolescents, whom they would then track and reinterview at 3-month intervals. The actual interviews were performed in a range of circumstances, from shelter interview rooms, outreach vans, and apartments where adolescents may be doubling up with friends or relatives to quiet corners of restaurants and outside.

The length of the baseline interview raised concerns about subject burden. Therefore, the first-wave interview was conducted in two parts. The first part consisted of a social history and symptom scales. The respondent was then asked to meet for a second interview during which the diagnostic interviews were conducted. Typically the two interviews were conducted in the same week. In some cases there was up to 2 weeks between the first and second interview. The respondents were paid $25 for the first interview and $25 for the second.

Informed consent procedures

The adolescents were informed that this was a longitudinal study, and the tracking protocols were explained. Informed consent was a two-stage process. First, the study was explained, and informed consent was obtained from the adolescent. They were assured that refusal to participate in the study, refusal of any question, or stopping the interview process would have no effect on current or future services provided by the outreach agency that provided office space and outreach support for the interviewer. Second, all adolescents were asked if we could contact their parents. If permission was granted, parents were contacted by telephone to gain informed consent. If the parent could not be reached or refused consent and the adolescent wished to continue in the study—or in the few cases where the adolescent was under 18 years, not sheltered, and refused permission to contact parents—the adolescents were treated as emancipated minors in accord with the Code of Federal Regulations (Title 45, Part 46) established by the National Institutes of Health (National Institutes of Health, 2005). If the adolescent was sheltered, we followed shelter policies for parental permission for placement and guidelines for granting such permissions. These policies were always based on state laws, which varied across the four states in which the study was conducted. A National Institute of Mental Health Certificate of Confidentiality was obtained to protect the respondent's statements regarding potentially illegal activities (e.g., drug use).

Tracking strategy

The tracking protocol involved a combination of collecting detailed tracking information at the time of each interview and providing incentives for continued participation in the study. At the time of baseline interviews, respondents were asked for detailed information regarding the locations they frequented, their informal and formal social networks, and any existing contact information such as telephone numbers, addresses, and relatives' names and addresses available at the time. This information was kept in a tracking file for the respondent that was updated at each follow-up interview. Interviewers also kept a daily log of any interactions they may have had with clients in which they recorded the type of interaction (e.g., phone call, street intercept) and the location of that interaction. If contact was lost with the respondent, interviewers were instructed to check locations of previous meetings, to call informal contacts and relatives, and to check all current contact information.

Respondents were provided a laminated photo identification listing project contact information for the individual conducting their interview. This identification card proved to be very popular among the adolescents who often had no other formal identification. At the time of the initial interview, respondents were informed that frequent contact with their interviewer could result in bonus reimbursements at the time of their follow-up interview. Youths were encouraged to call or contact the interviewer approximately every 2 weeks updating any changes in their tracking information and to check in to be eligible for a follow-up bonus of $10.

Recruitment and attrition rates

Those who did not complete the baseline assessment

Of the 455 adolescents who began the baseline assessment procedure, 428 (94.1%) completed both interviews (the study questionnaire and diagnostic interview). Of the 455 original participants, 27 did not complete the baseline procedure. Noncompleters had a significantly higher mean age at first run: Age 14.84 for noncompleters and age 13.41 for completers. Of completers, 85% identified themselves as heterosexual compared with 100% of those who did not complete the baseline report. Completers were more likely to report physical victimization than noncompleters. Of noncompleters, 42% reported experiencing some physical victimization while on their own compared with 63% of completers. Noncompleters, therefore, tended to be older and heterosexual and to have experienced less physical victimization when on their own.

Contact lost after baseline for all subsequent interviews

Of the 428 respondents completing the baseline procedure, contact was lost (no subsequent contact for any 3-month interview to date) with 84 (19.6%) participants. The mean age of those with whom we lost contact (17.17 years) was significantly lower than that for those who remained in the study (17.42 years). The mean number of days stayed in a group home was significantly lower for those who left the study (187.44 days) than those who remained in the study (347.57 days). Those who stayed in the study were significantly more likely to meet diagnostic criteria for PTSD than those with whom we lost contact. Of those who stayed in the study, 38% met diagnostic criteria for PTSD compared with 25% of those who left. Those who left the study after the first interview, therefore, tended to be younger, had spent less time on their own, and were less likely to have experienced severe trauma.

Attrition rates by year of study

Follow-up interviews were attempted every 3 months. A total of 60 adolescents (14%) completed all of the 13 follow-up interviews. The attrition rate at the end of year 1 was 44.6%; at the end of year 2 it was 54.6%; and by the final wave of the study it was 54%. The total number of adolescents who completed the final interview (Wave 13) was 197. Because of the transient nature of the population, participants who missed one of the follow-up interviews were not eliminated from the study, and attempts were made at each wave to contact all of the baseline participants. This resulted in variation in the number of waves completed by the participants.

Attrition rates by study site

Based on the number of respondents who completed both the initial baseline procedure and the final interview over the course of 3 years, we were able to retain 46% of the sample. There was considerable variability across the eight different interviewers, with retention rates ranging from 75% in one of the St. Louis locations to 5.1% in Kansas City. The Kansas City interviewer left the project at approximately the midpoint, and we were not able to replace her. This resulted in final interviews in Wave 13 with only three of the respondents from the area. The interviewer from the Cedar Rapids/Iowa City area also left the study at approximately the midpoint; however, we were able to add the Cedar Rapids/Iowa City caseload to that of the interviewer in Des Moines. With this adjustment we were able to retain 23.9% (11 of 46) of the respondents in the area. Figure 2.1 reports the retention rates by location.

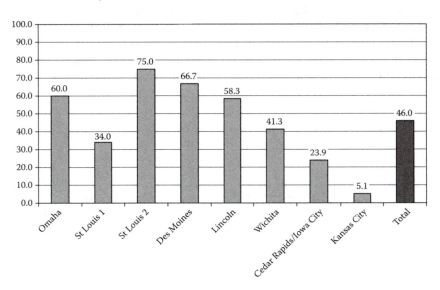

Figure 2.1 Final retention rates (in percent) by site.

Those who stayed in the study and those who left

To provide a reasonable comparison of those who remained in the study and those who left, we divided the sample into quartiles of completed interviews:

1. Those who completed less than 25%.
2. Those who completed 26% to 50%.
3. Those who completed 51% to 75%.
4. Those who completed 76% to 100%.

Figures 2.2 through 2.4 compare the completion rates by age (Figure 2.2), gender (Figure 2.3), and sexual orientation (Figure 2.4). Adolescents who were older (i.e., 19 years) at baseline were more likely to complete 76% to 100% of the interviews than their younger counterparts. Females were slightly more likely than males to have completed 76% to 100% of the interviews. The completion rates for heterosexuals and nonheterosexuals were nearly identical. The general trend was that younger adolescents were more easily recruited at baseline but were less likely to complete 76% or more of the interviews.

Figure 2.5, Figure 2.6, Figure 2.7, Figure 2.8, and Figure 2.9 reflect the completion rates by diagnosis. We were expecting that those who met diagnostic criteria for one of the mental or substance abuse disorders would be more difficult to track and more likely to leave the study. This was not the case. There were essentially no differences in completion rates between those who met diagnostic criteria and those who did not.

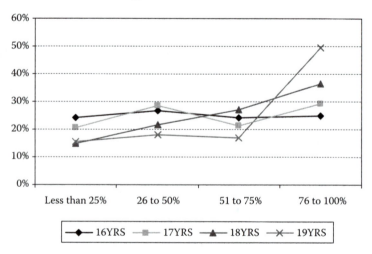

Figure 2.2 Completion rates by age.

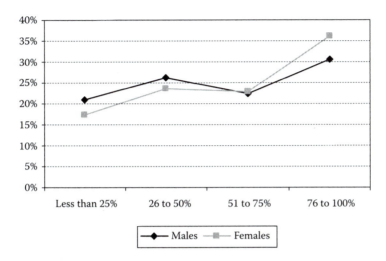

Figure 2.3 Completion rates by gender.

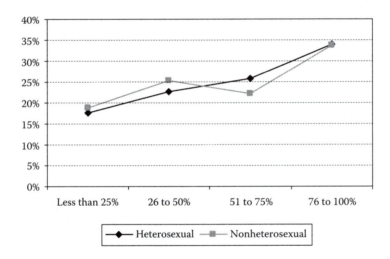

Figure 2.4 Completion rates by sexual orientation.

Imputation of missing values

Missing data are common analytic challenge in social science research. This challenge becomes more pronounced in longitudinal research studies where the standard sources of missing data, such as item nonresponse, are complicated with responses missing by wave of data collection and subject attrition. Traditional approaches to missing data have included case deletion (e.g., list-wise deletion in statistical analysis software) or

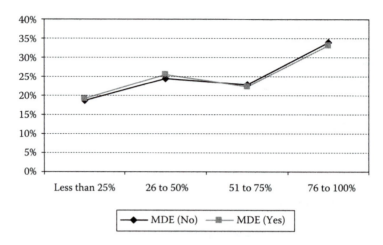

Figure 2.5 Completion rates by diagnosis: major depressive disorder.

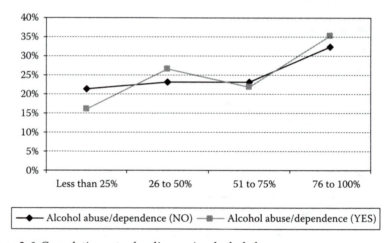

Figure 2.6 Completion rates by diagnosis: alcohol abuse.

simple mean imputation. These traditional approaches are likely to intro-
duce biases in most multivariate research applications and in recent years
have been replaced by a variety of more sophisticated imputation strategies. One common approach to missing data imputation that has been
incorporated into analytic software is based on the EM (Expectation-
Maximization) algorithm (Dempster, Laird, & Rubin, 1977; Little & Rubin,
1987). This single imputation method is used in some standard statistical software (e.g., SPSS MVA module). There are, however some limita-
tions associated with this approach, and the standard for missing data

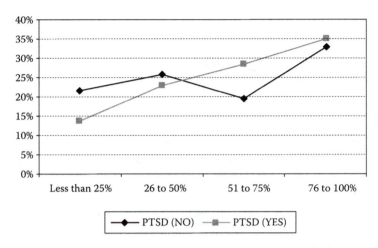

Figure 2.7 Completion rates by diagnosis: posttraumatic stress disorder.

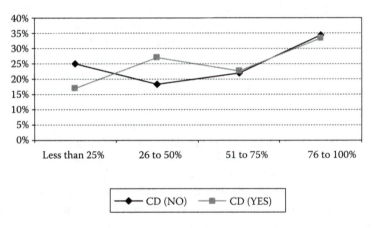

Figure 2.8 Completion rates by diagnosis: conduct disorder.

estimation has increasingly become based on multiple imputation strategies (Rubin, 1987; Schafer & Graham, 2002). We use multiple imputation to address the missing data in this study when appropriate.

The basic approach for multiple imputation was outlined by Rubin (Little & Rubin, 1987; Rubin, 1987). The initial step in the imputation is to estimate the missing data using a model that is appropriate for the data and incorporates random variation. This estimation is performed multiple times (typically three to five). The selected data analytic techniques are then applied to each of the imputed data files. Single-point estimates are calculated by averaging the estimates across the multiple analyses, and

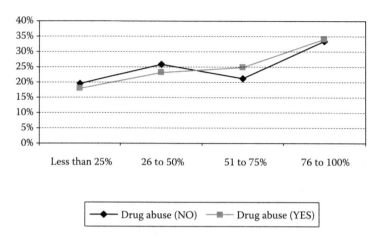

Figure 2.9 Completion rates by diagnosis: drug abuse.

appropriate standard errors are estimated. The advantages to this approach are that it (1) introduces random error into the imputation permitting approximately unbiased estimates of parameters, (2) provides good estimates of the standard errors from the repeated imputation, and (3) can be used with any type of data and analytic software (Allison, 2000).

Multiple imputation methods require the assumption that the data are missing at random (MAR). This term can be confusing, since it does not literally mean that there is no pattern to the missing data. What is required for the MAR assumption to hold is that, assuming a variable of interest Y, the probability of data being missing can be conditional on other X variables in the data set but not on the Y variable itself (Schafer, 1997). There is no way to verify that the assumption of MAR is appropriate, but recent research has shown that in many cases an incorrect assumption of MAR may have only minor impact on parameter estimates and standard errors (Collins, Schafer, & Kam, 2001).

The procedure for multiple imputation of missing data in this study required multiple steps. The exact imputation procedure varied for particular analyses since the single-point estimate approach requires that the method used in the imputation be consistent with the type of model used in the analyses. For certain models, such as those examining diagnostic estimates that were gathered only at the first and final interviews, the decision was made to impute values only if we had data for at least these two data points and at least two of the intermediate waves of data collection. Thus, a respondent would have to have participated in Wave 1, Wave 13, and two other interview waves. In this specification, 189 observations remained for the imputation.

Since the variables considered for the imputation in this context were categorical variables, logistic regression imputation was used, and we assumed that the data were missing at random. To generate the imputed data, we used the SAS procedure, PROC MI (SAS Institute, 2004, Cary, NC). To use PROC MI with a logistic option, it is required that the missing pattern is monotone. A monotone pattern is one typically associated with subject attrition in longitudinal studies, where once a subject drops out of the study he or she does not return. However, with this sample, some youths would be lost for a wave or two of data collection and then would return so that the pattern of the data is not naturally monotonic. Thus, we ran PROC MI variable by variable, wave by wave. For a given wave, we included all the variables that fit a monotonic pattern and then ran an additional imputation on the next set of monotonic variables. When that wave was completed, we moved to the next wave and repeated the process.

We generated five imputed data sets for each of the analyses. When we included imputed data in the analyses we used PROC MIANALYZE in SAS (SAS Institute, 2004, Cary, NC). PROC MIANALYZE does a separate statistical analysis for each imputed data set and combines the results from each analysis with adjustment using the estimate of increase in variance due to imputation.

Example of missing data imputation: survival analyses

An example of how we approached missing data estimation for a particular analytic model may be described in the context of survival analyses. In some of the chapters we present survival curves for behaviors across the 13 waves of data. Survival analysis indicates the proportions of participants who remain or "survive" from certain events, that is, the percentage of individuals at risk who have not experienced the event. For example, a survival analysis of physical victimization estimates the probability that an individual in the study would not experience physical victimization at any wave over the course of the study. Because the first wave asks, "Have you ever..." for many of the events of interest, there is a large amount of left censoring at Wave 1 (i.e., the respondent had already engaged in the behavior). The questions in Waves 2 through 13 ask, "Since the last interview..." Therefore, if a wave or two is missed but the answer is no when the individual is interviewed again, we know the answer is no at the missed points as well. However, if waves are missed and the response at the next point of contact is yes, we don't know when in the intervening time the event actually took place. For some events of interest (e.g., physical victimization, sexual victimization, rape) we used the imputed values to estimate survival. For other events (e.g., tried to kill self, thought about killing self, stealing, selling drugs, pregnancy) not in the imputation, when the individuals stopped responding they were considered right censored (Yamaguchi, 1991) at the last wave they responded.

The percentage surviving at a given wave $\hat{S}(i)$ was estimated using product-limit estimation (Kaplan & Meier, 1958) using estimated hazard rates $\hat{h}(i)$. Hazard rates were estimated as follows. $h(i) = d_i / Y_i$ where d_i is the number of individuals who report having the event of interest at wave i, Y_i is the number of individuals still under observation who still hadn't had the event just prior to wave i and where I = 1,2,...,13. Then

$$\hat{S}(i) = \hat{S}(i-1)^* (1 - h(i)) = \prod_{t=1}^{i}(1 - h(i))$$

where $\hat{S}(0) = 1$ (Klein & Moeschberger, 1997). Because we wanted to look at the survival of all the individuals in the study, we set the survival at Wave 1 as the percentage of all the respondents who had not yet experienced the event at the start of the study—that is, $\hat{S}(1) = 1 - \hat{h}(1) = (Y_1 - d_1) / Y_1$. In other words, Wave 1 survival is the percentage of individuals who said no to the "Have you ever…" questions. Then for each event of interest at each wave, a variable was created so that if the event had occurred before that wave it was 2, if it occurred at that wave it was a 1, if it had never occurred and the individual was in the study the variable was given a 0, and if the individual had stopped reporting the variable was missing. The count of the 1's in each variable were the d_i's and the count of the 0's and 1's were the Y_i's. These were used to estimate the survival rates at the different waves. In the figures the percentages were plotted and were connected by straight lines to show the change in survival over the 13 waves.

Measurement procedures, measures, and measurement issues

The adolescents' responses were entered on laptop computers using computer-assisted personal interviewing (CAPI) and then downloaded to a secure server at the university. There were several considerations that supported our use of this methodology. First, the skip patterns in the diagnostic interviews are complicated, and the use of CAPI minimizes the potential for interviewer error in administering this instrument. Second, the staggered sampling protocol implies that at a given time point in the data collection process a field interviewer will be working with up to four or five different interview forms (e.g., some respondents could be on their third follow-up while others are being administered the initial set of interviews). It would be cumbersome for an interviewer to be working with multiple copies of questionnaires. In addition, interview history and scheduling information were kept on the computer to ensure the selection of the correct interview protocol. Third, given the collection of the data in remote sites, the use of CAPI facilitates quick transmission of data to the university where it was edited, providing the opportunity for quick feedback to the interviewer on any clarification or quality control issues.

The interviewers underwent 2 weeks of intensive training regarding CAPI procedures and administering the four indices (i.e., major depressive episodes, posttraumatic stress disorder, alcohol use and abuse, and drug use and abuse) from the University of Michigan-Composite International Diagnostic Interview (UM-CIDI) (Kessler, 1994a, 1994b; Wittchen & Kessler, 1994) and the conduct disorder module from the Diagnostic Interview Schedule for Children-Revised (DISC-R). They then returned to their shelters and administered several "practice" interviews with staff and respondents 20 years or older. After completing their practice interviews the interviewers returned to the university for a second week of training and practice to assure interrater reliability.

The diagnostic measures

Because the baseline interviews were quite long and required two sessions to complete, we limited our baseline diagnostic assessments to five diagnostic categories to reduce subject burden. The UM-CIDI was used to assess major depressive episode, posttraumatic stress disorder, and the substance abuse disorders. The UM-CIDI is based on *Diagnostic and Statistical Manual of Mental Disorders,* third edition, revised (*DSM-III-R;* American Psychiatric Association, 1987) criteria and represents the University of Michigan revision of the CIDI (World Health Organization, 1990) used in the National Comorbidity Survey (NCS) (for information regarding the University of Michigan revisions see Kessler, 1994a, 1994b; Wittchen & Kessler, 1994). The CIDI (World Health Organization) from which the UM-CIDI is derived is a well-established diagnostic instrument (see Wittchen, 1994, for review) that has shown excellent interrater reliability, test–retest reliability, and validity for the five diagnoses that were used in this study.

The conduct disorder module was used from the DISC-R, which is a highly regarded, structured interview intended for use with trained interviewers who are not clinicians. It has been shown to have good to excellent interrater and test–retest reliability (Jensen et al., 1995; Shaffer et al., 1993). At Wave 13 the entire diagnostic interview was repeated with the exception that the conduct disorder module was replaced with the UM-CIDI module for antisocial personality disorder (Zhao, Kessler, & Wittchen, 1994, p. 34).

A note about statistical significance

We use the .05 level of statistical significance throughout this volume. However, sometimes in the multivariate analysis theoretically interesting coefficients will approach significance, and we do not believe their contribution to the explained variance should be completely overlooked (Daniel, 1998; Ziliak & McCloskey, 2007). When this occurs we note in the text that the coefficient was significant at the $p < .10$ level or give the actual significance level (e.g., $p = .07$).

The qualitative data

The qualitative data used throughout this book were supported by a University of Nebraska–Lincoln Faculty Seed Grant to Dr. Kimberly Tyler. Dr. Tyler used these funds to support semistructured interviews with a subsample of 40 (16 males and 24 females) of the project young people. Project interviewers conducted audiotaped interviews, which lasted about 1 hour. The interviews were then thematically coded by two reviewers, and the results were compared and reconciled.

Sample characteristics

The sample cohort was made up of 428 adolescents aged 16–19 years at baseline interview. Of the 428 young people, 187 were males and 241 were females; their mean age at baseline was 17.4 years. Three years later, 194 of the young people remained in the study (77 males and 117 females). Now aged 19–22 years, their mean age was 20.4 years at last contact. At baseline, slightly more than one half (58.8%) self-identified as White non-Hispanic, 21.6% said they were African American non-Hispanic, and 11.1% reported they were biracial. Only 4.5% self-identified as Hispanic, 3.3% Native American, and 0.7% Asian.

The majority of the young people (69.9%) came from cities with a population of 100,000 people or more or from suburbs of large cities. Fewer (16.1%) came from medium-sized cities, small cities, or towns of less than 100,000 people. Only 10.3% told us they were from small towns of 10,000 people or less, and a very small minority (1.4%) reported they had been raised in the country or on a farm.

All of the young people we interviewed met our criteria for being currently a runaway or currently homeless. For 14.3% of the adolescents (6.3%

males and 8.0% females), this was their first runaway episode, 13.6% (4.9% males and 8.7% females) had run away two times, and 72.1% (32.3% males and 39.8% females) had run away three or more times. At the time of their first runaway episode, 23.4% of the adolescents were living with two of their parents, 44.4% were living with mother only, and 10.3% were living with father only. Of those interviewed, 8.9% were living with a grandparent or other relative at the time of first runaway, 4.2% were living in a foster home, and 8.9% were in other living arrangements, such as group homes or institutions. At the baseline interview, nearly one half (48.6%) of the young people had spent at least one night on the streets. Of these, 22.4% had spent 1 night on the streets, 17.4% had spent 2 nights on the streets, and 60.2% had spent 3 or more nights on the streets.

Although there was considerable overlap in the reasons given for leaving home the first time, the majority (51.5%) gave "family conflict" as the primary reason for leaving home the first time, 21.7% said they left because of abuse by a caretaker, and only 9.9% said they had been told to leave or kicked out of the house the first time they left home, though an additional 2% told us they had been abandoned by their caretakers. Nearly 4% told us they left the first time because of caretaker substance abuse, and about 2% said they left home because of their own drug use.

Nearly all (88%) of the young people reported that at least one of their caretakers was employed at the time of their first runaway episode. Of those interviewed, 40% told us that their family was receiving some type of public assistance at the time they first left home. Almost 17% of the young people reported that a caretaker had not completed high school, 33.2% of the caretakers had finished high school or completed their GED, 15.2% had completed some college or vocational courses after high school, 22.9% had completed college, and about 7% had graduate school training.

The majority of the young people reported substance abuse by caretakers: 60% said that their fathers had a drug or alcohol problem, and 55.4% said their mothers had a drug or alcohol problem; 43.5% reported a sibling had a drug or alcohol problem. Nearly one half (47.7%) told us that a close family member had mental health problems, and 70.8% reported that a close family member had had "trouble with the law." Approximately two thirds (63.4%) reported that one of their caretakers had served time in jail or prison at some point in their lives.

As has been pointed out elsewhere (Holzer & Schwarz, 2004; Whitbeck, Johnson, Hoyt, & Cauce, 2004b), our lack of screening for psychoses is a major limitation of this study. Still, the rates of psychiatric disorders were very high. At baseline, approximately one third of the adolescents met lifetime criteria for major depressive episode (30.4%) or posttraumatic stress disorder (35.5%), 43.7% for alcohol abuse, 40.4% for drug abuse, 29.9% for alcohol dependence, and 75.7% for conduct disorder (Table 2.1). Nearly

Table 2.1 Lifetime Diagnoses Across Time

	Wave 1 (%) (N = 428)	Wave 13 (%) (N = 194)
Major depression	30.4	24.7
Posttraumatic stress disorder	35.5	29.4
Alcohol abuse	43.7	33.5
Alcohol dependence	29.9	19.1
Drug abuse	40.4	36.6
Conduct disorder	75.7	—
Antisocial personality disorder	—	67.5
At least one diagnosis	21.3	24.7
Two or more diagnoses	67.3	56.2

two thirds (67.3%) met lifetime criteria for two or more disorders and 21.3% met lifetime criteria for a single disorder. By Wave 13, among those with whom we were able to maintain contact, about one fourth (24.7%) met criteria for major depressive disorder, 29.4% for posttraumatic stress disorder, approximately one-third met criteria for a substance abuse disorder (33.5% alcohol abuse, 36.6% drug abuse) and 19.1% met criteria for alcohol dependence. Approximately two-thirds (67.5%) of the now young adults met criteria for antisocial personality disorder. At Wave 13, 24.7% met lifetime criteria for a single disorder, and 56.2% met criteria for two or more lifetime disorders. In the following chapters we closely consider the prevalence, comorbidity, and correlates of each of the six diagnoses for which the adolescents were screened at Waves 1 and 13.

section 2

Mental health and emerging adulthood among homeless and runaway adolescents

chapter 3

From conduct disorder to antisocial personality disorder

Disruptive behaviors from adolescence to early adulthood

With Devan M. Crawford

Criteria for conduct disorder (CD) comprise a number of disruptive behaviors. The basic requirement for the disorder is that children must "manifest a lot of these behaviors if they are to be given the diagnosis" (Angold & Costello, 2001, p. 126). This corresponds to the developmental histories of the majority of runaway and homeless adolescents. Most exhibit multiple behavioral problems prior to and after their first runaway episode (Hagen & McCarthy, 1997; Kipke, Simon, Montgomery, Unger, & Iverson, 1997; Whitbeck & Hoyt, 1999; Whitbeck, Hoyt, Yoder, Cauce, & Paradise, 2001). Many will meet lifetime diagnostic criteria for CD. Indeed, the diagnostic criteria for CD in the *Diagnostic and Statistical Manual of Mental Disorders,* third edition, revised (*DSM-III-R;* American Psychiatric Association, 1987) includes "repeated running away from home overnight" (p. 48) and the *Diagnostic and Statistical Manual of Mental Disorders,* fourth edition (*DSM-IV;* American Psychiatric Association, 2000) for CD includes "has run away from home overnight on at least two occasions while living in a parental or parental surrogate home or once without returning for a lengthy period" (p. 99).

However, there is considerable diversity of types of behaviors and combinations of behaviors that can be attributed to the disorder. A recent review article points out that estimating prevalence of CD is difficult in that "we have no agreement on what constitutes a 'true' case of CD" (Angold & Costello, 2001, p. 141). Various attempts have been made to account for the multidimensional characteristics of the diagnosis, resulting in discussions of subtypes based on clusters of similar behaviors. Although these have varied between two-factor (Quay, 1986) and three-factor models (Loeber & Coie, 2001), the most fundamental underlying

43

structure is between high-aggression conduct problems and low-aggression conduct problems (Angold & Costello). This fundamental dichotomy is based on a long history of research indicating separate developmental paths for behavior problems involving aggressive and nonaggressive behavioral problems (e.g., Achenbach, Conners, Quay, Verhulst, & Howell, 1989; Coie & Dodge, 1998; Dodge, Lochman, Harnish, Bates, & Pettit, 1997; Lipsey & Derzon, 1998; Loeber & Coie).

In this chapter, we first report the prevalence and correlates of CD among the homeless and runaway adolescents at Wave 1. We then investigate the diversity of behavioral characteristics we found among the conduct disordered adolescents. The chapter concludes with a description of characteristics of those with CD who went on to meet criteria for antisocial personality disorder (APD) at Wave 13.

Factors associated with conduct disorder in adolescence

Disruptive behavior represents the oldest and most common childhood mental health problem (Hill, 2002) and accounts for more than one half of child referrals to mental health clinics (Waschbusch, 2002). Recent reviews agree that between 5% and 10% of children and adolescents in Western industrialized societies manifest persistent aggressive, disruptive, oppositional, and noncompliant behaviors that would meet diagnostic criteria for CD (Angold & Costello, 2001; Hill; Waschbusch).

Because of its costs to society, no other childhood mental disorder has received more research attention. Numerous developmental studies have shown poor outcomes for behaviorally disruptive children including interpersonal and relationship difficulties, low academic achievement, employment problems, low socioeconomic status, and antisocial behaviors as adults (for recent reviews see Caspi & Moffitt, 1995; Hill, 2002; Hill & Maughan, 2001; Lipsey & Derzon, 1998). Although various theoretical interpretations regarding the development of CD in children and adolescents have emerged over time, they all share common predictive factors.

The severity and chronicity of CD are strongly associated with age of onset (Caspi & Moffitt, 1995; Lahey et al., 1998; Loeber, 1982, 1991). The effects of age, however, vary by type of behavioral problem. With the exception of a small percentage of highly aggressive young people whose aggressive behaviors increase and become more diverse (Loeber & Coie, 2001) aggression tends to be negatively associated with age (Cairns & Cairns, 1994; Tremblay et al., 1996). Neurological characteristics (e.g., attention deficit hyperactivity) and predisposing temperament (Lahey, Waldman, & McBurnett, 1999) interact with environmental factors for continuity and exacerbation of antisocial behaviors as children move into adolescence (Moffitt, 1997; Reid, Patterson, & Snyder, 2002). However, environmental effects are not straightforward. For example, parent–child effects tend to be reciprocal where child behaviors evoke parent responses and parent responses reinforce child behaviors (Patterson, 1982). Moreover, numerous environmental contingencies influence parent and child behaviors (e.g., stressors, daily hassles, alcohol use, economic stress; for a recent review, see Maughan, 2001).

As children move into adolescence, peer associations become increasingly influential and may be a major factor in late-onset behavioral problems (Bartusch, Lynam, Moffitt, & Silva, 1997; Fergusson, Lynskey, & Horwood, 1996). Deviant children and adolescents may be rejected by conventional peers and select into deviant peer groups where their behaviors are reinforced (Cairns & Cairns, 1994; Vitaro, Tremblay, & Bukowski, 2001).

Conduct disorder among homeless and runaway adolescents

Because running away is often preceded by or accompanied by other types of serious violations of rules (e.g., staying out at night despite parental prohibitions, truancy) and other behavioral problems, runaway and homeless adolescent are very likely to meet criteria for CD. Although we are aware of no studies that include possible neurological impairments, runaways have been shown to run from or drift out of families that are highly disorganized (Whitbeck & Hoyt, 1999), with ineffective parenting (Daddis, Braddock, Cuers, Elliott, & Kelly, 1993; Schweitzer, Hier, & Terry, 1994; Whitbeck, Hoyt, & Ackley, 1997b), and where many have experienced neglect or physical or sexual abuse (Janus, Burgess, & McCormack, 1987; Silbert & Pines, 1981; Kurtz, Kurtz, & Jarvis, 1991; Pennbridge, Yates, David, & MacKenzie, 1990; Tyler, Hoyt, Whitbeck, & Cauce, 2001a). Most have been or are experiencing academic difficulties due to previous or current truancy (Whitbeck & Hoyt), and many have histories of delinquent behaviors and alcohol and drug use prior to and concurrent with running away (Hagen & McCarthy, 1997; Kipke, Montgomery, & MacKenzie, 1997; Koopman, Rosario, & Rotheram-Borus, 1994).

We were unable to locate any study that investigated age of onset of CD among runaways; however, often adolescents run the first time at a very young age (i.e., 12–13 years) indicating an early onset of conduct problems (Whitbeck & Hoyt, 1999). We also know little about peer networks prior to running away, but there is extensive evidence that points to deviant peer associations while the adolescents are on their own (Bao, Whitbeck, & Hoyt, 2000; Hagen & McCarthy, 1997; Johnson, Whitbeck, & Hoyt, 2005a;

Kipke, Montgomery, Simon, Unger, & Johnson, 1997; Whitbeck & Hoyt). In concert with deviant peer group affiliation, almost all runaway adolescents are sexually active and at high risk for sexually transmitted disease and sexual exploitation (Kipke, Montgomery, Simon, Unger, et al., 1997; Rotheram-Borus et al., 1992; Tyler, Hoyt, Whitbeck, & Cauce, 2001b; Tyler, Whitbeck, Hoyt, & Yoder, 2000).

In summary, because of runaways' propensity for multiple behavioral problems, most of the research focuses on the antisocial behaviors in which they are involved. However, there appears to be a broad spectrum of runaways, some of whom engage in many antisocial behaviors, some who engage in few, some who may be highly aggressive, and others who are much less so. Although many will meet diagnostic criteria for CD, the diagnosis does not capture this diversity of experience and risk.

Diagnostic studies of conduct disorder among homeless and runaway adolescents

We were able to locate only five studies of homeless and runaway adolescents that employed diagnostic indices or complete diagnostic interviews for CD. Each of these was confined to one site, usually a single shelter in a large city. In all but one, only sheltered young people were interviewed (no street intercepts); sample sizes were usually very small.

Feitel and colleagues used the complete Diagnostic Interview for Children and Adolescents-Revised (DICA-R) based on the *DSM-III-R* (American Psychiatric Association, 1987) to assess 150 New York City Covenant House adolescents (mean age = 18.5 years) in eight diagnostic categories. Of the sample, 59% met criteria for CD (Feitel, Margetson, Chamas, & Lipman, 1992).

Based on the Diagnostic Interview Schedule for Children-Revised (DISC-R), Booth and Zhang (1997) reported that 54% of adolescents (60% of females; 50% of males) from a sample of 219 runaway and homeless adolescents (mean age = 17.4 years) interviewed in a single drop center met *DSM-III-R* (American Psychiatric Association, 1987) criteria for CD.

Buckner and Bassuk (1997) conducted diagnostic interviews using the Diagnostic Interview Schedule for Children (DISC-2.3) with a very small sample of 41 homeless adolescents (mean age = 11.8 years) who were part of a controlled diagnostic study (housed and never homeless vs. homeless) in Worcester, Massachusetts. Of the homeless adolescents surveyed, 17% met lifetime criteria for CD or oppositional defiant disorder.

A Detroit area study (McCaskill, Toro, & Wolfe, 1998) provided diagnostic (DISC 2.3) comparisons between 118 housed and 118 "homeless" adolescents (mean age = 14.7 years). However, of those designated to be "homeless," two thirds (66%) had been away from home 1 week or less and had never been homeless before this episode (McCaskill et al., p. 311). Moreover, 27% of the shelter sample were not runaways; rather, they were "seeking some type of temporary intervention services from the shelter" (McCaskill et al., p. 311). Prevalence rates based on the DISC-R (*DSM-III-R* [American Psychiatric Association, 1987] criteria) were 39% for "disruptive behavior." The adolescents designated as homeless were significantly more likely to meet criteria for disruptive behavior than the housed comparison group.

The largest diagnostic study of homeless and runaway adolescents to date was conducted by Cauce and colleagues (Cauce et al., 2000). Using the DISC-R, 364 adolescents (mean age = 16.4 years) were interviewed in shelters and on the streets in Seattle, Washington, and in two nearby communities. More than one half of the sample (53%) met criteria for CD. Prevalence rates for CD in the samples of adolescents who could be confidently classified as "homeless" were very similar: 54% in the Booth and Zhang (1997) study, 59% in the New York City study (Feitel et al., 1992), and 53% in the Seattle area sample.

Prevalence and comorbidity of conduct disorder among runaway and homeless adolescents

Slightly more than three fourths (75.7%) of the runaway and homeless adolescents in our study met lifetime criteria for CD (Table 3.1). Males (82.9%) were significantly more likely than females (70.1%) to meet criteria for the disorder. Because all of the adolescents were runaways, we were curious to know how much of the prevalence was accounted for by endorsing criteria that had to do with running away. Deleting the runaway item from the diagnostic criteria resulted in a loss of 9.3% in total prevalence. The decrease in prevalence from the deletion of running away from the diagnostic criteria was greater for females (13.3%) than for males

Table 3.1 Conduct Disorder (CD) Lifetime Diagnosis Among Homeless and Runaway Adolescents at Wave 1 ($N = 428$)

	Total (%)	Male (%)	Female (%)
CD	75.7	**82.9***	70.1
CD without runaway items	66.4	**78.6***	56.8
CD 10 years or younger	47.0	**58.8***	37.8
Aggressive CD	51.9	**60.6***	43.8

* $p < .01$ between males and females.

(4.3%), indicating that males were more likely to be engaged in a wider array of disruptive behaviors other than running away. Nearly one half (47%) of the adolescents met criteria for CD at age 10 years or before. Males (58.8%) were significantly more likely to report early onset CD than were females (37.8%).

High and low aggression among adolescents meeting criteria for CD

To investigate whether the adolescents' behaviors grouped them into high- and low-aggression subgroups, latent class analyses were performed on the aggression items from the DISC-R Conduct Disorder criteria (Clogg, 1995; McCutcheon, 1987). This procedure allowed us to see if there were respondents who shared similar patterns of responses to the nine aggressive behavior indicators. The analysis starts by examining a one-cluster solution, followed by a two-cluster solution, until the number of clusters emerges that provides an optimal solution. The criteria for selection of the best-fitting model involve examining the model fit likelihood ratio chi-squared statistic (L^2) as well as the model Bayesian information criterion (BIC) (Rafferty, 1996). The optimal solution is one where we obtain an acceptable model fit (L^2 criteria) and where moving to a model estimating an additional cluster does not significantly improve on the fit of the prior model (change in L^2 and BIC criteria). The BIC takes into account the parsimony of the model in the context of the overall fit. Using these criteria, the best-fitting model for the current data was obtained for a two-cluster solution.

The adolescents almost equally split between the clusters (51.9% in Cluster 1, 48.1% in Cluster 2). Males (60.6%) were significantly more likely to be included in the high-aggression subgroup than were females (43.8%). The pattern found in the high-aggression cluster (Cluster 1) is characterized by significantly higher proportions reporting affirmative responses to 7 of the 9 aggressive behaviors (Table 3.2). The only dimensions where there were not significant differences were for the very low incidence behaviors of sexual assault and purposeful cruelty to humans. The differences between the low- and high-aggression clusters are particularly strong for starting fights (25.5% compared with 77.5%), trying to hurt others (25.9% compared with 79.6%), and assaulting another with a weapon (8.5% compared with 56.8%).

Comorbidity

Among conduct disordered adolescents, only 18% met criteria for CD alone. Table 3.3 presents comorbidity patterns by gender and age of onset of CD. We designated those who met criteria at age 10 years or below as "early onset." There were no statistically significant differences in patterns of

Table 3.2 Percent With Affirmative Responses to
Aggression by Cluster

Item	Cluster 1 (%)	Cluster 2 (%)
Animal	**33.0***	12.0
Sexual	1.9	0.0
Bully	**53.3***	27.6
Threat	**71.0***	41.2
Fight	**100.0***	75.9
Start fight	**77.5*****	25.5
Try hurt	**79.6*****	25.9
Cruel	5.9	1.5
Weapon	**56.8*****	8.5

* $p < .05$.
** $p < .01$.

Table 3.3 Comorbidity of Early Versus Late Conduct Disorder (CD) at Wave 1

	All ($N = 324$)		Male ($n = 155$)		Female ($n = 169$)	
	Early CD (%)	Late CD (%)	Early CD (%)	Late CD (%)	Early CD (%)	Late CD (%)
CD and MDE	36.8	30.4	29.5	28.8	44.2	31.7
CD and PTSD	42.5	36.3	34.1	23.4	51.2	47.6
CD and alcohol abuse	56.3	51.1	54.5	55.0	58.1	47.6
CD and drug abuse	47.1	48.5	43.2	54.1	51.2	43.7
Any disorder	29.9	28.7	36.4	36.9	23.3	21.4
Two or more disorders	56.3	51.9	47.7	46.8	65.1	56.3

comorbidity by age of onset among the adolescents. Rates of comorbidity with CD were very high, particularly with the substance abuse disorders. About one half of CD runaways and homeless adolescents also met criteria for alcohol or drug abuse regardless of gender. A breakdown of patterns of comorbidity between the high-aggression and low-aggression clusters of conduct-disordered adolescents (not shown in tables) indicated no statistically significant differences between the clusters. The comorbidity percentages were essentially the same as those for early and late onset CD.

Problem behaviors among CD and non-CD adolescents

As one would expect, conduct-disordered adolescents account for the majority of problem behaviors and street crime among the runaways (Table 3.4). The magnitude of the differences in problem behaviors was often very great, particularly among the girls. The one area where behaviors converged for CD and non-CD adolescents and for boys and girls was fighting. Nearly all of the CD males (94.8%) and females (81.7%) had been involved in a fight where someone was hurt or could have been hurt, and more than one half of non-CD males and females had also fought. The differences had to do with who started the fight. About one half of CD males (56.8%) and females (46.7%) reported they had started a fight where someone was hurt or could have been hurt compared with 15.6% of non-CD males and 9.7% of non-CD females. The gender patterns of problem behaviors suggest that CD boys are highly aggressive and that CD girls are much more aggressive than non-CD girls.

The reported behaviors from in-depth interviews add even more evidence that the lives of homeless and runaway adolescents can be very violent and that day-to-day interactions are often coercive. For example, one 18-year-old male runaway recounted his experiences while in a group home. He told us that he "got in a fight every week at least for 3 and a half months [when he] was there the first time." He was both physically restrained and medicated to control his physical aggression. Another told us that he was "kicked out" of a foster home for "starting fights with other people in the apartment complex" (male, aged 19 years). For some, there is the potential that threats of violence can become very serious. For example, one young man (aged 18 years) with a history of violent outbursts threatened his teacher at a group home and ended up in jail:

> I snapped and told her that one day I might just show up on her doorstep, since I knew where she lived, with a baseball bat and I might just bludgeon her to death, and I believe I went directly to jail after that.

The levels of various kinds of property crimes were very high, particularly among CD runaway and homeless males. As one 20-year-old male put it:

> I'm a thief from way back. I steal anything—anything under the sun, you name it, I could probably steal it and get away with it. (Laughs) You know, there's no end to the list of things I can steal; I can steal cars, you just name it. I just know how to and that's not

Table 3.4 Problem Behaviors Among Conduct-Disordered Adolescents at Wave 1

Deviant Behavior	Total (N = 428)		Male (n = 187)		Female (n = 241)	
Have you ever ...	Non CD (%)	CD (%)	Non CD (%)	CD (%)	Non CD (%)	CD (%)
Secretly stolen money or other things from people you lived with?						
Yes	29.8	**62.0*****	28.1	**61.9*****	30.6	**62.1*****
Shoplifted, that is, stolen something from a store when you thought no one was looking?						
Yes	40.4	**84.9*****	43.8	**88.4*****	38.9	**81.7*****
Stolen from anyone else when they weren't around or weren't looking?						
Yes	13.5	**49.4*****	15.6	**58.7*****	12.5	**40.8*****
Faked someone's name on a check or used someone's credit card without permission?						
Yes	3.8	**19.8*****	6.3	**20.0**	2.8	**19.5*****
Snatched someone's purse or jewelry?						
Yes	0.0	**9.0****	0.0	**12.9***	0.0	**5.3***
Held someone up or attacked somebody to steal from them?						
Yes	0.0	**7.4****	0.0	**14.2***	0.0	1.2
Threatened someone in order to steal from them?						
Yes	0.0	**9.9*****	0.0	**17.4***	0.0	3.0
Lied to get money or something else that you wanted?						
Yes	24.0	**72.2*****	15.6	**72.9*****	27.8	**71.6*****
Lied so that you wouldn't have to pay back money or to get out of something important?						
Yes	20.2	**64.2*****	18.8	**67.1*****	20.8	**61.5*****
Broken into a house, building, or car?						
Yes	6.7	**43.8*****	12.5	**59.4*****	4.2	**29.6*****
Broken something or messed up some place on purpose?						
Yes	8.7	**55.2*****	15.6	**71.0*****	5.6	**40.8*****
Broken or damaged someone else's things on purpose?						
Yes	7.7	**56.2*****	3.1	**63.9*****	9.7	**49.1*****
Started a fire that caused damage or hurt someone?						
Yes	5.8	**16.7****	12.5	21.9	2.8	**11.8***

— continued

Table 3.4 Problem Behaviors Among Conduct-Disordered Adolescents at Wave 1

Deviant Behavior	Total (N = 428)		Male (n = 187)		Female (n = 241)	
	Non CD (%)	CD (%)	Non CD (%)	CD (%)	Non CD (%)	CD (%)
Have you ever …						
Been physically cruel to animals or hurt them on purpose?						
Yes	2.9	22.5***	6.3	36.1***	1.4	10.1*
Had a sexual experience with another person?						
Yes	83.5	95.4***	77.4	95.5***	86.1	95.3*
Hurt or threaten someone to make them do something sexual that they didn't want to do?						
Yes	0.0	0.9	0.0	1.9	0.0	0.0
Bullied someone?						
Yes	16.3	50.3***	9.4	53.5***	19.4	47.3***
Threatened or frightened someone on purpose?						
Yes	16.3	68.2***	15.6	73.5***	16.7	63.3***
Been in a physical fight in which someone was hurt or could have been hurt?						
Yes	57.7	88.0***	56.3	94.8***	58.3	81.7***
Started a physical fight in which someone was hurt or could have been hurt?						
Yes	11.5	51.5***	15.6	56.8***	9.7	46.7***
Tried to hurt someone badly or been physically cruel to someone?						
Yes	16.3	52.8***	12.5	57.4***	18.1	48.5***
Hurt someone with a weapon like a bat, brick, broken bottle, gun, or knife?						
Yes	1.9	32.7***	0.0	43.2***	2.8	23.1***
Threatened someone with a weapon like a bat, brick, broken bottle, gun, or knife?						
Yes	12.5	49.4***	21.9	61.3***	8.3	38.5***

* $p < .05$ between CD and non-CD.
** $p < .01$ between CD and non-CD.
*** $p < .001$ between CD and non-CD.

> 'cause I'm a hardened criminal; that's because I was
> kicked on the street and I had to learn. I had to learn
> a way to survive and survive fast, and that's what
> you catch on to is stealing and selling drugs.

Some of the criminal behaviors involved survival strategies: "When I was on the run, I stole. I used to steal from grocery stores and stuff to get food" (female, aged 19 years). Young women were also involved in deviant survival strategies. One woman (aged 19 years) reported, "Yeah I've stole some people's cars…. (and) like CDs, sunglasses if they look expensive…. Uh, have sex for money." A young woman (aged 21 years) told us:

> Because after three weeks of living with the acquain-
> tances, I had been thrown out of the place so I was
> living on the streets. I was living underneath the
> bridges, um, so the only way that I could get my food
> was to steal it. The only way I could get the clothing
> was to steal it. Well when I went into Younker's I
> end up stealing a belt, a wallet and sunglasses and
> got caught, and, come to find out, I had a warrant.
> That's when I found out about the warrant.

But at other times the motive seemed to be the thrill or the expression of anger: "It was me and couple of my friends, and we just, I don't know, this car was left on down in west Omaha, and we stole it and we wrecked it off a bridge" (male, aged 19 years). For the most part, criminal behavior was viewed as how one survived in a difficult environment. It was partly a survival strategy and partly protective. One 20-year-old male summed it up very succinctly:

> I tell you that's a quick way to make yourself safe on
> the street to gain respect from people on the streets.
> That's the way to do it, you know; I mean you can't
> live on the streets without being ruthless. If you're
> not ruthless you're fucked, that's just the way it
> works. Because living on the streets it's basically a
> game. You always got to be under the assumption
> that the people that you're trusting are out to get
> you. That's just the way it works. If you don't live
> with that reality, if you don't think about that real-
> ity, you're going to end up getting screwed.

Victimization of homeless and runaway adolescents

With high rates of delinquent behaviors come high rates of victimization (Tyler, Whitbeck, Hoyt, & Cauce, 2004; Whitbeck et al., 2001). The adolescents who met criteria for CD were about two times as likely as non-CD adolescents to be beaten up (39.5% vs. 18.3%), robbed (31.5% vs. 16.3%), threatened with a weapon (53.4% vs. 28.8%), or assaulted with a weapon (28.1% vs. 11.5%) (Table 3.5). Conduct-disordered girls (34.3%) were nearly twice as likely to report sexual assault than non-CD girls (18.1%). What is noteworthy about these comparisons is not so much the rates of victimization among the highly delinquent adolescents but the high rates among those who did not meet criteria for CD. Among the non-CD runaway males, nearly one half (40.6%) reported having been threatened with a weapon at some point, one fourth had been beaten up when on the streets, and 21.9% had been robbed on the streets. Being on the streets is a dangerous regardless of the adolescents' behaviors, but it is clear that engaging in delinquent acts increases the risk for victimization among both male and female runaways.

Street gangs and conduct disordered runaways

One half of male runaways and approximately one third of female runaways told us that they were aware of street gangs. There were no

Table 3.5 Victimization by Conduct Disorder (CD) and Gender at Wave 1

	All (N = 428)		Male (n = 187)		Female (n = 241)	
	Non-CD (%)	CD (%)	Non-CD (%)	CD (%)	Non-CD (%)	CD (%)
Beat up	18.3	**39.5***	25.0	39.4	15.3	**39.6***
Robbed	16.3	**31.5**	21.9	31.0	13.9	**32.0**
Threatened weapon	28.8	**53.4***	40.6	**59.4†**	23.6	**47.9***
Assaulted weapon	11.5	**28.1***	15.6	**36.8***	9.7	**20.1***
Sexual favors	26.0	**37.2***	25.0	20.8	26.4	**52.1***
Sexually assaulted	13.5	19.8	3.1	3.9	18.1	**34.3***

† *p* < .10 between CD and non-CD.
* *p* < .05 between CD and non-CD.
** *p* < .01 between CD and non-CD.
*** *p* < .001 between CD and non-CD.

significant differences between males who met criteria for CD and those who did not. However, conduct-disordered females (55.6%) were much more likely than non-CD females (36.1%) to be aware of gangs (Table 3.6). Similarly, CD females (26.6%) were nearly three times more likely than non-CD females (9.7%) to say they had been threatened or bothered by a street gang. There was no significant difference in regards to gang threats between CD and non-CD males. Both CD males (44.5%) and CD females (34.9%) were more likely to report that they had participated in gang activities than non-CD males (28.1%) and females (9.7%). Nearly two thirds (61.9%) of the CD males and approximately one half of the CD females (53.8%) had been asked to join a gang. A full 31% of CD males and 21.3% of CD females had been through a gang initiation, with 21.9% of CD males and 10.7% of CD females reporting that they currently considered themselves gang members.

Although rates of gang activities were quite low among non-CD females, the amount of gang contact and involvement among non-CD

Table 3.6 Gang Participation by Conduct Disorder (CD) and Gender at Wave 1

	All (N = 428)		Male (n = 187)		Female (n = 241)	
	Non-CD (%)	CD (%)	Non-CD (%)	CD (%)	Non-CD (%)	CD (%)
Aware of gangs						
Yes	**40.4****	57.4	50.0	59.4	**36.1****	55.6
Threatened or bothered by gangs						
Ever	**17.3*****	36.1	34.4	46.5	**9.7****	26.6
Participated in gang activity						
Yes	**15.4*****	39.5	**28.1**[a]	44.5	**9.7*****	34.9
Asked to join gang						
Yes	**26.9*****	57.7	**40.6***	61.9	**20.8*****	53.8
Been through gang initiation						
Yes	**11.5****	25.9	28.1	31.0	**4.2*****	21.3
Member of gang						
Yes	8.7[b]	16.1	18.8	21.9	4.2[c]	10.7

* $p < .05$ between CD and non-CD.
** $p < .01$ between CD and non-CD.
*** $p < .001$ between CD and non-CD.
[a] $p = .087$, $n = 78$ between CD and non-CD
[b] $p = .059$, $n = 61$ between CD and non-CD
[c] $p = .10$, $n = 21$ between CD and non-CD

males was considerable. It appears that gangs are ubiquitous in the street life of young men. There were no significant differences between CD and non-CD males for awareness, threats, gang initiation, and gang membership. This raises questions about the role of gangs for males on the streets. They could serve as a mechanism for delinquent activity but also be viewed as protective among those less prone to delinquent behaviors. For example, one young man (aged 21 years) told us:

> I was in a gang their gang name is Bloods. This was while I was in the group home. Never did stick nobody or shoot nobody or anything like that. But mainly what I did was I covered my other gang partners' backs when they had trouble I'd back them up. Mainly I was like a bodyguard for them. If someone started hitting on them I'd knock the person out that did it. Really wasn't in a lot of riots or anything. I was in one riot. And that was because the gal that was in our gang a guy had threatened to hit her and me and my other gang members was like you hit her and we'll be on you basically white on rice. And he didn't take us seriously he hit her and um we pounced on him and then his friend got involved and ended up being like around 20 or 30 people fighting all together. We won, but that's not the point. I'm not proud of it but I've hurt people and I can't even count how many. For no reason just because they looked at me wrong. I'd get up in their face and you know they would start yelling at me and now they're down you know. Really don't like talking about it because then people think that I brag about it.

From conduct disorder to antisocial personality disorder

The prevalence of antisocial personality disorder (APD) in the general population is between 4% (Moran, 1999; Robins, Tipp, & Przybeck, 1991) and 6% (Moran, 1999; Newman, Moffitt, Caspi, Magdom, Silva, & Stanton, 1996; Swanson, Bland, & Newman, 1994). Among homeless adults the lifetime prevalence for APD has been estimated at about one fifth, or 21% (Koegel, Burnam, & Farr, 1988) to one fourth, or 25% (North, Smith, & Spitznagel, 1993) of homeless males. Almost 80% of National Comorbidity

Table 3.7 Percent Who Report Antisocial Personality
Disorder (APD) at Wave 13

	All (%)	Male (%)	Female (%)
Conduct disorder (N =146)	87.9	86.2	89.3
Early conduct disorder (N =41)	85.4	84.2	86.4
High aggression (N = 72)	87.5	84.2	91.2

Survey respondents with APD met criteria for a lifetime substance abuse disorder (Kessler, Nelson, McGonagle, Edlund, Frank, & Leaf, 1996). Approximately 50% of those who meet criteria for a personality disorder have two or more co-occurring personality disorders (Loranger, Susman, Oldham, & Russakoff, 1987; Pfohl, Coryell, Zimmerman, & Stangl, 1986; Oldham, Skodol, Kellman, Hyler, Rosnick, & Daves, 1995).

In general population studies about 30% to 50% of adolescents who meet criteria for CD will meet criteria of antisocial personality disorder as adults (Loeber, Burke, & Lahey, 2002; Robins, 1991; Robins et al., 1991). There are numerous conceptualizations of pathways to antisocial personality, the most influential of which posit early onset of CD symptoms (Moffitt, Caspi, Dickson, Silva, & Stanton, 1996; Swanson et al., 1994), aggression (Loeber, 1988a; Lynam, 1996; Moffitt et al., 1996), attention deficit hyperactivity disorder (Loeber, 1988b; Schachar, Rutter, & Smith, 1981), callousness and lack empathy (Loeber et al., 2002), and comorbid substance abuse (Bukstein, Brent, & Kraminer, 1989; Myers, Stewart, & Brown, 1998) as important predictors of developing APD in early adulthood.

Although we were aware that the runaways and homeless adolescents in our study exhibited multiple risks for later APD, we were surprised to find that 87.9% of those who met criteria for CD at Wave 1 met criteria for APD at final evaluation (Table 3.7). The percentages of the CD adolescents who met criteria for APD as young adults did not vary significantly by age of onset at 10 years or younger (85.4%) or by inclusion in the high-aggression cluster of adolescents (87.5%), nor did the percentages vary significantly by gender of adolescent. In fact, the CD males (86.2%) were slightly less likely than CD females (89.3%) to meet APD criteria in young adulthood.

Comorbidity with APD

About one third (32.1%) of the Wave 13 APD young adults also met criteria for MDE (Table 3.8). The APD young women (40.5%) were more likely than

Table 3.8 Comorbidity With Antisocial Personality Disorder (APD) at Wave 13 ($N = 131$)

	Total (%)	Male (%)	Female (%)
APD and MDE	32.1	26.3	36.5
APD and PTSD	32.8	22.8	**40.5***
APD and alcohol abuse	40.5	47.4	35.1
APD and drug abuse	49.6	63.2	**39.2****
APD and one disorder	21.4	24.6	18.9
APD and two or more disorders	55.7	57.9	54.1

* $p < .05$ between CD and non-CD between male and female.
** $p < .001$ between CD and non-CD between male and female.

the APD young men (22.8%) to also meet criteria for PTSD. Nearly one half (47.4%) of the APD males also met criteria for alcohol abuse compared with one third of the APD females (35.1%). Approximately three fifths (63.2%) of the APD males also met criteria for drug abuse, as did 39.2% of the APD females. Nearly all of the APD young adults (77.1%) met criteria for at least one of the other study disorders, and slightly more than one half (55.7%) met criteria for two or more of the other disorders.

Summary and discussion

The stability of problem behaviors among the runaway and homeless adolescents was remarkable. About 83% of the adolescent males and 70% of the adolescent females met criteria for CD at ages 16–19 years. Of those who remained in the study until they were 19–22 years, 87.9% of the conduct-disordered adolescents met criteria for APD as young adults. Because nearly all of the CD adolescents later met criteria for APD, there was so little variance in the CD–APD relationship that we could not fit predictive regression models for APD at Wave 13. Although the CD adolescents scored higher on almost every measure of problem behaviors and associated victimization at baseline, there was no distinction between those in the high- and low-aggression clusters in adult outcomes. The stability of behavioral problems from adolescence to early adulthood among runaway and homeless adolescents was about twice that expected among CD adolescents in the general population.

The full-sample prevalence rate for APD (CD and non-CD adolescents) was 67.5%. This prevalence rate is higher than projections of APD from prison samples where prevalence ranges from 63% to 33% (Moran, 1999), higher than rates for adolescents from clinical samples of inpatient substance abusers (61%), and two to three times higher than rates from diagnostic studies for homeless adults (Koegel et al., 1988; North et al., 1993).

Theoretical implications

This evidence of the stability of problem behaviors from adolescence into young adulthood among runaway and homeless adolescents is disturbing. In a later chapter we examine the possibility that the context of homelessness at this stage of life inflates the prevalence estimates for various diagnoses including CD and APD. Regardless, the pattern is clearly one of high stability of antisocial behaviors among the adolescents. The findings are congruent with several theories of the stability of maladaptive behaviors across time but in our opinion come closest to Moffitt's (1997) conceptualization of life course persistent antisocial behaviors and our own life course based amplification of problem behavior models (Whitbeck & Hoyt, 1999; Whitbeck, Hoyt, & Yoder, 1999). Chronic running away or homelessness may be an important indicator of life course persistent antisocial behaviors. The break from adult supervision and influence is often early and irreversible. Although we show in subsequent chapters that for some there may be a renewal of family relationships in early adulthood, by the time reconciliation occurs these relationships have evolved from supervisory to adult child–parent relationships. Running away appears to be a critical step in a self-reinforcing trajectory that is difficult to overcome and that will shape the course of early adult lives. As we continue to show in the following chapters, experiences on streets and during periods of independence amplify early developmental deficits and contribute to the continuity of problem behaviors and psychological difficulties.

Policy implications

Kessler and colleagues pointed out that the social burden of mental illness derives primarily from those who have early onset disorders and comorbid disorders (Kessler, Berglund, Demler, Jin, & Walters, 2005). Given the poor prognosis for APD (Loeber, Green, & Lahey, 2003) and the high levels of comorbidity, these young people will require substantial resources over the course of their lives. These findings are indicative of the urgent need for early and effective prevention efforts for high-risk children (see Farrington & Coid, 2003). As we work through the various psychiatric diagnoses and symptoms in this volume and describe the social contexts of these young people it will become clear that the societal burden of current national and state policies of benign neglect is very great. It should also become apparent that what we have been doing is not working. As we point out, chapter by chapter, the current child protection, foster home, group home, juvenile justice approaches make the wrong assumptions about runaways, provide the wrong solutions, and often contribute to the negative chains of events that shape the lives of these young people.

Conclusions

Conduct-disordered adolescents who self-identify as runaways or homeless at 16–19 years may well be the most at-risk population of young people in our nation. They are ensnared in a developmental trajectory where the accumulated consequences of a disorganized often abusive family environment, lack of adult influence and attachment, and early independence make change very difficult. Moreover, innovative adaptations necessary for survival on the streets increase the likelihood of negative adult outcomes by reinforcing and adding to existing repertoires of antisocial behaviors (Whitbeck et al., 1999).

As dismaying as these findings may be, the following chapters attest that focusing simply on antisocial behaviors among these young people is far from the whole story. Depression, PTSD, and substance use all affect their attempts to adapt to life on their own in difficult circumstances, their ability to establish adult relationships and to enter the labor force as they make the transition to young adulthood. These varying influences may affect the type and duration of antisocial behaviors. For example, internalization symptoms may moderate antisocial behaviors, and hard drug use may increase its likelihood. Other influences such as forming stable intimate relationships and finding conventional means of self-support may also mitigate problem behaviors. The stories of these adolescents are complex and individual; their hopes and aspirations are those of any other adolescent. If we focus only on their antisocial trajectories we miss the traumatic effects of running away and potential points of intervention.

chapter 4

Adolescent major depressive episodes and emerging adulthood

With Devan M. Crawford

Although there have been no national epidemiological studies focusing specifically on adolescents, numerous small community samples and clinical studies provide estimates of prevalence of depressive disorders among this age group. Nearly one in six children and adolescents admitted to psychiatric hospitals has an intake diagnosis of depressive disorder (Silver, 1988). Community studies indicate lifetime prevalence rates of 10% to 20% of adolescents in the general population (Reynolds, 1992; 1994). There is also evidence that rates of depression among children and adolescents are rising (Klerman, 1988; Klerman & Weissman, 1989). Moreover, depressive disorders rarely occur alone (Angold & Costello, 1993), and comorbidity may exacerbate the severity of both depression and co-occurring mental disorders (Angold & Costello, 2001).

Recent symptom studies have indicated high rates of depressive symptoms and co-occurring conduct and substance abuse problems among runaway and homeless adolescents (Whitbeck, Hoyt, & Bao, 2000). However, diagnostic studies are few and sometimes conflicting regarding the extent of depressive disorders among this population. This chapter presents lifetime and 12-month prevalence rates of major depressive episode (MDE) and comorbidity rates. We also investigate depressive symptoms across time and use multivariate analyses to investigate factors associated with meeting criteria for MDE in early adulthood.

Adolescent depressive disorders

Once a topic of controversy (e.g., Cytryn & McKnew, 1972; Glazer, 1967; Lefkowitz & Burton, 1978; Rie, 1966), studies of child and adolescent depression have proliferated over the past 2 decades. Now considered essentially equivalent to adult depression (Ambrosini & Puig-Antich, 1985), work has progressed to estimating prevalence and risk factors for adolescent depressive disorders. Diagnostic studies indicate a range of lifetime prevalence rates. Deykin and associates found a prevalence of 6.8% for depressive disorders among adolescents aged 16–19 years (Deykin, Levy, & Wells, 1987). Kashani and colleagues reported a prevalence rate of 8% for major depressive disorder among younger adolescents aged 14–16 years (Kashani et al., 1987). Lewinsohn and associates found a lifetime prevalence rate of 20.4% in a community sample of 1,170 adolescents aged 15–18 years (Lewinsohn, Rohde, Seeley, & Hops, 1991). Findings from the National Comorbidity Survey (NCS) indicate lifetime prevalence rates of major depressive episodes of 11% for males and 20.8% for females aged 15–24 years (Blazer, Kessler, McConagle, & Swartz, 1994).

According to a review of studies pertaining to comorbidity and depression among adolescents the "presence of depression increases the likelihood of another disorder up to 100-fold; in most cases, the increase is of the order of 20-fold" (Angold & Costello, 1993, p. 1783). Rates for comorbidity of depression and conduct/oppositional defiant disorder ranged from 22% to 83% and for depression and anxiety disorder 30% to 75%. Biederman and colleagues found that of 136 children who met criteria for major depression, 95% had at least one comorbid disorder, and more than 80% had two or more comorbid disorders. The most likely dual diagnoses were for behavioral disorders (e.g., 74% attention deficit hyperactivity disorder [ADHD], 73% oppositional defiant disorder, and 27% conduct disorder [CD]) (Biederman, Faraone, Mick, & Lelon, 1991). Simonoff and colleagues found that approximately 77% of depressed children and adolescents met criteria for one other disorder and that 27% of the subjects met criteria for two or more disorders (Simonoff et al., 1997). Results from the NCS indicate that comorbidity is most likely among the youngest cohort (15–24-year-olds), with the highest levels among those with early onset (Blazer et al., 1994). Patterns of comorbidity appear to differ by gender. Adolescent males are more likely to be comorbid for oppositional defiant disorder and conduct disorder. Depressed adolescent females are more likely to manifest comorbid eating disorders (Rohde, Lewinsohn, & Seeley, 1991).

Factors associated with adolescent depression

Numerous factors have been found to be associated with adolescent depression and depressive symptoms in the past 2 decades. There is evidence that early-onset depressive disorders are particularly more likely among adolescents with first-degree relatives with major depression (for reviews see Beardslee & Wheelock, 1994; Harrington et al., 1997). Potential hereditary effects are enhanced by effects of parental psychopathology on the parent–child relationship and family environment (Downey & Coyne, 1990). Rejecting or emotionally unavailable parents (Burge & Hammen,

1991) and living in families with high levels of marital or family conflict (Burbach & Borduin, 1986; Forehand, McCombs, Long, Brody, & Fauber, 1988; Puig-Antich et al., 1993) increase risk for depressive symptoms. Children, particularly girls, whose parents are divorced are at greater risk (Feldman, Rubinstein, & Rubin, 1988; Wallerstein & Corbin, 1991), as are children in lower socioeconomic environments (Garrison, Schlucter, Schoenbach, & Kaplan, 1989) and children in economically distressed families (Conger, Conger, Elder, Lorenz, Simons, & Whitbeck, 1992; 1993). Children with histories of maltreatment and physical or sexual abuse are at particular risk for depressive symptoms (Downey & Walker, 1992; Finkelhor, 1984; Kaufman, 1991). Young people with depressive symptoms report more negative life events in their own lives and in those of family members (Compas, Howell, Phares, Williams, & Ledoux, 1989) and more daily stressors (Wagner, Compas, & Howell, 1988). They also report lower levels of social support available to them to help cope with stressful events (Daniels & Moos, 1990). Depressed adolescents often view themselves as unpopular with peers and as having poor relationships with peers (Puig-Antich, Lukens, Davies, Goetz, Brennen-Quattrock, & Todak, 1985).

Risk factors for depression among homeless and runaway adolescents

Runaway and homeless adolescents fall into nearly all of the risk categories enumerated in the adolescent depression literature. Recent work has shown convincingly that runaways experience high rates of family disorganization, ineffective parenting, and physical or sexual abuse. Homeless and runaway adolescents have few social resources, low levels of social support (Johnson, Whitbeck, & Hoyt, 2005a), and high levels of daily stressors associated with being on their own alone (Whitbeck, Hoyt, & Ackley, 1997b) or coping with life in a homeless and runaway youth shelter. Running away is in itself a major source of stress for young people. Leaving even a disorganized family and losing familiar routines of school and home are extremely disruptive for young lives. Time spent on the streets or shelters exposes the adolescents to novel situations, unfamiliar and threatening surroundings, hunger, lack of sleep, and new, often unpredictable, associates.

As noted in Chapter 1, the stress associated with homelessness induces externalizing problematic behaviors associated with survival strategies and internalizing symptoms in response to exposure to dangerous situations, such as a heightened sense of vulnerability, hypervigilance, anxiety, and fear (Goodman, Saxe & Harvey, 1991). Interrupted sleep patterns because of the lack of a secure place to rest along with irregular meals and poor nutrition may result in fatigue and lack of energy. Loss of support systems, absence of nurturing adults, and loneliness may contribute to a sense of low self-worth and hopelessness. All of these situational factors should serve to induce depressive symptoms that are largely situational and may remit when the adolescent is securely housed, safe, and in a familiar routine.

Diagnostic studies of depression among homeless and runaway adolescents

We located only four studies of homeless and runaway adolescents that employed diagnostic indices or complete diagnostic interviews for depressive disorders. Each of these was confined to one site, usually a single shelter in a large city. In all but one, only sheltered young people were interviewed (no street intercepts), and sample sizes were usually very small. Several of the studies report prevalence of depressive disorders, but only one addresses comorbidity. Probably because of the wide variation in samples and methods, these studies often report conflicting prevalence rates, lending confusion regarding the extent and seriousness of depressive disorders among these young people.

Using indices from the Diagnostic Interview Schedule (DIS), Mundy and colleagues interviewed 96 homeless youth (mean age = 16.1) in shelters and on the streets of Los Angeles (Mundy, Robertson, Robertson, & Greenblatt, 1990). They found that 20% scored above the clinical cutoff on the Childhood Depression Inventory (CDI) (Kovacs, 1981). Based on individual items from the DIS depression index, 62% reported suicidal ideation, and 46% had attempted suicide. Feitel and colleagues used the complete Diagnostic Interview for Children and Adolescents-Revised (DICA-R) based on the *Diagnostic and Statistical Manual of Mental Disorders*, third edition, revised (*DSM-III-R*; American Psychiatric Association, 1987) to assess 150 New York City Covenant House adolescents (mean age = 18.5 years) in eight diagnostic categories (Feitel, Margetson, Chamas, & Lipman, 1992); 49% met criteria for major affective disorder.

Buckner and Bassuk (1997) conducted diagnostic interviews using the Diagnostic Interview Schedule for Children (DISC-2.3) with a very small sample of 41 homeless adolescents (mean age = 11.8 years) who were part of a controlled diagnostic study (housed and never homeless vs. homeless) in Worcester, Massachusetts; 10% of the homeless adolescents met lifetime criteria for major depression.

A Detroit area study (McCaskill, Toro, & Wolfe, 1998) provided diagnostic (DISC-2.3) comparisons between 118 housed and 118 "homeless" adolescents (mean age = 14.7 years). Twenty-seven percent of the shelter sample were not runaways; rather, they were "seeking some type of temporary intervention services from the shelter" (McCaskill et al., p. 311). Prevalence rates based on the Diagnostic Interview Schedule for Children-Revised (DISC-R) (*DSM-III-R* [American Psychiatric Association, 1987] criteria) were 33% for depression/dysthymia. The homeless and housed comparison groups did not differ statistically for prevalence of depressive disorders.

The largest diagnostic study of homeless and runaway adolescents to date was conducted by Cauce and colleagues (2000). Using the DISC-R, 364 adolescents (mean age = 16.4 years) were interviewed in shelters and on the streets in Seattle, Washington, and two nearby communities. More than two thirds of the sample met criteria for a mental disorder. Of these, 21% met criteria for major depression.

Extant studies indicate that although we have information from various sites (i.e., Los Angeles, New York City, Detroit, and Seattle) there is little agreement regarding prevalence of depressive disorders, and little attention is given to comorbidity among runaway and homeless adolescents. Issues of sampling (e.g., sample size, location, definition of *homeless*), differences in age ranges of subjects, differences in measurement (e.g., 6-month vs. lifetime prevalence, screeners vs. diagnostic assessments), and vague reporting of prevalence rates have generated widely varying results that are difficult to interpret. Prevalence rates for depressive disorders range from 49% in the New York City study (Feitel et al., 1992) to 10% in the Worcester, Massachusetts, study (Buckner and Bassuk, 1997). These diverse findings lend confusion to our attempts to understand mental health status of this understudied, high-risk population.

Prevalence and comorbidity of major depressive disorder among homeless and runaway adolescents

Almost one third (30.4%) of the study adolescents met criteria for lifetime MDE (Table 4.1). Adolescent females (33.6%) were significantly ($p \leq .10$) more likely to meet lifetime criteria for MDE than were males (26.2%), and 23% of the adolescents (19.8% males; 26.1% females) met criteria for 12-month prevalence of MDE. The University of Michigan-Composite International Diagnostic Interview (UM-CIDI) provides information regarding timing of first episode of major depression. About 12.1% of the runaway and homeless adolescents (9.6% males; 14.1% females) met criteria for MDE prior to first running away, and 15% (12.3% males; 17.4% females) met criteria for MDE at the time of or after their first runaway episode.

Table 4.1 Prevalence of Major Depressive Disorder (MDE) at Wave 1 (N = 428)

	All (N = 428)		Male (n = 187)		Female (n = 241)	
	Lifetime (%)	12-Month (%)	Lifetime (%)	12-Month (%)	Lifetime (%)	12-Month (%)
MDE	30.4	23.4	**26.2†**	19.8	33.6	26.1
MDE prior to first run	12.1	—	9.6	—	14.1	—
MDE after first run	15.2	—	12.3	—	17.4	—

† $p \leq .10$ between males and females.

When you hear their stories, most of the adolescents view their depressive symptoms as situational and stress related. For example, one young man (aged 19 years) expressed feelings of being emotionally overwhelmed:

> Stress goes back to earlier, like the whole no stability thing going on. And the depression I don't—I've started being sober recently and so I actually have like to deal with the fact that sometimes things are shitty instead of just being able to ignore it. And so like I've had like a lot of like built-up shit not really as much stuff to think about but more emotions I chose not to deal with…. So they all backlash and I was like really depressed for like a week and shit. It's like I'm still kind of depressed but it's like I'm starting to curve it.

A young woman (aged 19 years) enumerated the "top five" reasons for being depressed:

> I can think of top five. I can only think of about 10 like really easy. They're all like related to each other. I don't have a decent job. I don't have my GED yet. And I've been trying to get my GED since I was 15. It's going on almost 5 years and I'm trying to get my GED and I still have not taken the test. I don't have my own place. If I had my own place I'd have my own phone. I could have Jason call me which would

be a good thing but I don't so it's a bad thing. I've been working on getting my own place since I was 15, well I might jump that up to 17 because I was in a group home for a year…. No matter what I say I have not been able to stay in one place longer than 6 months. And now I'm here now I always say I want to settle down. I want to do this I want to do that. And I always end up leaving. I'm thinking about going up to New York now. Because I don't have nothing tying me down keeping me from moving.

The pervasive theme that emerged was what one the young man called the "whole no stability thing going on." Another young woman (aged 20 years) summed it up very poignantly:

Right now I'm not depressed. In the past generally in a period of about 4 years I'd say about 2 and a half if not more being depressed. I can't speak for nobody but myself but I know that my situation makes my mood, you know what I'm saying? If I'm in a stable environment than I will become stable. if all hell breaks lose than I don't crumble but I have no hope of anything. You know if like I might smile and be nice but I don't really feel like that inside you know. When you are homeless you lose all hope for real. When you just straight ain't got no where to go you ain't got no family. Your friends can't help you you know what I'm saying. You ain't got nothing. It's not a good feeling it's really not. You know and I don't know nobody that's going to say I went through my life being homeless and I enjoyed it or I was never depressed, cause I always know it's going to get better I mean I believe in God, but you know sometimes you wonder is there really a God to make me go through all this. You know do I really have to suffer like this? It's hard it really is. You start to lose track of what's important and you feel like like I said all hope is gone you know. I don't have nothing so maybe I shouldn't look forward to nothing you know. My life is not going to get better. You just start letting all these negative things across your mind. Once you find yourself in a stable environment like I said this is

> for me you know I get better I start to build off that
> and as long as I can stay in a stable environment
> I be cool.

The majority of the adolescents who discussed being depressed believed that a change of circumstances and stabilization of their chaotic lives would alleviate their depressive symptoms. But even though they seem to believe the feelings are situational, there was an underlying sense of hopelessness that things will get better soon. As one young woman (aged 19 years) put it:

> I think life sucks. I think life sucks and I want to get
> to a point in my life where I don't feel like it sucks
> anymore. Right now it stinks pretty much; I don't
> really have a whole lot going for me right now.

There was the sense that no matter how hard they tried they weren't going to make it:

> I try my fucking hardest with what I have you know.
> I'm the type of person that can make something out
> of nothing and that's still not good enough. You
> know that's what gets depressing. (male, aged 20
> years)

> My life is going nowhere; I don't see anything
> right now. I don't feel anything in the future; I
> don't see myself anywhere, doing anything right
> now. I don't hope. I just live day by day. (female,
> aged 19 years)

Comorbidity

Of the adolescents who met criteria for MDE, 95.3% also met criteria for at least one other disorder; 71.5% met criteria for two or more other disorders (Table 4.2). Among those who met criteria for MDE, 80% also met criteria for conduct disorder, more than one half (56.2%) also met criteria for post-traumatic stress disorder (PTSD), and about one half also met criteria for alcohol abuse (53.1%) and drug use (46.9%). Depressed females were more likely than depressed males to meet criteria for PTSD (65.4% vs. 40.8%). Depressed males were more likely than depressed females to meet criteria

Table 4.2 Comorbidity of Major Depressive Disorder (MDE) at Wave 1
(*N* = 130)

	Total (%) (*N* = 130)	Male (%) (*n* = 49)	Female (%) (*n* = 81)
MDE and CD	80.0	91.8	**72.8***
MDE and PTSD	56.2	40.8	**65.4***
MDE and alcohol abuse	53.1	63.3	**46.9†**
MDE and drug abuse	46.9	57.1	**40.7†**
MDE and one disorder	23.8	24.5	23.5
MDE and two or more disorders	71.5	75.5	69.1

† p ≤. 10 between male and females.
* *p* ≤.01 between males and females.

for conduct disorder (91.8% vs. 72.8%), alcohol abuse (63.3% vs. 46.9%), and drug abuse (57.1% vs. 40.7%).

Variation in MDE and depressive symptoms by sexual orientation

Gay and bisexual males reported significantly higher levels of depressive symptoms and were more likely to meet diagnostic criteria for MDE than were their heterosexual counterparts (Figure 4.1). On the Center for Epidemiologic Studies-Depression Scale (CES-D) (Radloff, 1991), nonheterosexual males were nearly two times more likely to have cutoff scores at 16 or above (94.4% vs. 58.9%) or 28 or above (50% vs. 27.4%) than were heterosexual males. They also were nearly twice as likely to meet criteria for MDE than were heterosexual males (44.4% vs. 24.4%). There was little difference in CES-D scores or prevalence of MDE among nonheterosexual females and heterosexual females.

Depression in emerging adulthood

Prevalence and comorbidity of MDE in early adulthood

At Wave 13, when the adolescents were 19–22 years, 24.4% met criteria for major depressive episode, 18.8% of males and 28.2% of females (not shown in tables). All of the males who met criteria for MDE also met criteria for antisocial personality disorder (APD), as did 81.8% of the females (Table 4.3). One half of the MDE females (51.5%) and one third of the MDE males (33.3%) also met criteria for PTSD, and about one half of males (46.7%) and females (54.4%) who were depressed also met criteria

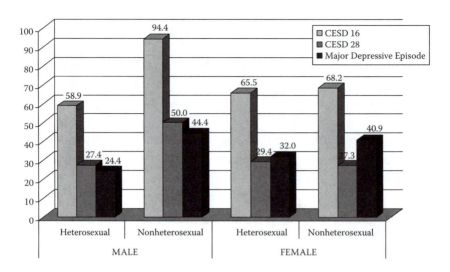

Figure 4.1 Percent reporting depression by gender and sexuality.

Table 4.3 Comorbidity of Major Depressive Disorder (MDE) at Wave 13 (N = 48)

	Total (%) (N = 48)	Male (%) (n = 15)	Female (%) (n = 33)
MDE and APD	87.5	100.0	81.8†
MDE and PTSD	45.8	33.3	51.5
MDE and alcohol abuse	52.1	46.7	54.4
MDE and drug abuse	47.9	60.0	42.4
MDE and one disorder	12.5	20.0	9.1
MDE and two or more disorders	83.3	80.0	84.8

† $p \leq .10$ between male and female

for alcohol abuse. Nearly two thirds (60.0%) of the depressed males and 42.4% the depressed females also met criteria for drug abuse. Among the depressed young adults all of the males and almost all of the females (93.9%) met criteria for one of the other mental disorders, and in excess of 80% met criteria for two or more of the other disorders.

In summary, MDE rarely occurred alone among the runaway and homeless young adults and was particularly likely to occur among APD and drug-abusing young men and APD young women. The majority of

the depressed young men and women also engaged in serious externalizing behaviors.

The persistence of depressive symptoms across time

We graphed depressive symptoms across the 3 years of the study using
cutoff scores of 16 and 28 for the CES-D (Figure 4.2). There was remarkable consistency in depressive symptoms scores across all 13 waves of the
study. Females were more likely to have higher scores than males in both
cutoff groups. Approximately one third of the young women had CES-D
scores of 28 or above across time, as did about one fifth of the young men.
The cutoff of 28 is very stringent, marking the 95th percentile of inpatients
who were hospitalized for depression. It is noteworthy that the percentages of those at or above the cutoff of 28 closely approximate the percentages that met diagnostic criteria for MDE. The more usual cutoff for the
CES-D is 16. More than one half of males and females scored above the
less conservative CES-D cutoff. Depressive symptoms were quite common
among the runaway and homeless adolescents and in consistent proportions across time.

Predicting MDE among the young adults at wave 13

We used logistic stepwise regression analyses to investigate MDE among
the Wave 13 young adults while controlling for lifetime MDE at Wave 1.
The models also controlled for age, gender, and sexual orientation of the
young people. Victimization was assessed with a count of victimization
occurrences reported during Waves 2–13. Meeting lifetime diagnostic criteria for alcohol abuse, drug abuse, PTSD, and meeting criteria for two or
more disorders were also included in the regression model.

The multivariate analyses indicated that being female increased the
likelihood of meeting criteria for MDE at Wave 13 two and one-half times
(Model b Exp(b) = 2.62) (Table 4.4). Victimization during Waves 2–13 was
statistically significant at the .10 level with only the control variables in the
model (Model 2), but lost significance when meeting criteria for MDE at
Wave 1 was added to the equation in Model 3. Those depressed at Wave 1
were twice as likely to meet criteria for MDE at Wave 13 than those who
were not depressed at Wave 1 (Exp(b) = 2.08). Meeting criteria for two or
more disorders increased the likelihood of MDE at Wave 13 nearly four
times (Exp(b) = 3.99).

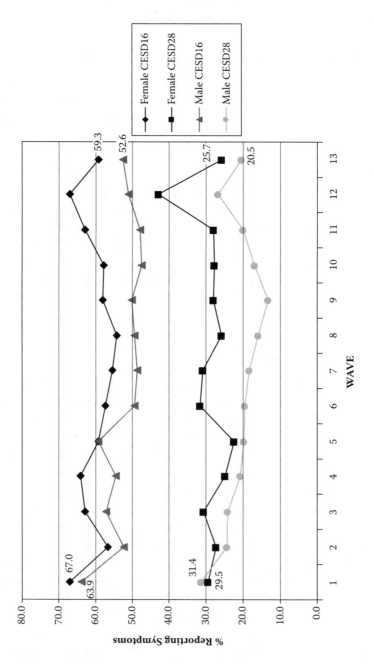

Figure 4.2 Depressive symptoms across time.

Table 4.4 Logistic Regression Model Predicting Meeting Major Depression Criteria at Wave 13 (N = 194)

	Model 1		Model 2		Model 3		Model 4		Model 5		Model 6	
	b	Exp(b)	b	Exp(b)	b	Exp(b)	b	Exp(b)	b	Exp(b)	b	Exp(b)
Age	0.29	1.34†	0.27	1.31	0.24	1.26	0.20	1.22	0.21	1.23	0.23	1.26
Female	0.75	2.13*	0.81	2.25*	0.72	2.05†	0.78	2.19*	0.85	2.33*	0.96	2.62*
Heterosexual	-0.18	0.84	-0.12	0.89	-0.15	0.86	-0.11	0.89	-0.14	0.87	-0.14	0.87
Victimization			1.337	3.81†	1.14	3.13	0.98	2.67	1.10	3.01	0.95	2.59
MDE Wave 1					0.64	1.90†	0.65	1.91†	0.73	2.08*	0.73	2.08†
Alcohol abuse							0.39	1.48	0.43	1.54	-0.02	0.98
Drug abuse							0.27	1.31	0.28	1.32	-0.20	0.82
PTSD									-0.32	0.73	-0.73	0.48†
Two or more diagnoses											1.38	3.99*
Constant	-6.61	0.00*	-6.56	0.00*	-6.04	0.00†	-5.78	0.00†	-5.93	0.00†	-6.68	0.00*
Nagerlkerke	0.05		0.07		0.09		0.11		0.11		0.15	
Cox & Snell	0.03		0.05		0.06		0.07		0.08		0.10	

† $p \le .10$.
* $p \le .05$.
** $p \le .01$.

Co-occurring conduct disorder and major depressive episode

Some have suggested that the co-occurrence of depression and CD represents a special group of adolescents who differ in types of depressive symptoms and externalizing behaviors from those with either disorder alone (Puig-Antich et al., 1989). To further examine this we compared the comorbid depressed CD adolescents with their nondepressed CD counterparts. Depressed CD males were more likely to indicate same-sex sexual orientation ($p < .02$) and to have been physically victimized on the streets ($p < .09$) than nondepressed CD males. Depressed CD females were more likely to report physical victimization on the streets ($p < .08$) than nondepressed CD females.

Summary and discussion

About one third of the homeless and runaway adolescents met criteria for MDE at Wave 1, as did about one fourth at Wave 13. In accord with numerous findings on depression among adolescents and young adults, the young women were more likely to meet criteria for MDE than young men at both Waves 1 and 13. Those who were depressed at Wave 1 were likely to remain depressed 3 years after the first assessment. The proportion of those with depressive symptoms was very consistent across all 13 waves of data collection.

Comorbidity patterns were congruent with other findings that suggest that depression among adolescents seldom occurs alone. In fact, by Wave 13, all of the young men and 94% of the young women who met criteria for MDE also met criteria for another disorder. The levels of co-occurrence of depression with externalizing disorders were particularly striking. Of the depressed young men at Wave 1, 92% also met criteria for CD and of the depressed young men at Wave 13, 100% met criteria for APD. Three fifths of depressed young adult males also met criteria for drug abuse at Wave 13.

We found little evidence that depressed, conduct-disordered runaways differed from nondepressed CD adolescents in levels or type of externalizing behaviors. The primary difference between depressed CD runaway adolescents and nondepressed CD adolescents, aside from sexual orientation among males, was experiencing street victimization. The findings regarding same-sex sexual orientation among depressed CD male adolescents are in accord with those reported earlier in this chapter indicating that gay and bisexual males are generally more at risk for depressive symptoms and MDE than are heterosexual males. They also are congruent with our earlier report regarding differences in victimization and emotional well-being among sexual minority runaway and homeless adolescents (Whitbeck, Chen, Hoyt, Tyler, & Johnson, 2004). There is considerable evidence that male runaways who are sexual minorities are more likely to engage in risky sexual behaviors and are at greater risk for victimization than heterosexual male runaway and homeless youths (Cochran, Stewart, Ginzler, & Cauce, 2002; Whitbeck et al.).

Theoretical implications

These results challenge media portrayals of depressed, victimized runaways. Even when they met criteria for depression, the majority of these young people were engaging in problem behaviors in great enough numbers and of sufficient severity to qualify them for a diagnosis of conduct disorder. This pattern does not change among the depressed homeless young adults. Nearly all also met criteria for APD; some two thirds of the depressed males and one half of the depressed females were also drug abusers. This could prove to be a lethal combination of disorders, increasing risk for suicide and other risky behaviors associated with feeling worthless, self-punitive, and hopeless about the future (Yoder, Longley, Whitbeck, & Hoyt, 2008).

One young woman's (age 19 years) statement summarizes this point:

> I just felt like nobody believed me, nobody wanted to believe me, nobody cared about me, just another kid, just, just you know just another chapter of life. You know just a social worker's another paycheck, that's it that's how I felt I felt like nobody cared. Just send her to wherever you know; I guess you don't know, you don't know…. It's when you're stressed out and you're depressed that you sometimes you have good days, most times you have bad days. You cry all the time. Either you just like eat and get fat like me or you just don't eat at all or you think about killing yourself and sometimes you act upon it. And sometimes you don't.

Underlying depressive symptoms that affect self-worth, energy levels (already depleted due to fatigue and nutrition), and the tendency to self-medicate with alcohol, nicotine, and drugs likely reinforce life course persistent developmental trajectories. Low energy and feelings of helplessness increase the likelihood of "drifting" and decrease motivation and hope for change.

Policy implications

Although it is well known that depression and, indeed, all adolescent psychiatric disorders are highly comorbid, the extent to which depression and antisocial behaviors overlap among runaways is striking. Almost all of the depressed adolescents met criteria for CD at Wave 1 and APD at Wave 13 (although only about one third of CD adolescents and APD young adults met criteria for MDE; Chapter 3). Our results indicate that these depressed externalizers may not be any less aggressive than their nondepressed counterparts; however, they are certainly at greater risk for drug abuse, perhaps as a form of self-medication, and may be more impulsive, exposing them to greater risk for victimization and self-injury than their depressed, non-CD adolescents.

The clinical message is that runaways are not only "bad" but also "sad." The positive aspect of this combination is that sadness is highly treatable. Identifying and treating depressive symptoms may be a clinical "hook" to engaging and maintaining a therapeutic relationship with these clinically challenging adolescents. Also, if the depressive symptoms are indeed situational as the adolescents believe, they will moderate with stabile housing and safety. Resolving some of the depressive symptoms also may contribute to reducing anger, irritability, and co-occurring substance abuse.

Conclusions

As is abundantly illustrated in the following chapters, the patterns of psychopathology among runaway and homeless adolescents are complex and overlapping. Although runaways will typically present externalizing behaviors, these results show that a significant proportion will also manifest serious internalizing symptoms. Some of these young people may be caught in a vicious cycle where risky behaviors result in victimization, and victimization increases the likelihood of depressive symptoms. In turn, depressive symptoms may lead to self-medication with drugs and alcohol, which promote risky behaviors and risk of victimization. In the next chapter we explore the prevalence and correlates of PTSD, a highly related internalizing disorder associated with high-risk behaviors and victimization that may be part of this externalizing–internalizing cycle.

chapter 5

Traumatic histories and adult transitions

With Devan M. Crawford

Aside from experiencing combat or living in a war zone, the vulnerability of homelessness may pose the greatest single situational risk for adolescent posttraumatic stress disorder (PTSD). Living life in public places or not knowing where you will sleep on a given night is extremely stressful for adults (Goodman, Saxe, & Harvey, 1991), and it is even more so for adolescents whose vulnerability is increased by developmental and societal norms of adult protection and supervision (Whitbeck & Hoyt, 1999). The first diagnostic criterion for PTSD in the *Diagnostic and Statistical Manual of Mental Disorders*, third edition, revised (*DSM-III-R*; American Psychiatric Association, 1987) is that the individual has been involved in a traumatic event that is "outside of the range of usual human experience" (p. 236). In the *Diagnostic and Statistical Manual of Mental Disorders*, fourth edition, text revision (*DSM-IV-TR*; American Psychiatric Association, 2000), the first two criteria are as follows (p. 467):

1. The person experienced, witnessed, or was confronted with an event or events that involved actual or threatened death or serious injury or a threat to the physical integrity of self or others.
2. The person's response involved intense fear, helplessness, or terror.

Examples of what would constitute a traumatic event include experiences such as rape, sexual molestation, being threatened with a weapon, witnessing a traumatic event, being in a bad accident, and being the victim of a physical attack (Kessler, Sonnega, Bromet, Hughes, & Nelson, 1995). The lives of runaway and homeless youth are characterized by atypically high frequencies of these types of traumatic experiences (Kipke, Simon, Montgomery, Unger, & Iverson, 1997; Whitbeck & Hoyt, 1999). In this chapter we investigate factors associated with meeting criteria for PTSD among homeless and runaway adolescents, comorbidity, rates of victimization across time among the young people, and factors that predict PTSD in emerging adulthood.

PTSD among adolescents: prevalence and risk factors

Although rates of lifetime PTSD vary dramatically by exposure to traumatic events and environments, general population estimates range between 10% and 12% for adult women and 5% to 6% for men (Breslau, Davis, Andreski, & Peterson, 1991; Kessler et al., 1994; Resnick, Kilpatrick, Dansky, & Saunders, 1993). Generally, rates tend to be lower for younger persons, reflecting less cumulative risk exposure for traumatic events. For example, PTSD rates for young persons aged 15 to 24 years from the National Comorbidity Survey were 10.3% for young women and 2.8% for young men (Kessler et al., 1994). Using data from a national probability sample, Kilpatrick and colleagues reported rates of 3.7% for adolescent boys and 6.3% for adolescent girls aged 12–17 years (Kilpatrick, Ruggerio, Acierno, Saunders, Resnick, & Best, 2003). However, rates for adolescents exposed to traumatic events may be as high as 100% (e.g., Terr, 1979). There is an emerging consensus that about one third of young people will develop PTSD after experiencing life-threatening accidents. Higher rates may be expected for particularly distressing incidents (Silverman & Treffers, 2001).

Adolescents may be especially vulnerable to PTSD symptoms after exposure to traumatic events in that most have not yet experienced serious health emergencies, life-threatening illnesses, serious injury, death, or personal trauma or loss. Traumatic experiences teach young people that life is extremely fragile and may make them prematurely aware of their own mortality. Also, because at this age adolescents begin to define risk, danger, and estimates of their need for protection based on peer group appraisals and responses, they are at once more vulnerable and more risk taking. National health statistics indicate that compared with other age groups, adolescents have high rates of unintentional injuries and physical violence including injuries from fights, threats or injury with a weapon, dating violence, and sexual assault (Grunbaum et al., 2004).

The magnitude of the stressor (for a review, see March, 1993), the degree of exposure to it (Pynoos, Frederick, Nader, & Arroyo, 1987; Vernberg, La Greca, Silverman, & Prinstein, 1996), and type of stressor (e.g., its severity and gruesomeness) will affect the likelihood of developing PTSD. Some children are at increased risk of PTSD dispositionally, particularly those who have histories of anxiousness, attention problems, and poor academic attainment (La Greca, Silverman, & Wasserstein, 1998). There also is a subjective component to vulnerability that involves the individual's response to the stressor. Most important is the perceived threat of death or serious injury and how terrified the adolescent was in response to the traumatic event.

Childhood experiences of physical and sexual abuse either may result in PTSD symptoms or may increase vulnerability for PTSD in later life when exposed to other traumatic events (Briere & Runtz, 1993; Browne & Finkelhor (review), 1986; Finkelhor, 1990; Follette, Polusny, Bechtle, & Naugle, 1996). Family histories characterized by neglect or spousal violence also affect vulnerability to PTSD (Kessler, 2000; Kessler, Sonnega, Bromet, Hughes, Nelson, & Breslau, 2005) as does spending time in foster care even among those who had no confirmed abuse (Dubner & Motta, 1999). Children whose parents meet lifetime diagnostic criteria for PTSD, depression, or anxiety also are at increased risk for PTSD following trauma exposure.

PTSD during adolescence may be especially injurious in that it can have long-term developmental consequences. Symptoms may delay or permanently impair accomplishing important developmental tasks such as establishing a sense of self-efficacy, developing critical social skills, and launching independence. Like most disorders of childhood and adolescence, PTSD rarely occurs alone. PTSD is known to increase risk for substance abuse and depressive symptoms (Deykin & Buka, 1997; Jacobsen, Southwick, & Kosten, 2001), which also may interfere with important developmental processes.

Risk factors for PTSD among homeless and runaway adolescents

It is well documented that runaway and homeless adolescents often come from physically and sexually abusive family environments (Janus, Burgess & McCormack, 1987; Kipke, Montgomery, Simon, & Iverson, 1997; Kufeldt & Nimmo, 1987; Tyler, Hoyt, Whitbeck, & Cauce, 2001b; Whitbeck & Hoyt, 1999). Compared with housed youth, reports from both the parents and the youth indicate that the early home experiences of homeless youth are characterized by caretaker neglect, abuse, and violence (Whitbeck, Hoyt, & Ackley, 1997a). Runaway and homeless youth who have been maltreated by caretakers are about twice as likely as those who were not maltreated to manifest serious psychological and learning disabilities (Sullivan & Knutson, 2000). Once on their own, the adolescents are exposed to sexually predatory behaviors of adults and other street youth, to violence, or to the witnessing of violence. Self-reported victimization rates are extremely high (Hagen & McCarthy, 1997; Hoyt, Ryan, & Cauce, 1999; Whitbeck &

Hoyt, 1999), as is the almost constant fear of victimization (Kipke, Simon, et al., 1997). This fear of victimization is accompanied by stresses associated with shelter life, loss of protective supervision of adults, and the loss of routine and predictability in everyday life (Goodman, Saxe, & Harvey, 1991). Street life may amplify existing stress symptoms among those with histories of victimization (Whitbeck, Hoyt, & Yoder, 1999).

Diagnostic studies of PTSD among homeless and runaway adolescents

Very few studies have addressed PTSD among homeless adolescents. Among those that do, several included only PTSD symptom measures (Buckner & Bassuk, 1997; Mundy, Robertson, Robertson, & Greenblatt, 1990); others estimated PTSD among sheltered adolescents who had never spent time directly on the streets (McCaskill, Toro, & Wolfe, 1998), thus excluding those particularly at risk. We could locate only two prior studies that included diagnostic assessments of PTSD in samples of homeless youth who have actually spent time on the streets. Feitel and colleagues used the Diagnostic Interview for Children and Adolescents-Revised (DICA-R) to assess 150 New York City adolescents (Feitel, Margetson, Chamas, & Lipman, 1992). Nearly one third (32%) of the adolescents met lifetime criteria for posttraumatic stress disorder. Cauce and colleagues (2000) used the Diagnostic Interview Schedule for Children-Revised (DISC-R) to interview 364 youths in the Seattle metropolitan area and concluded that 12% met criteria for posttraumatic stress disorder. They point out that this was likely to be a lower-bound estimate due to a protocol that omitted the PTSD module for interviews where the earlier modules of the Diagnostic Interview Schedule for Children (DISC) had taken longer than 2 hours to administer. This occurred in 7% of the interviews. The length of the other diagnostic components is likely associated with meeting criteria for one or more disorders, and, considering the general population estimates of high comorbidity between PTSD and other disorders (Kessler, 2000), it is logical to assume the lifetime PTSD rates in the Seattle sample may have been higher. These two diagnostic studies based on samples of street youth provide mixed evidence regarding prevalence of lifetime PTSD.

In summary, homeless adolescents often leave situations where they have been victimized (Janus et al., 1987; Kipke, Montgomery, Simon, & Iverson, 1997; Kufeldt & Nimmo, 1987; Tyler et al., 2001b; Whitbeck & Hoyt, 1999) only to experience traumatic stress associated with living in public places (Goodman et al., 1991), fear (Kipke, Simon, et al., 1997), and further victimization when they are on their own (Hagen & McCarthy, 1997; Hoyt et al., 1999; Whitbeck & Hoyt, 1999). The experiences of street life exacerbate existing psychological symptoms and do little or nothing to ameliorate them (Whitbeck et al., 1999). Indeed, if the adolescent is not already symptomatic, street life may induce many PTSD symptoms as a natural response to the environment (Whitbeck & Hoyt, 1999).

Prevalence and comorbidity of PTSD among homeless and runaway adolescents

In all, more than one third (35.5%) of the adolescents in our study met lifetime criteria for PTSD at Wave 1 (Table 5.1). Females (44.8%) were nearly twice as likely as males (23.5%) to meet lifetime criteria. A total of 20% of the adolescents met 12-month criteria for PTSD. The prevalence of 12-month PTSD among the female runaways (26.5%) was almost twice that for males (12.8%). Nonheterosexual females were more likely to meet lifetime criteria and 12-month criteria for PTSD than were heterosexual females.

PTSD rarely occurred alone (Table 5.2). Almost all (92.1%) of the adolescents who met criteria for PTSD also met criteria for at least one of the other four diagnoses. Adolescent males (97.8%) were slightly more likely to be comorbid than were females (89.8%). Nearly all of the males (93.2%) and three fourths (75.9%) of the females who met criteria for PTSD also met criteria for conduct disorder (CD). Almost one half of the runaways (48%) who met criteria for PTSD also met criteria for major depressive episode (MDE). About one half of the adolescents who met criteria for PTSD also met criteria for alcohol abuse (51.3%) and drug abuse (48.7%). PTSD males (59.1%) were more likely than PTSD females to meet criteria for alcohol and drug abuse. Of the females with PTSD, 48% also met criteria for alcohol abuse, and 44% also met criteria for drug abuse.

Table 5.1 Prevalence of Posttraumatic Stress Disorder (PTSD) by Sexuality at Wave 1

	All (N = 428)		Male (n = 187)		Female (n = 241)	
	Lifetime (%)	12-Month (%)	Lifetime (%)	12-Month (%)	Lifetime (%)	12-Month (%)
All	35.5	20.0	23.5	12.8	**44.8***	**26.5***
Heterosexual	33.4	19.3	23.8	14.1	**41.6***	**24.3***
Nonheterosexual	48.4	25.6	22.2	0.00	**59.1****	**37.9****

* *p* ≤ .05 between males and females.
** *p* ≤ .01 between males and females.
*** *p* ≤ .001 between males and females.

Table 5.2 Comorbidity of Posttraumatic Stress Disorder (PTSD) at Wave 1

	Total (%) (N = 152)	Male (%) (n = 44)	Female (%) (n 108)
PTSD and CD	80.9	93.2	**75.9***
PTSD and MDE	48.0	45.5	49.1
PTSD and alcohol abuse	51.3	59.1	48.1
PTSD and drug abuse	48.7	59.1	**44.4†**
One disorder	20.4	20.5	20.4
Two or more disorders	71.7	77.3	69.4

† $p \leq .10$ between males and females.
* $p \leq .01$ between males and females.

Traumatic experiences among PTSD adolescents

We were careful to designate traumatic experiences in terms of the *DSM-III-R* and *DSM-IV-TR* criteria of being "outside of the usual range of usual human experience" (American Psychiatric Association, 1987, p. 236) or as those involving either actual or threatened death, serious injury, or a threat to the physical integrity of self or others and a response of intense fear, helplessness, or terror (American Psychiatric Association, 2000, p. 467). Of the runaway adolescents who met criteria for PTSD, nearly two thirds (63.8%) had experienced severe physical abuse by a caretaker (e.g., hit with fist, beaten, threatened or assaulted with a weapon; Table 5.3). Males (79.6%) were significantly more likely to report severe caretaker physical abuse than were females (57.4%). One half of the adolescent PTSD females had experienced caretaker sexual abuse compared with 20.5% of the PTSD males. About one half (51.2%) of those who met lifetime criteria for PTSD had run away at age 14 years or younger.

Some of the young people who had experienced severe caretaker abuse tended to minimize their experiences. For example, one young woman (aged 19 years) told us:

> I don't know, not really that much just like whenever somebody's drunk or really ticked off or whatever that they just tend to like hit people. Like physically it would be like my mom or my dad or just people, friends that were living with us or whatever. And then like sexually it was my brother.

Table 5.3 Experience of Trauma Among Those With Lifetime Posttraumatic Stress Disorder (PTSD) at Wave 1

	Total (%) (N = 152)	Male (%) (n = 44)	Female (%) (n = 108)
Ever experience severe parental abuse	63.8	79.6	**57.4****
Ever experience parental sexual abuse	41.5	20.5	**50.0****
Early runaway (< 14 years old)	51.2	59.1	49.1
Physically assaulted with weapon on own	32.9	45.5	**27.8***
Sexually assaulted on own	29.6	0.0	**41.7****

* $p \leq .05$ between males and females diagnosed with lifetime PTSD (one-way analysis of variance; ANOVA).
** $p \leq .01$ between males and females diagnosed with lifetime PTSD (ANOVA).

A young man (aged 19 years) who fought with his father wasn't sure he had been abused:

> Not really abused like as in the sense where like I got beat or anything like that but I've been like beat up where we ended up throwing punches at each other and I got beat up like that but not really. I didn't even really ever get spanked when I was a kid like nothing like that.

The young women were particularly susceptible to sexual abuse and the sense of helplessness associated with it.

> I was 12, almost 13, it happened for a whole summer every night after he got off work. And sometimes during the day my mom would leave and go somewhere then he'd do it. I guess my stepdad felt as if he wasn't being loved by my mom and he didn't know how to show my mom affection so he took it out on me. And at night he pretty much raped me or play with me with his fingers and fondle me. (female, aged 19 years)

Sexual acts with my little brother and I. Very physi-cally abusive and neglectful like sticking me in a closet and not giving me any food and putting like an open bottle of bleach in the little closet so that it would stink and I would end up barfing and puking and all that good stuff. As well as certain sickos that she [maybe] knew. She would have them do things to me and then she would in turn like get sexually aroused by it so she was a very sick, sick woman. (female, aged 22 years)

Yeah because my mom she would like go out and stay with one of her boyfriends and leave me and my brother there with him and I would be like I don't want to stay here because he's doing this and this and this to me and she was like you're just a liar you're just saying that.... I just wonder if I'm ever going to have a mother–daughter relationship with my mom. That's all I ever wonder about. (female, aged 19 years)

Besides caretaker abuse, many of the young people had experienced significant trauma when on the streets. Nearly one half (45.5%) of the PTSD males and 27.8% of the females had been assaulted with a weapon (Table 5.3). For example, one of the young men (aged 20 years) told us about hav-ing been shot at in a gang drive-by:

I think the other people I think they were some hard-core gang members or something. We were all sitting around this picnic table in one of those shelters and this car comes by and just starts shooting at us. You know (laughs) I don't think they were shooting at me but the gunfire was heading my way so I'm calling it shooting at me. You know, that was pretty scary.

For the young men, physical victimization on the streets was usually related to fighting:

I don't know, I get in fights all the time, once a week, I've been like assaulted to the point where like I had my seatbelt on in the car and the car door didn't open and I just had somebody run up and just start punching me through the open window and I couldn't get out. (male, aged 19 years)

These young women were more likely to have been assaulted by a boyfriend:

> I was over at a friend's house drinking. Well, he called me a cunt, and, and, well, I got mad and he knocked over a shot glass and then pushed back into my chair, my right foot came out from underneath me and I cut the bottom of my foot open I thought it was just a little inky dinky little cut cause it didn't hurt. And so I hear him go there's too much blood and then I found out my foot wasn't as fixable as I thought it was.... I cut the ligaments, the tendons, the nerves, the muscles, and the blood vessels. So nonrepairable. (female, aged 20 years)

> Well I was dating this guy off and on for the last 5 to 6 years and then he wants, he pretty much is my son's father and he used to hit me all the time. And he's tried to kill me. And he'd make me spend money on him. Money I didn't have that I should be spending on my son. And he would just do things that would hurt me emotionally really. He would use stuff against me. Tell me I was stupid because I didn't finish school, I dropped out and got my GED. (female, aged 19 years)

A total of 42% of the females had been sexually assaulted when on the streets (Table 5.3). Sometimes the sexual assaults were in the context of trying to find a place to stay:

> He said I could stay with him for awhile and all he ever wanted to do was you know—try to have sex with me and... I told him no I told him no and then he smoked crack and he flipped out. I was sleeping ... and he just raped me. And then after it was all said and done with and after I told him I wouldn't tell nobody, I left. I told my mom and then she didn't do nothing about it but she just called the children's home so I got placed with the children's home again because I turned myself in. And that's what happened the first time. (female, aged 19 years)

Prevalence and comorbidity of PTSD in early adulthood (Wave 13)

Prevalence rates for PTSD at Wave 13 were much the same as those at baseline (Table 5.4). Nearly one third (29.4%) met lifetime criteria for PTSD. The now young adult females (37.7%) were much more likely than males (17.5%) to meet lifetime criteria. The young women (13.2%) also were twice as likely to meet 12-month criteria for PTSD as the young men (6.3%). About three fourths (75.4%) of the PTSD runaways also met criteria for antisocial personality disorder (APD) at Wave 13 (Table 5.5). As was the case with CD at Wave 1, almost all of the young adult males (92.9%) also met lifetime criteria for APD, as did 69.8% of the PTSD females. About one third of the young adults who met criteria for PTSD also met criteria for MDE (38.6%) and alcohol abuse (31.6%), with no significant differences between men and women. One half (50.0%) of the PTSD young adult males also met criteria for drug abuse, as did one third (32.6%) of the PTSD young adult females. Nearly all of the PTSD young adults were comorbid with at least one of the other four disorders (92.9% males; 81.4% females), and two thirds were comorbid with two or more of the other disorders (78.6% males; 60.5% females).

Table 5.4 Prevalence of Posttraumatic Stress Disorder (PTSD) at Wave 13

	Total (%) (N = 194)	Male (%) (n = 80)	Female (%) (n = 114)
PTSD 12 month	10.3	6.3	13.2
PTSD lifetime	29.4	17.5	37.7*

* $p \le .01$ between males and females.

Table 5.5 Comorbidity of Posttraumatic Stress Disorder (PTSD) at Wave 13

	Total (%) (N = 57)	Male (%) (n = 14)	Female (%) (n = 43)
PTSD and APD	75.4	92.9	69.8†
PTSD and MDE	38.6	35.7	39.5
PTSD and alcohol abuse	31.6	35.7	30.2
PTSD and drug abuse	36.8	50.0	32.6
One disorder	19.3	14.3	20.9
Two or more disorders	64.9	78.6	60.5

† $p \le .10$ between males and females.

Predictors of PTSD at wave 13

To better understand the propensity among the young adults (aged 19–22 years) to meet criteria for PTSD, we regressed known correlates of PTSD against meeting criteria for the disorder at Wave 13 controlling for meeting diagnostic criteria for PTSD at Wave 1 (Table 5.6). We also controlled for age, gender, and sexual orientation of the young people. Wave 1 physical abuse was measured by taking the average of the three severe caretaker abuse questions including being physically hit with fists and being threatened or physically wounded with a weapon. Wave 1 sexual abuse was measured by summing two questions: if a caretaker had asked the respondent to do something sexual or forced the respondent to do something sexual. Sexual victimization was a sum of victimization occurrences (i.e., forced sexual contact) in Waves 2–13 and was weighted by the number of waves in which the respondent participated.

In Model 1, females and nonheterosexual young people were more likely to meet criteria for the disorder than their male and heterosexual counterparts. Young women were approximately three times as likely as males to meet criteria for PTSD at Wave 13 than were young men. Similarly, nonheterosexual young people were almost three times as likely to meet criteria at Wave 13 compared with heterosexuals. In Model 2, sexual abuse by a caretaker more than doubled the odds of meeting criteria for PTSD at Wave 13, and in Model 3, sexual assault when on the streets also increased the odds of Wave 13 PTSD about two times. In Model 4, with all of the variables in the equation, those with a diagnosis of PTSD at Wave 1 were 2.6 times more likely to meet criteria at Wave 13 than those who did not meet criteria for PTSD at Wave 1. Female young people and nonheterosexuals were each about two times more likely to meet criteria for PTSD at Wave 13, even with Wave 1 PTSD in the equation. When meeting criteria for PTSD at Wave 1 was added in Model 4, all of the other predictors became nonsignificant.

Summary and discussion

As would be expected, this is a highly vulnerable and highly victimized population. Two thirds of the homeless and runaway young people had histories of severe caretaker physical abuse, and one half of the young women had histories of caretaker sexual abuse. High rates of severe caretaker physical and sexual abuse among the PTSD young people increase the potential for systematic patterns of revictimization (Koenig, Doll, O'Leary, & Pequegnat, 2004). Nearly one half of the young men had been assaulted with a weapon, and almost one half of the young women had been sexually assaulted since being on their own. It is noteworthy that

Table 5.6 Predictors of Posttraumatic Stress Disorder (PTSD) at Wave 13 (N = 193)

	Model 1		Model 2		Model 3		Model 4	
	b	Exp(b)	b	Exp(b)	b	Exp(b)	b	Exp(b)
Age	0.19	1.21	0.12	1.13	0.11	1.12	0.07	1.7
Female	1.08	2.95**	0.91	2.49*	0.83	2.29*	0.70	2.02†
Heterosexual	-1.03	0.36*	-0.89	0.41*	-0.88	0.42*	-0.85	0.43†
Physical abuse Wave 1 (0.1)			0.23	1.27	0.23	1.26	0.09	1.10
Sexual abuse Wave 1 (0.1)			0.84	2.33*	0.78	2.19*	0.58	1.80
Sexual victimization					0.75	2.13†	0.62	1.86
PTSD Wave 1							0.95	2.59**
Constant	-4.03	0.02	-3.20	0.04	-3.09	0.05	-2.63	0.07
Cox & Snell		0.08		0.11		0.12		0.15
Nagelkerke		0.12		0.16		0.18		0.22

† $p \le .10$.
* $p \le .05$.
** $p \le .01$.

more than one half of those who ran away prior to age 14 years met criteria for PTSD, an indicator of the long-term consequences of early trauma. The odds of meeting criteria for PTSD accumulate with caretaker victimization and later victimization when on the streets.

As a consequence of this vulnerability and victimization, nearly one third of the young people make the transition to early adulthood meeting criteria for PTSD. The prevalence rate for PTSD for the young women in this sample was approximately three times that expected in the general population. Moreover, PTSD almost always co-occurred with another disorder. Rates of co-occurrence with depression ranged from 38% to 50%, depending on the year of evaluation (Tables 5.2 and 5.5). At Wave 13, more than 90% of the PTSD males and about 70% of the PTSD females also met criteria for APD.

Early traumatic experiences increase vulnerability to later PTSD in response to contemporary traumatic events. And, although symptoms of PTSD are typically time limited, if there is continuing threat exposure they are apt to persist. Although we can't predict lifelong consequences, we do know that PTSD increases risk for substance abuse and depressive symptoms (Deykin & Buka, 1997; Jacobsen et al., 2001). There also is significant overlap between PTSD symptoms and other serious adolescent behaviors such as self-mutilation (Sutton, 2004) and dissociation (Bremmer & Brett, 1997), which are addressed in Chapters 7 and 9, respectively.

Theoretical implications

In terms of life course development, traumatic events are important links in the self-reinforcing chains of negative events that build momentum across time. Caretaker abuse changes how children view themselves and other people, their ability to trust, and their interaction styles. Subsequent victimization on the streets confirms their perceptions of others. Recall the young man in Chapter 3 who told us, "You can't live on the streets without being ruthless. If you're not ruthless you're fucked you know that's just the way it works."

As PTSD symptoms persist, the traumatized young people may relive these experiences over and over again in response to triggers. This may affect their ability to form intimate relationships, to concentrate in academic settings, and to hold a job. Self-medication through alcohol and drugs may be additional links in chains of negative behaviors and events. Finally, there is the possibility of the vicious cycle of victimization, aggressive behaviors, self-medicating alcohol and drug use, and revictimization (discussed in Chapter 4).

Policy implications

As pointed out in Chapter 4, many, if not most, of the "bad" kids on the streets also are seriously injured kids. Just as soldiers experience PTSD from combat trauma, these young people carry their own scars from witnessing and experiencing violence. Unfortunately, our present societal response typically comes through the criminal justice system in reaction to criminal behaviors such as drug use, drug dealing, or theft. This punitive societal response is one more link in the chain: Aggression is met with aggression; the most powerful aggressor "wins." Would responding to the trauma work as an intervention? We need randomized controlled studies to test this. However, we are convinced that the most immediate and cost-effective policy response is to prevent further trauma. This means a rapid response system for runaways to protect them on the streets. As we discuss in subsequent chapters, this may involve changing the way shelters work and revising our response to runaways by acknowledging their "too early" entrance into adulthood. We can't make them children again, but perhaps we can guide them into adulthood.

Conclusions

It is our belief that this chapter and our later chapter on victimization tell the true story of runaway and homeless adolescents. The vast majority of these young people are not "adventurers" or "nomads," although they may tell the media this. Rather, their lifestyles are largely the consequences of severe harm and their attempts to take control of untenable and, many times, dangerous situations. They are trying to make their way in the world as they know it using the tools they have been given.

chapter 6

Substance abuse patterns among homeless and runaway adolescents across time

With Devan M. Crawford

Substance abuse pervades almost every aspect of the lives of the majority of homeless and runaway adolescents. Often they come from families where relatives and caretakers are substance abusers (Whitbeck & Hoyt, 1999). Once on their own, alcohol and drugs are ubiquitous. Whether in shelters, on the streets, or living on their own, they are exposed to alcohol and drug users (Hagen & McCarthy, 1997; Johnson, Whitbeck, & Hoyt, 2005b) and the high-risk behaviors associated with substance abuse. Affiliation with substance abusers and engaging in substance abuse themselves place them at special risk for physical and sexual victimization (Tyler, Hoyt, Whitbeck, & Cauce, 2001a; Tyler, Whitbeck, Hoyt, & Cauce, 2004), high-risk sexual behaviors (Booth & Zhang, 1997; Kipke, Montgomery, Simon, Unger, & Johnson, 1997; Kipke, O'Conner, Palmer, & MacKenzie, 1995; Koopman, Rosario, & Rotheram-Borus, 1994; Rotheram-Borus, Luna, Marotta, & Kelly, 1994), suicidal ideation (Yoder, 1999; Yoder, Hoyt, & Whitbeck, 1998), hunger and malnutrition (Whitbeck, Chen, & Johnson, 2006), health problems (Yates, MacKenzie, Pennbridge, & Cohen, 1988), and mental health problems (Whitbeck, Johnson, Hoyt, & Cauce, 2004a). Alcohol and drug use also are strongly associated with externalizing behaviors resulting in arrests (Chen, Thrane, Whitbeck, & Johnson, 2006), victimizing behaviors (Hagen & McCarthy, 1997; Whitbeck & Hoyt, 1999), and survival sex (Rotheram-Borus et al., 1992).

There is a general consensus that addictive disorders emerge during late adolescence and early adulthood (Kessler, 2000; Kessler, Berglund, Demler, Jin, & Walters, 2005) and that comorbid mental disorders, with the exception of posttraumatic stress disorder (PTSD), typically occur first (Chilcoat & Menard, 2003; Kessler, Nelson, McGonagle, Edlund, Frank, & Leaf, 1996). In this chapter, we document the prevalence and correlates of substance use and substance abuse disorders (SUDs) among runaway and homeless adolescents. In addition, we investigate predictors of emergent alcohol dependence between Wave 1 and Wave 13 and address the question of preexisting psychiatric disorders among those who became alcohol dependent across the 3 years of the study.

Substance abuse disorders among homeless and runaway adolescents

Every study of homeless and runaway adolescents has documented rates of alcohol and drug use in excess of that found among nonrunaway adolescents. Repeat runaways surveyed in the National Longitudinal Survey of Youth were 7 to 12 times more likely to have used drugs than their nonrunaway counterparts (Windle, 1989). Kipke and colleagues reported high rates of drug use among their sample of Hollywood street youth: Almost all had used alcohol and marijuana, approximately two thirds had used speed or LSD, and about one half had used cocaine, mushrooms, and crack cocaine (Kipke, Montgomery, & MacKenzie, 1997). Cauce and colleagues reported that 72% of a sample of 361 homeless and runaway adolescents in Seattle, Washington, had used alcohol, 62% had used marijuana, and 32% had used hard drugs (Cauce et al., 2000). These rates are substantially higher than those reported for 8th, 10th, and 12th graders in the most recent Monitoring the Future Survey. Lifetime prevalence rates for any illicit drug use excluding marijuana in 2005 were 12.1% among 8th graders, 18% among 10th graders, and 27.4% among 12th graders (Johnston, O'Malley, Bachman, & Schulenberg, 2005).

There are very few studies that have used diagnostic criteria to evaluate SUDs among homeless and runaway adolescents. Kipke and colleagues used diagnostic interviews to assess prevalence of SUDs in a sample of youth recruited from both homeless service agencies and the streets of Los Angles; 71% of the adolescents met *Diagnostic and Statistical Manual of Mental Disorders,* third edition (*DSM-III;* American Psychiatric Association, 1980) criteria for alcohol or "illicit drug use disorder" (Kipke, Montgomery, Simon, & Iverson, 1997). Based on Diagnostic Interview Schedule for Children-Revised (DISC-R) criteria, Feitel and colleagues reported that 41% of runaway adolescents interviewed in a shelter met clinical criteria for alcohol and drug abuse (Feitel, Margetson, Chamas, & Lipman, 1992). Among 96 youth from shelters and the streets of Los Angeles interviewed by Mundy and associates, 39% met *DSM-III* diagnostic criteria for drug use or dependency, and 48% met criteria for alcohol abuse or dependency (Mundy, Robertson, Robertson, & Greenblatt, 1990). A Detroit area study that compared diagnostic assessments of 118 housed and 118 homeless adolescents reported prevalence rates of 24%

drug abuse/dependence and 21% alcohol abuse/dependence based on the DISC-R (*Diagnostic and Statistical Manual of Mental Disorders,* third edition, revised [*DSM-III-R;* American Psychiatric Association, 1987] criteria) for the homeless adolescents (McCaskill, Toro, & Wolfe, 1998).

In summary, prevalence rates of SUDs among homeless and runaway adolescents range from 71% to 24% for drug abuse. The variation in rates reflects differences in age groups and sampling strategies that beleaguer research efforts with this population. However, the range of findings is well above the prevalence rates of 16.7% for any SUD among those 18–29 years in the National Comorbidity Survey Replication (NCSR) (Kessler, Berglund, et al., 2005). Perhaps a better comparison would be with populations more at risk for SUDs. Aarons and colleagues reported SUD prevalence rates of 62.1% among youth in the juvenile justice system, 40.8% among those in mental health settings, 23.6% among those who are severely emotionally disturbed, and 19.2% among adolescents in the child welfare system (Aarons, Brown, Hough, Garland, & Wood, 2001). Most of these fall within the range of prevalence rates of SUDs reported for homeless and runaway adolescents in the available diagnostic studies.

Alcohol and drug use among homeless and runaway adolescents across time

Wave 1 rates of lifetime alcohol and drug use

Our rates of alcohol use were very similar to those reported in Cauce et al.'s (2000) Seattle study: 69% had drunk beer, and 66% had drunk hard liquor (Table 6.1). Males were significantly more likely than females to have drunk hard liquor. A similar proportion had smoked marijuana (67.5%). Males (77%) were significantly more likely than females (60.2%) to have used marijuana, and many used the drug frequently:

> Maybe 5 times a week. Five days out of a week and it's been some, sometimes I … went months straight every day smoking weed. It depends on how much money I got to spend on it or who gots the shit you know what I'm saying? (male, aged 20 years)

Alcohol and drugs relieve the stress of street life. The young people were unambiguous about self-medicating with alcohol and drugs:

> I would say about 4 or 5 grams a day. Smoking weed makes me feel all cloudy and carefree almost. Not carefree but it makes me think about situations

Table 6.1 12-Month Substance Use by Gender at Wave 1

	Total (%) (N = 428)	Male (%) (n = 187)	Female (%) (n = 241)
Beer	69.2	72.7	66.4
Hard liquor	66.4	71.1	62.7†
Marijuana	67.5	77.0	60.2***
Crank	14.6	18.4	11.6*
Amphetamines	11.4	12.3	10.8
Cocaine	15.0	15.5	14.6
Opiates	8.2	12.8	4.6**
Hallucinogens	21.7	24.6	19.5
Barbiturates	8.9	11.2	7.1
Inhalants	6.1	5.9	6.2
Intravenous drugs	9.6	13.4	6.6*
Any hard drug besides marijuana or alcohol	34.8	40.6	30.3*

† $p \leq .10$ between males and females.
* $p \leq .05$ between males and females.
** $p \leq .01$ between males and females.
*** $p \leq .001$ between males and females.

like when I have to think about those situations. It stretches them out and blocks out all the other bullshit going on in me.... Weed just makes me sit down, just kind of like a hyperactive medicine like Ritalin or something. (male, aged 19 years)

It depends on the alcohol or drug, but it pretty much it enables you to not take life not so seriously and kind of introvert yourself... within your own mind most of the time. Just like in kind of create your own little world and shit. (male, aged 19 years)

Like I'm worth something. That I'm not I'm not depressed I just feel happy. I don't think about anything but being happy at that moment while I'm high. All I can think about is being happy for that time. I don't try to focus on my problems. (female, aged 19 years)

Rates of lifetime use for harder drugs were much lower than those for alcohol or marijuana. About one third of the adolescents had used hard drugs (i.e., drugs other than marijuana) (Table 6.1). Males (40.6%) were significantly more likely to have used hard drugs than were females (30.3%). About one fourth of males (24.6%) and one fifth of females (19.5%) had used hallucinogens. This was followed by cocaine use, at about 15% of the adolescent males and females, and crank (14.6%), where males (18.4%) were significantly more likely to have used the drug than were females (11.6%).

Crack was the hard drug most mentioned in the in-depth interviews:

> I had several guys, you know, I had gone through several of them while I was with, was living with her [girlfriend]. And yeah, everything went downhill from there. Started smoking crack. Getting, see I had been sober off and on this whole time. You know, so many months here, a year or two here, days here. And I got back into drugs when I met him. And I ended up losing my job. I was suspended pending investigation for drug trafficking. (female, aged 20 years)

> If I gave him money to go get crack, he would hold on to it. You know, he wouldn't just let me have the crack that I bought, he was holding it. He would break me off a piece when he felt I needed it. Half the time, he'd take it over to his friend's house, smoke it all with them and then come back with like a little piece for me. Then, which would leave me more pissed off then I was before. And I really got into the addiction part, to where I would cry and scream and yell whenever I couldn't get any. Whenever he had it, and I knew he had it, and he wasn't giving any to me and he was just smoking it like it was all his. I would get violent and I would start cussing him out and I didn't care who I was in front of. I didn't care if I was in front of my friends, and I don't care if they thought I was stupid. (female, aged 20 years)

> Well, crack was an everyday thing. Weed and alcohol were to come down from the crack. Crystal was, pretty much, just everyday thing also. But of course, like the trailer park we lived in was all dealing methamphetamines. So we'd have to go out of the county into the city to get what we wanted,

> which was crack or coke. And bring it back. So we
> would bring it back and deal it to the people in our
> neighborhood. Or smoke it all, one of the two. And
> in return for some of theirs, so we'd [have] some of
> this and some of this, you know? (female, aged 20
> years)

Rates for lifetime use of opiates, barbiturates, and intravenous (IV) drugs were similar, at about 8% of the adolescents. Males (13.4%) were about two times more likely to have engaged in IV drug use than females (6.6%):

> Because I used to do heroin I used to smoke cream
> rolls. I used to do a lot of things but when I came
> to [name of group home] I stopped smoking cream
> rolls and then I was still dipping and dabbing with
> the heroin. I came a long way from there I totally
> quit that you know. I still smoke my little weed or
> whatever. That helps, but whether people believe it
> or not is them. Because they say us kids shouldn't
> have stress and matters, we do. I mean it's like when
> you're smoking marijuana for that period of time or
> you're being high you have no worries no stress you
> ain't got no problems and then you can think about
> how to get piece of mind. (male, aged 19 years)

> We'd always go to bars and pick up some people
> there who we'd never met before and who were, you
> know, heroin and, just anything. And even though
> I didn't protect myself that well with the whole sex
> thing, the needles isn't going to happen, you know?
> Just wasn't going to happen. I've used them before
> and I used them frequently when I was out there,
> but I wasn't going to use somebody else's. (female,
> aged 20 years)

Prevalence of lifetime and 12-month substance use disorders

At ages 16–19 years (Wave 1) almost one half of the males (48.1%) and 40.2% of the females met lifetime criteria for alcohol abuse (Table 6.2). This conrasts to lifetime prevalence rates of 14.3% among individuals aged 18–29 years in the NCSR (Kessler, Berglund, et al., 2005). About one third (32.7%) of the adolescents met 12-month criteria for alcohol abuse. The lifetime

Table 6.2 Substance Abuse Disorders by Gender at Wave 1

	Total (%) (N = 428)	Male (%) (n = 187)	Female (%) (n = 241)
Alcohol abuse lifetime	43.7	48.1	40.2
Alcohol abuse 12 month	32.7	35.8	30.3
Alcohol abuse currently	0.7	1.1	0.4
Alcohol dependence lifetime	29.9	31.0	29.0
Alcohol dependence 12 month	21.5	23.0	20.3
Alcohol dependence currently	2.1	2.7	1.7
Drug abuse lifetime	40.4	47.1	**35.3***
Drug abuse 12 month	25.7	32.6	**20.3****

* $p \leq .05$ between males and females.
** $p \leq .01$ between males and females.

rate for alcohol dependence at ages 16–19 years (29.9%) was nearly five times that for those 18–29 years in the NCSR (6.3%). The 12-month prevalence for alcohol dependence was 21.5%.

Almost the same percentages of adolescents met lifetime criteria for drug abuse (40.4%) as for alcohol abuse (43.7%), four times the prevalence rate for drug abuse among the 18–29-year age category in NCSR (10.9%). A total of 47% of the males and 35.3% of the females met lifetime criteria of drug abuse. Nearly one third of the males (32.6%) and 20.3% of the females met 12-month criteria for drug abuse. Unfortunately, the length of the drug-screening protocol and our limited interview window with the runaway adolescents precluded screening for both drug abuse and drug dependence.

Comorbidity at Wave 1

Alcohol abuse (97.3%), alcohol dependence (98.4%), and drug abuse (96%) almost always co-occurred with at least one other disorder (Table 6.3). There was one important gender pattern of comorbidity. The female adolescents were more likely than males to manifest co-occurring substance abuse and PTSD. More than half of substance-abusing females also met criteria for PTSD (e.g., PTSD and alcohol abuse [53.6%], PTSD and alcohol dependence [54.3%], and PTSD and drug abuse [56.5%]). Also, drug-abusing females

Table 6.3 Comorbidity of Lifetime Substance Abuse Disorders at Wave 1

	Total (%)	Male (%)	Female (%)
	(n = 187)	*(n = 90)*	*(n = 90)*
Alcohol abuse and MD	36.9	34.4	39.2
Alcohol abuse and CD	90.9	94.4	87.6
Alcohol abuse and PTSD	41.7	28.9	**53.6*****
Alcohol abuse and drug abuse	62.0	64.4	59.8
Alcohol abuse and additional disorder	19.8	27.8	**12.4****
Alcohol abuse and two or more additional disorders	77.5	72.2	**82.5**†
	(n = 128)	*(n = 58)*	*(n = 70)*
Alcohol dependence and MD	43.8	44.8	42.9
Alcohol dependence and CD	93.8	91.4	95.7
Alcohol dependence and PTSD	44.5	32.8	**54.3***
Alcohol dependence and drug abuse	63.3	75.9	**52.9****
Alcohol dependence and additional disorder	16.4	12.1	20.0
Alcohol dependence and two or more additional disorders	82.0	86.2	78.6
	(n = 173)	*(n = 88)*	*(n = 85)*
Drug abuse and MD	35.3	31.8	38.8
Drug abuse and CD	90.2	89.8	90.6
Drug abuse and PTSD	42.8	29.5	**56.5*****
Drug abuse and alcohol abuse	67.1	65.9	68.2
Drug abuse and additional disorder	16.8	21.6	**11.8**†
Drug abuse and two or more additional disorders	79.2	71.6	**87.1****

† $p ≤ .10$ between males and females.
* $p ≤ .05$ between males and females.
** $p ≤ .01$ between males and females.
*** $p ≤ .001$ between males and females.

were more likely than drug-abusing males to meet criteria for other disorders, although rates of comorbidity were very high for both genders.

Patterns of drug use across time

The proportions of runaway and homeless adolescents who were marijuana users and who abused drugs other than marijuana were very consistent across the 3 years of data collection. As Figure 6.1 indicates, marijuana users tended to group by frequency of use from those who said they used "never" used marijuana, those who reported having used "a few times" during the previous 3 months (about 20%), and those who reported being weekly users (around 10%) or daily users (around 15%).

Hard drug use (other than marijuana) was much less prevalent across time (Figure 6.2). The proportion of those who reported hard drug use a "few times" in the preceding 3 months fluctuated at or slightly above 10%. The proportion of "regular users"—those who used hard drugs weekly or daily in the preceding 3-month intervals—hovered at around 5% or lower across the 13 interviews. These findings suggest small cores of persistent marijuana and hard drug users who may differ from the rest of the runaways in the sample.

Emerging alcohol dependency

By Wave 13, when the young people were 19–22 years, 19.1% met lifetime criteria for alcohol dependence. We were interested in risk factors for emergent alcohol dependence between Wave 1 and Wave 13 of the study. Table 6.4 presents a stepwise logistic regression analysis of factors predicting alcohol dependence at Wave 13 when controlling for alcohol dependence at Wave 1. The models controlled for age, gender, and sexual orientation of the young people. Subsistence strategies were separated into nonsexual and sexual strategies. Engaging in nonsexual subsistence strategies was measured in each wave by summing six questions that asked if respondents had panhandled, spare changed ("spainging"), broke into stores or houses to steal, stole or shoplifted, or dumpster dived. Respondents must have answered four of six questions to be included in the scale. The scale was dichotomized at each wave to indicate whether respondents had engaged in any of the reported behaviors. The final scale was computed by summing scores across Waves 2 through 13. Respondents must have answered at least one wave to be included in analyses.

Engaging in sexual subsistence strategies (i.e., survival sex) was assessed by three questions asking if respondents had traded sex for money, drugs, or food and shelter. Respondents must have answered two

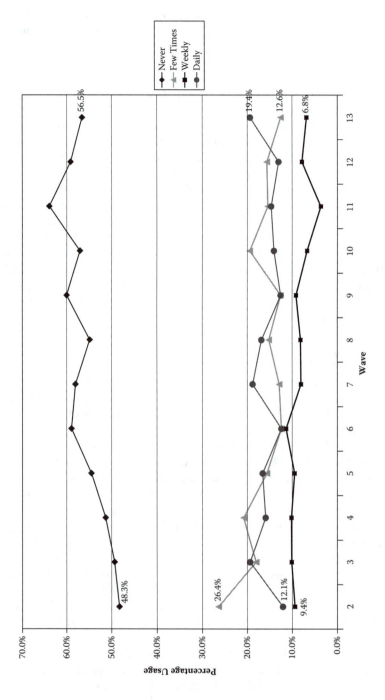

Figure 6.1 Marijuana use, Waves 2–13.

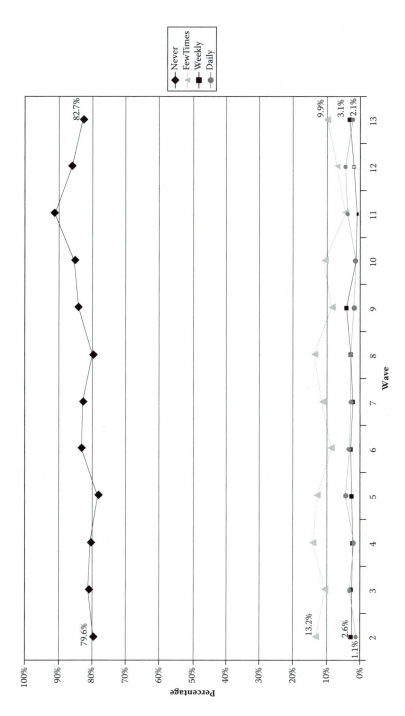

Figure 6.2 Drug use (other than marijuana and alcohol), Waves 2–13.

Table 6.4 Logistic Regression Model Predicting Alcohol Dependence at Wave 13 (N = 194)

	Model 1		Model 2		Model 3		Model 4		Model 5		Model 6	
	b	Exp(b)	b	Exp(b)	b	Exp(b)	b	Exp(b)	b	Exp(b)	b	Exp(b)
Age	0.27	1.31	0.25	1.29	0.27	1.31	0.26	1.29	0.23	1.26	0.37	1.45†
Female	0.07	1.08	0.10	1.11	0.39	1.47	0.28	1.32	0.12	1.13	0.29	1.34
Heterosexual	−0.04	0.96	0.08	1.08	0.28	1.32	0.28	1.32	0.31	1.37	0.55	1.72
Alcohol dependence Wave 1			1.03	2.81**	1.03	2.80**	1.09	2.99**	0.70	2.02†	0.63	1.88
Nonsexual subsistence					1.12	3.06†	0.87	2.38	0.41	1.51	−0.01	0.99
Sexual subsistence							0.92	2.50†	0.74	2.09	0.29	1.34
Comorbidity									2.34	10.39**	2.20	9.02**
Daily alcohol use											1.55	4.70***
Constant	−6.27	0.00†	−6.42	0.00†	−7.28	0.00†	−7.11	0.00*	−8.23	0.00**	−11.27	0.00**
Nagerlkerke		0.02		0.08		0.10		0.12		0.24		0.32
Cox & Snell		0.01		0.05		0.06		0.08		0.15		0.20

† $p \le 0.10$.
* $p \le 0.05$.
** $p \le 0.01$.
*** $p \le 0.001$.

vof three questions to be included in the analysis. The scale was dichoto-mized at each wave to indicate whether respondents had engaged in any of the reported behaviors. The final scale was computed by summing scores across Waves 2 through 13 and then dichotomizing to indicate whether respondents had engaged in any of the reported behaviors in any of the waves. Respondents must have answered at least one wave to be included in analyses. Comorbidity was assessed by the presence of two or more disorders other than alcohol dependence. Daily alcohol use was measured with a sum of the number of waves respondents said they drank alcohol or hard liquor daily. The scale was then dichotomized to indicate whether respondents had engaged in any of the reported behav-iors. Respondents must have answered the question at least at one wave to be included in analyses. Both the nonsexual subsistence and alcohol use scales were divided by the number of waves respondents answered to correct for overresponse by specific individuals.

In Model 1, none of the control variables significantly predicted Wave 13 alcohol dependence. When we added Wave 1 alcohol dependence in Model 2, it increased the likelihood of Wave 13 alcohol dependence nearly three times. Nonsexual deviant survival strategies during Waves 2–13 (Model 3) were associated with the emergence of alcohol dependence at Wave 13 until the sexual subsistence strategies measure was added in Model 4 ($p < .10$). In Model 5, meeting diagnostic criteria for two or more psychiatric disorders (other than alcohol dependence) strongly predicted Wave 13 alcohol dependence increasing the odds of meeting criteria more than 10 times. Daily alcohol use during Waves 2–13 was added to the equa-tion in Model 6 and increased the likelihood of meeting criteria for alco-hol dependence at Wave 13 nearly five times. In the final model (Model 6), Wave 1 alcohol dependence lost significance. The strongest predictor of Wave 13 alcohol dependence was not preexisting dependence but meet-ing criteria for two or more co-occurring psychiatric diagnoses other than alcohol dependence.

To further understand the relationship between Wave 1 psychiat-ric diagnoses and the emergence of alcohol dependence at Wave 13, we checked for overlap between Wave 1 diagnoses and those who became alcohol dependent at Wave 13. All of the young adults who became alcohol dependent at Wave 13 had at least one other psychiatric disorder at Wave 1. This is congruent with Kessler et al.'s (1996) findings that other psychiatric disorders typically occur prior to addictive disorders in young adulthood. About two thirds (67.6%) of those who met criteria for alcohol dependence at Wave 13 had met criteria for alcohol abuse at Wave 1. Similarly, among those who were alcohol dependent at Wave 13, 45.9% had met criteria for major depressive episode (MDE) at Wave 1, and 51.4% had met criteria for PTSD. Nearly two thirds (62.2%) of those who met criteria for alcohol dependence at Wave 13 met lifetime criteria for drug abuse at Wave 1, and 91.9% % had met Wave 1 criteria for conduct disorder (CD).

Summary and discussion

As has been previously documented (Cauce et al., 2000; Feitel et al., 1992; Johnston et al., 2005; Kipke, Montgomery, Simon, & Iverson, 1997), the rates of alcohol and drug abuse among homeless and runaway adolescents are very high. The rates of drug use reported here are very similar to those reported by Cauce and colleagues and are higher than for 12th graders in the Monitoring the Future Study (34.8% vs. 27.4%). The important distinction between runaways and nonrunaways appears to be chronic use versus experimental use and meeting diagnostic criteria for substance abuse disorders. The rate of alcohol abuse disorder reported here is three times that of similarly aged young people in the NCSR, the rate of alcohol dependence is five times that found in the NCSR, and the prevalence of drug abuse disorder is four times that found in the NCSR (Kessler, Berglund, et al., 2005).

Theoretical implications

Becoming substance dependent occurs across time. Among the homeless and runaway adolescents the propensity to become alcohol dependent was profoundly affected by preexisting psychiatric disorders. All of the adolescents who became alcohol dependent over the 3 years of the study met criteria for another psychiatric disorder at Wave 1. This, along with the young people's own statements from our in-depth interviews, lends support to self-medication explanations of emerging alcohol dependence among these young people. In their own words, the adolescents made it very clear that alcohol and drugs were stress reducing and served to remove them from unpleasant situations. For some they were antidepressants; they made them feel happy for a little while. This daily self-medication process may well explain the process through which some eventually become drug and alcohol dependent.

There also is some evidence for gateway theories of drug use. Clearly, alcohol and marijuana were the substances of choice, and even those who had moved on to harder drugs still reported using both. One young man who no longer used hard drugs admitted to continuing marijuana use as if it were not a drug at all; another spoke of using alcohol and marijuana to come down from hard drug highs. For hard drug users, marijuana and alcohol are considered benign.

In the context of life course theory, substance abuse plays a critical role in negative chains of life events. Drugs were the reason one young woman left school. As we saw in the in-depth interviews and document in subsequent chapters, drugs are strongly associated with abusive and violent intimate relationships. Drug use often leads to dabbling in drug dealing to friends and may lead to serious drug dealing with concomitant exposure to violence and, as one young woman told us, criminal charges.

Policy implications

For good reasons, alcohol and drugs are a ubiquitous part of street culture. The young people need them to feel better and to block out the pervasive stress and vulnerability of their situations. Our most controversial policy recommendations are based on accepting the reality of alcohol and drug use in the street culture. We believe that the first and most critical intervention is to keep the runaway from being further harmed. To accomplish this we need shelters that accept young people who are using or currently high as long as they are not violent. Adolescents need a safe place that they can go even when—especially when—they are high. "Crash pads" existed in the 1960s. Similar places may help protect young people on the streets today. They also may provide a critical opportunity for drug education (e.g., dangers of needle sharing, potentially lethal drug combinations, overdose information) and an opportunity for interventions such as Brief Motivational Interviews that have been shown to be effective in drug treatment (D'Amico, Miles, Stern, & Meredith, 2007).

Conclusions

As we show in subsequent chapters, alcohol and drug abuse is associated with increases in other high-risk behaviors such as risky survival strategies (Chapter 12), risky sexual behaviors (Chapter 10), the likelihood of victimization (Chapter 7), and self-harm (Chapters 8 and 9). Indeed, substance abuse plays a role in nearly every negative event or outcome. Although pervasively documented in the literature on homeless and runaway adolescents along with all of its consequences, it is our opinion that our current response is not working. By requiring that homeless young people be sober to be sheltered, we are refusing services to those most at risk and perhaps even missing an intervention opportunity. Being high is part of street life. We cannot continue to ignore it.

chapter 7

Dissociative symptoms

Prevalence, correlates, and association with other mental disorders and problem behaviors

With Katherine A. Johnson

Dissociation has been described as a psychological "gift" to children exposed to severe traumatic events such as emotional, physical, and sexual abuse or experiencing or witnessing severe injuries (Sutton, 2004). The term refers to "a psychological mechanism that allows the mind or body to split off or compartmentalize traumatic experiences or disquieting thoughts from normal consciousness" (Sutton, p. 24). Although the propensity to dissociate in childhood varies (Irwin, 1994), it is considered a normal developmental process of childhood imagination. Intense "pretending" where the child enters fully into an altered state of consciousness is typical in imaginative play (Shirar, 1996). Dissociative experiences are very common (Ross, Joshi, & Currie, 1990) but most prevalent among children up to about age 10 years (Putnam, 1991). There is general consensus that normative dissociation tends to peak in late childhood or early adolescence and then to steadily decline through adolescence into early adulthood (Putnam, Hornstein, & Peterson, 1996; Wallach & Dollinger, 1999 (review)).

When exposed to severe trauma in childhood or early adolescence, this normal psychological mechanism becomes a means of coping. The traumatized child may respond to severe or repeated trauma by "(a) automatization of certain behaviors; (b) resolution of irreconcilable conflicts; (c) escape from the constraints of reality; (d) isolation of catastrophic experiences; (e) cathartic discharge of certain feelings; (f) analgesia; and (g) alteration of sense of self so that a traumatic event is experienced as if 'it is not really happening to me'" (Putnam, 1993, p. 40). These dissociative symptoms are learned in an effort to defend against trauma, but with repetition they may become automatic and uncontrollable responses to stress (Kirby, Chu, & Dill, 1993; Putnam, 1993; Terr, 1991).

Prevalence of dissociative symptoms among adults and adolescents

The prevalence of dissociative symptoms typically is reported as median or mean scores on the Dissociative Experiences Scale (DES) (Berstein & Putnam, 1986). Although there are two recognized versions of the scale (i.e., DES and the DES II), the scoring cutoffs are the same for each version. Psychologically healthy individuals typically score below 20 on the DES (Carlson & Putnam, 2000). Median scores for five nonclinical community populations ranged from 4.4 to 7.8 (Carlson & Putnam, 1993). A recent population study in Finland reported mean DES scores of 8.0 (Maaranen, Tanskanen, Honkalampi, Haatainen, Hintikka, & Viiamaki, 2005).

Prevalence of symptoms varies by the focus of particular measures. For example, using only measures of derealization and depersonalization, Aderibigbe and colleagues reported that about 23% of rural North Carolina adults had experienced one or both of the two symptoms in the past year (Aderibigbe, Bloch, & Walker, 2001). Mulder and colleagues reported that 6.3% of a random sample of New Zealand adults reported three or more frequently occurring dissociative symptoms (Mulder, Beautrais, Joyce, & Fergusson, 1998).

Although the DES median scores are quite low in nonclinical samples, the rates are much higher and vary widely among clinical samples. For example, individuals who meet diagnostic criteria for multiple personality disorder tend to have median DES scores in the 40s and 50s (Carlson & Putnam, 1993; Ross, Norton, & Anderson, 1988). Median DES scores among those who meet criteria for posttraumatic stress disorder (PTSD) range from the high 20s to the low 40s. Those who meet criteria for borderline personality disorder have median scores in the high teens or low 20s, and those with affective disorders tend to have median scores similar to those in the general population or a little higher at 6.0–12.7 (Carlson & Putnam, 1993).

Prevalence rates among children and adolescents

Most of what we know about dissociative symptoms and dissociative disorders among children and adolescents comes from studies of adults who were victimized children or from clinical samples (Diseth, 2005). Studies of maltreated children report the prevalence of dissociative symptoms ranging from 19% to 73% (Silberg, 2000 (review), p. 126). Typically, the more severe and ongoing the maltreatment, the more severe the symptoms (Gershuny & Thayer, 1999 (review); Van Den Bosch, Verheul, Langeland, & Van Den Brink, 2003). Special populations of adolescents such as juvenile offenders and children and adolescents in residential treatment tend to show elevated scores on measures of trauma and dissociation (Brosky & Lally, 2004; Carrion & Steiner, 2000; Kisiel & Lyons, 2001), very likely as a consequence of trauma exposure.

Correlates of dissociative symptoms among children and adolescents

Findings regarding gender distribution of dissociative symptoms have been mixed, probably due to variations in samples and measurement. Available evidence indicates that dissociative disorders are diagnosed for male and female young children at essentially the same rates but that there is a progressive increase in females meeting diagnostic criteria for the disorders from school age to late adolescence (Putnam et al., 1996). In adulthood, females are about nine times more likely to be diagnosed with a dissociative disorder than are males, though this ratio has been called into question and is likely the result of selection bias (Putnam, 1993).

Research based on DES scores indicates no gender differences in prevalence among community samples or clinical samples (Ross et al., 1990; Van IJzendoorn & Schuengel, 1996). Where gender variation has been reported, it appears to be a function of the particular symptoms measured. For example, Aderibigbe and colleagues found that females scored higher on measures of depersonalization and derealization than males in a rural population sample (Aderibigbe et al., 2001). Spitzer and colleagues also found that although there was no gender variation in total DES scores in a large clinical sample made up of various diagnostic groups, women scored significantly higher than males on measures of derealization and depersonalization (Spitzer et al., 2003). A recent study of homeless youth in Seattle found no gender differences in DES scores (Tyler, Cauce, & Whitbeck, 2004).

The most important correlate of dissociative symptoms is the experience of trauma. Although extreme trauma such as combat, serious accidents, physical assaults, or experiencing natural catastrophes can evoke dissociative symptoms (Creamer, O'Donnell, & Pattison, 2003; Elklit & Brink, 2004; Feeny, Zoellner, & Foa, 2000; Kozaric-Kovacic & Borovecki, 2005), by far the most prevalent and researched traumatic events are associated with maltreatment in childhood. Multiple studies have shown insidious acute and chronic effects of childhood sexual abuse on dissociative symptoms among children and adults (Briere & Runtz, 1988; Chu & Dill, 1990; Collin-Vezina & Hebert, 2005; Gershuny & Thayer, 1999 (review); Haugaard, 2004 (review); Irwin, 1994; Kirby et al., 1993; Kisiel & Lyons, 2001; Mulder et al., 1998; Putnam, 1993; Silberg, 2000 (review); Sutton, 2004 (review)). Sexual abuse is probably the single most significant predictor of dissociative symptoms, particularly if there was an early age of onset (Kirby et al., 1993), if it involved a family member as perpetrator (Plattner et al., 2003), if there was penetration (Kirby et al., 1993), or if there was use of force (Sandberg & Lynn, 1992). Physical abuse, especially if it is severe and chronic, has been linked to dissociative symptoms (Carrion & Steiner, 2000; Mulder et al., 1998) as has chronic emotional abuse (Simeon, Guralnik, Schmeidler, Sirof, & Knutelska, 2001).

There is also evidence of family linkages. Children whose parents manifest dissociative symptoms are likely to exhibit symptoms as well (Mann & Sanders, 1994). However, it is unclear whether family linkages are explained by heredity or whether dissociative parents are more likely to maltreat or neglect their children (Egeland & Sussman-Stillman, 1996) and to manifest inconsistent, rejecting parenting styles (Mann & Sanders, 1994). Although several studies have shown that adolescents in the criminal justice system are at risk for dissociative symptoms (Brosky & Lally, 2004; Carrion & Steiner, 2000; Plattner et al., 2003), the single common factor in all of these reports is that adjudicated children are more likely to have experienced significant maltreatment.

The experience of trauma and risk of dissociative symptoms among homeless and runaway adolescents

The high rates of caretaker physical abuse, sexual abuse, neglect, and rejection consistently reported by runaway and homeless adolescents place them at great risk for dissociative symptoms (Janus, Burgess, & McCormack, 1987; Kurtz, Kurtz, & Jarvis, 1991; Pennbridge, Yates, David, & MacKenzie, 1990; Silbert & Pines, 1981; Tyler, Cauce, et al., 2004). Both caretakers and runaways report high levels of family violence (Whitbeck, Hoyt, & Ackley, 1997b). Moreover, the rates of traumatic victimization when the adolescents are on their own are very high (Hagen & McCarthy, 1997; Tyler, Whitbeck, Hoyt, & Cauce, 2004; Whitbeck & Hoyt, 1999); in fact, the rates of physical victimization over the 3 years of the present study were more than 80% (Chapter 8, this volume). There is also constant fearfulness and anxiety of street violence (Kipke, Simon, Montgomery, Unger, & Iverson, 1997) and the inherent stress and anxiety associated with being homeless (Goodman, Saxe, & Harvey, 1991). Such exposures to nontraumatic but threatening stressors can trigger dissociative responses among those who have developed these defensive mechanisms earlier in their lives.

As noted previously, dissociative symptoms are highly associated with PTSD (Bremmer & Brett, 1997; Briere, 2006; Carlson & Putnam, 1993;

Collin-Vezina & Hebert, 2005; van der Hart, Nijenuis, & Steele, 2005). Rates of PTSD among the adolescents in this sample are very high (Chapter 5, this volume; Whitbeck, Johnson, Hoyt, & Cauce, 2004a). There is also evidence that dissociative symptoms are associated with affective disorders (Feeny, Zoellner, Fitzgibbons, & Foa, 2000; Putnam, Carlson, et al., 1996) and psychopathy among adult offenders (Poythress, Skeem, & Lilienfeld, 2006). Significant proportions of the adolescents in this study meet criteria for major depressive disorder (MDE) (Chapter 4, this volume) and antisocial personality disorder (APD) (Chapter, 3, this volume). Moreover, dissociative symptoms are strongly linked to self-mutilating behaviors (Low, Jones, MacLeod, Power, & Duggan, 2000; Saxe, Chawla, & van der Kolk, 2002), which were very prevalent among the adolescents in this sample (Chapter 9, this volume).

In summary, runaway and homeless adolescents meet numerous risk factors for dissociative symptoms. They are highly likely to have been maltreated as children, victimized when on the streets, and exposed to chronic stressors that may trigger memories of maltreatment and victimization. In addition, many meet criteria for psychiatric diagnoses that feature dissociation as part of the diagnostic criteria (e.g., PTSD) or diagnoses where dissociative features have been documented (e.g., APD, MDE). A significant proportion of the runaways also engage in self-mutilating behaviors, which are linked to various dissociative states such as numbing, depersonalization, and derealization. The prevalence of dissociative symptoms, their links to other psychiatric disorders, and their affects on runway and homeless adolescents are essentially unknown.

Prevalence of dissociative symptoms among homeless and runaway adolescents

The Dissociative Experiences Scale-II (DES-II; Carlson & Putnam, 1993) was used to assess dissociative symptoms among the runaway and homeless adolescents at Wave 13. The DES-II has 28 questions and an 11-point response format that ranges from 0% to 100% of the time. Scores for each item range from 0% to 100%. The DES-II score is the sum of all the items divided by the number of items. Carlson and Putnam indicate that psychologically healthy individuals generally score under 20 on the scale. Based on 11 studies, the sample-size weighted mean score for healthy individuals was 11.05 (Van IJzendoorn & Schuengel, 1996).

We assessed dissociative symptoms only at Wave 13 of the study, when the homeless and runaway young people were 19–22 years old. All of the mean DES-II scores, except those for heterosexual females, were 20 or above. The mean scores ranged from 18.5 for heterosexual females to

Table 7.1 Descriptive Statistics for Dissociation by Gender and Sexuality

	Total (%) (N = 192)	Heterosexual		Nonheterosexual	
		Male (%) (*n* = 72)	Female (%) (*n* = 91)	Male (%) (*n* = 8)	Female (%) (*n* = 21)
Mean	21.7	23.4	18.5	33.4	24.9
Median	18.6	21.4	14.3	30.7	21.4
Standard deviation	16.0	16.0	15.2	19.2	15.9
Minimum	0	0	0	1.4	1.8
Maximum	75.7	75.8	72.1	64.3	53.2

33.4 for nonheterosexual males (Table 7.1). There were no statistically significant differences in mean DES-II scores by gender or sexual orientation. Another way to consider DES-II scores is the percentage of the sample that exceed cutoffs of 20, 30, and 40 (Carlson & Putnam, 2000). Approximately one half (48.1%) of the adolescents had DES-II scores of 20 or above, 26.4% had scores of 30 or above, and 16.8% had scores of 40 or above with no significant differences by gender or sexual orientation (not shown in tables).

Table 7.2 shows psychiatric diagnoses and self-mutilating behaviors by DES-II cutoff scores. Among young people who scored 20–29 on the DES-II, approximately three fourths (77.5%) met lifetime criteria for APD, and nearly one half met criteria for alcohol (45%) or drug abuse (47.5%). Those with MDE were more likely to score 20–29 than 30 or above. As the scores increased to 30–39, the percentage of young people who met criteria for PTSD increased, particularly among the young women. More than one half of young women with DES-II scores of 30–39 and 40–49 met criteria for PTSD. Of the women who scored 30–39, 100% met criteria for APD. Two thirds to three fourths of those who met criteria for two or more disorders had scores above the cutoffs for all three scoring categories. Self-mutilating behaviors were most common among those who scored 20–29 and 40 and above on the DES-II. Of the women who scored 40 or above, 50% engaged in self-mutilating behaviors.

Correlates of DES-II scores of 20 or higher

Following Carlson and Putnam (2000), we set a cutoff for dissociation at a DES-II score of 20 or above and used logistic regression to investigate correlates of clinically significant dissociative symptoms among the adolescents at Wave 13 (Table 7.3). Caretaker physical abuse was measured

Table 7.2 DES Scores by Diagnoses and Self-Mutilation

	DES 20–29 (n = 40)			DES 30–39 (n = 18)			DES 40+ (n = 31)		
	Total (%)	Male (%)	Female (%)	Total (%)	Male (%)	Female (%)	Total (%)	Male (%)	Female (%)
Alcohol abuse	45.0	42.1	47.6	38.9	44.4	33.3	35.5	33.3	37.5
Alcohol dependence	30.0	31.6	28.6	16.7	22.2	11.1	35.5	33.3	37.5
Drug abuse	47.5	57.9	38.1	44.4	44.4	44.4	45.2	53.3	37.5
Major depression	40.0	31.6	47.6	16.7	0.0	33.3	32.3	26.7	37.5
Posttraumatic stress	25.0	10.5	38.1	44.4	33.3	55.6	38.7	20.0	56.3
Antisocial personality	77.5	78.9	76.2	88.9	77.8	100.0	71.0	80.0	62.5
Comorbidity	72.5	73.7	71.4	66.7	55.6	77.8	71.0	73.3	68.8
Self-mutilation	33.3	38.9	28.6	11.8	12.5	11.1	38.7	26.7	50.0
Cutting or carving	5.1	5.6	4.8	5.9	12.5	0.0	9.7	0.0	18.8

Table 7.3 Logistic Regression Model Predicting Dissociation ($N = 184$)

	Model 1		Model 2		Model 3		Model 4		Model 5		Model 6		Model 7		Model 8	
	b	Exp(b)	b	Exp(b)	b	Exp(b)	b	Exp(b)	b	Exp(b)	b	Exp(b)	b	Exp(b)	b	Exp(b)
Age	0.31*	1.36	0.22	1.25	0.25	1.29	0.20	1.22	0.17	1.18	0.16	1.17	0.17	1.19	0.16	1.17
Female	-0.40	0.67	-0.63†	0.53	-0.64†	0.53	-0.54	0.59	-0.61	0.54	-0.60	0.55	-0.53	0.59	-0.55	0.58
Heterosexual	-0.74†	0.48	-0.53	0.59	-0.38	0.68	-0.43	0.65	-0.51	0.60	-0.52	0.60	-0.42	0.66	-0.40	0.67
Sexual abuse			0.20*	1.23	0.21*	1.24	0.14	1.15	0.17†	1.19	0.17†	1.19	0.15	1.16	0.16	1.17
Physical abuse			0.03	1.03	0.03	1.03	0.00	1.00	-0.01	0.99	-0.01	0.99	0.00	1.00	-0.01	1.00
Cutting and carving					1.38	3.97	1.64†	5.13	1.52†	4.58	1.32	3.75	1.57†	4.82	1.45	4.24
Physical victimization							0.55**	1.74	0.56**	1.75	0.51**	1.67	0.52**	1.68	0.49**	1.63
Sexual victimization							0.35†	1.42	0.34	1.40	0.32	1.37	0.36†	1.44	0.32	1.38
Major depression									0.83†	2.30	0.75†	2.11				
Conduct disorder									-0.01	0.99	-0.04	0.96				
Posttraumatic stress disorder									-0.26	0.77	-0.19	0.83				
Alcohol abuse											-0.07	0.93				
Alcohol dependence											0.56	1.74				
Drug abuse											0.08	1.08				
Single diagnosis													-0.52	0.59		
Two or more diagnoses															0.60†	1.82
Constant	-4.66		-3.65		-4.34		-3.982		-3.32		-3.22		-3.38		-3.50	
Nagelkerke	0.07		0.14		0.15		0.27		0.29		0.30		0.28		0.29	
Cox & Snell	0.05		0.10		0.12		0.20		0.22		0.23		0.21		0.22	

† $p \le .10$.
* $p \le .05$.
** $p \le .01$.

by the sum of seven physical abuse items. The items included incidents such as having objects thrown at them, being pushed shoved or grabbed, being slapped, being hit with an object, being beaten with fists, and being threatened or wounded with a weapon. Caretaker sexual abuse was measured by the sum of two sexual abuse items: being asked to do something sexual or being made to do something sexual. Cut/carve skin was measured with a single item at Wave 13 that asked respondents if they had cut or carved their skin in the past 12 months. Sexual and physical victimization were a sum of the respective victimization occurrences from Waves 1 to 13. Each was weighted by the number of waves in which the respondent participated. PTSD, MDE, and APD were stepped into the equation in Model 5, and the substance abuse disorders (SUDs) were added in Model 6. Meeting criteria for a single disorder and for two or more co-occurring disorders was added in the final model.

In Model 1 with only age of adolescent, gender, and sexual orientation in the model, older adolescents and nonheterosexuals were more likely to score 20 or higher on the DES-II than younger adolescents and heterosexuals. Caretaker physical and sexual abuse were added in Model 2. Experiencing sexual abuse by a caretaker increased the likelihood of scoring 20 or above on the DES-II by 23%. Age and sexual orientation became nonsignificant in Model 2. Cutting and carving was added to the regression equation in Model 3 and was nonsignificant. However, when physical and sexual street victimization were added to the equation in Model 4, cutting and carving emerged as marginally significant ($p <$ .10) and increased the odds of exceeding the cutoff of 20 on the DES-II fivefold. Having experienced physical victimization when on the streets increased the odds of exceeding the cutoff of 20 on the DES-II measure by 74% and having experienced sexual abuse increased the odds 42%. In Model 5, meeting criteria for MDE increased the odds of a DES-II score of 20 or above more than two times. When the substance abuse disorders were added to the equation in Model 6, none was statistically significant. Meeting criteria for any single psychiatric disorder (Model 7) was added in a separate equation not including any of the individual diagnoses and was not significantly associated with a DES-II cutoff score of 20 or above. Similarly, a separate equation for meeting criteria for two or more psychiatric disorders (Model 8) indicated that comorbid psychiatric disorders increased the odds DES-II scores of 20 or above nearly two times ($p <$ .10).

Summary and discussion

The mean DES-II scores for the adolescents in our sample were several times those reported in population studies (Maaranen et al., 2005) and higher than those reported in some clinical samples (Carlson & Putnam,

1993; Silberg, 2000). According to Carlson and Putnam (2000), DES-II scores of 20 or above are clinically significant, and, as scores increase, the likelihood of significant mental health consequences becomes greater. This was certainly true among the runaway and homeless adolescents. High DES-II scores were particularly evident among those meeting criteria for APD, SUDs, MDE, and PTSD. Scores of 40 or greater are indicative of dissociative disorders such as multiple personality disorder (Carlson & Putnam, 1993; Ross, Norton, & Anderson, 1988). The young people with scores of 40 or higher who met criteria for one of the psychiatric disorders are very likely to have a co-occurring dissociative disorder.

The profile of the young adult homeless or runaway with clinically significant dissociative symptoms is that of a young woman who has experienced sexual abuse by a caretaker and later victimization when on the streets. She is likely to engage in self-mutilating behaviors, to be depressed, to abuse substances, and to meet criteria for APD. She is also likely to meet criteria for co-occurring disorders. The rates of DES-II scores 20 or above for both men and women suggest that many of these young people have clinically significant dissociating symptoms and that these symptoms should be taken into account by street workers, therapists, criminal justice professionals, and emergency room workers who encounter homeless young people.

Theoretical implications

Dissociation, alone and in combination with substance abuse, may be an important coping mechanism for homeless and runaway adolescents. Although it plainly decreases as the adolescents age, simply "spacing out" when high or imagining a safer, happier place may alleviate stress and decrease fear. The quantitative findings suggest that dissociation is strongly linked to substance use, and this is supported by some of the qualitative interviews quoted in Chapter 6. At this point we need to learn more about the extent of dissociative symptoms among homeless young people, the precise sequence of the origin of symptoms, and the degree to which they interrelate and contribute to other psychiatric symptoms.

Policy implications

Although these findings are highly intriguing, they indicate the need for more thorough diagnostic screenings for homeless people that include consideration of dissociative disorders, comorbidty, and Axis II disorders such as borderline personality disorder where dissociation is part of the diagnostic criteria. Multiple measures of dissociative symptoms are in order rather than relying completely on the DES-II. We may be underreporting an important subgroup of psychiatric symptoms and perhaps underdiagnosing Axis II disorders such as borderline personality disorder. We are aware of no studies of homeless people that screened for this disorder.

Conclusions

Dissociation may well be an overlooked means of coping with the enormous stresses associated with homelessness. Also, many of the young people arrive on the streets with dissociative symptoms deriving from early caretaker abuse, and street experiences may exacerbate the tendency to use this coping mechanism. Others may learn to separate themselves from difficult situations by psychologically removing themselves from traumatic events or uncomfortable environments, often with the aid of alcohol and drugs. Regardless, the amount of dissociative symptoms among these young people suggests we may be overlooking significant psychopathology in our work with them.

section 3

Unintentional and intentional injuries from adolescent to early adulthood

chapter 8

Victimization and revictimization among homeless and runaway adolescents

With Devan M. Crawford

Probably more has been written about the victimization of homeless and runaway adolescents than any other aspect of their lives. High rates of victimization among homeless adolescents have been reported for more than 2 decades (e.g., Janus, Burgess, & McCormack, 1987; Kufeldt & Nimmo, 1987; Saltonstall, 1984; Silbert & Pines, 1981; Pennbridge, Yates, David, & MacKenzie, 1990). Runaways leave home largely as a consequence of overt emotional, physical, and sexual abuse in families of origin or as victims of neglect in disorganized families where they have lacked basic needs and adult monitoring and support. Once on their own, because of their age and lifestyle exposure they are highly vulnerable to subsequent personal victimization on the streets (Kipke, Simon, Montgomery, Unger, & Iverson, 1997; Whitbeck, Hoyt, Yoder, Cauce, & Paradise, 2001).

This sequence of early caretaker maltreatment and subsequent street victimization exacts cumulative psychological tolls (Whitbeck & Hoyt, 1999; Whitbeck, Hoyt, & Yoder, 1999). Victimization of homeless adolescents has been linked to psychological and behavioral outcomes such as deviant behaviors (Hagen & McCarthy, 1997; Whitbeck et al., 2001), posttraumatic stress disorder (PTSD; Stewart, Steiman, Cauce, Cochran, Whitbeck, & Hoyt, 2004), alcohol and drug abuse (Chen, Tyler, Whitbeck, & Hoyt, 2004; McMorris, Tyler, Whitbeck, & Hoyt, 2002; Rew, Taylor-Seehafer, & Fitzgerald, 2001), and depressive symptoms (Whitbeck, Hoyt, & Bao, 2000). However, a lack of prospective studies of runaways has limited our ability to investigate important causes and consequences of victimization, particularly associations between early caretaker abuse and subsequent street victimization among runaway and homeless adolescents. Although we have correlational evidence for the effects of early caretaker abuse on revictimization when on the streets (e.g., Tyler, Hoyt, & Whitbeck, 2000; Tyler, Hoyt, Whitbeck, & Cauce, 2001b), we do not understand the causal relationships or the specific mechanisms through which early victimization affects later victimization among this high-risk population. In this chapter we revisit self-reported rates of caretaker abuse and street victimization among homeless and runaway adolescents and investigate the effects of caretaker maltreatment reported at Wave 1 on later street victimization reported in Waves 2–13.

Caretaker and street victimization of homeless and runaway adolescents

Caretaker maltreatment

Evidence for caretaker victimization of runaways has been accumulating for years. Rates of caretaker victimization vary widely, ranging from 28% (Kurtz, Kurtz, & Jarvis, 1991) to 71.5% (Janus et al., 1987) depending on sample characteristics. For example, the high rates reported by Janus and colleagues are from a single shelter sample of male runaways, whereas the lower rates reported by Kurtz and associates are from shelters in eight southeastern states. Even among multistate samples, caretaker victimization rates vary widely; the National Network of Runaway and Youth Services reports that 70% of runaways in shelters have been physically or sexually abused (Kennedy, 1991). Southern California and Seattle samples show rates of 40% to 50% (Cauce et al., 1998).

At least one study has shown that parents/caretakers of runaways confirm the high levels of violence and abuse in families of origin reported by their offspring (Whitbeck & Hoyt, 1999; Whitbeck, Hoyt, & Ackley, 1997b). Although adult caretakers recounted lower rates of abusive treatment than did their adolescent offspring particularly for the most severe types of abuse, they confirmed serious levels of maltreatment. For example, two thirds of the adult caretakers reported that the adolescent had been slapped, 80% said that an adult caretaker had thrown something at the adolescent in anger, and one third of the adults reported that a caretaker had hit the adolescent with a fist (Whitbeck & Hoyt).

Caretaker sexual abuse of runaways also has been widely reported with rates ranging from a high of 60% among juvenile and adult street prostitutes (Silbert & Pines, 1981) to 47% of females and 19% of males in Seattle (Cauce et al., 1998). Rates vary by how *sexual abuse* is operationalized. If the construct includes behaviors other than actual sexual assault, rates tend to be higher. For example, in the Seattle study, 28.8% of the young women said that an adult had them "do something sexual," 29.5% reported that an adult had touched them sexually, and 16.2% said that an adult had attempted or engaged in penetration (Tyler et al., 2001b).

As with physical abuse, rates of sexual abuse also vary by reporter. In a matched caretaker–runaway adolescent sample, caretakers were about one half as likely as the runaway adolescents to report that the child had experienced some type of sexual abuse (18% vs. 30%). A total of 15% of the caretakers (compared with 35% of the children) reported that their child had been forced to have sex (Whitbeck & Hoyt, 1999).

Street victimization

For adolescents on the streets, the environment is essentially a combat zone. Rates of physical and sexual assaults are extremely high and, at least in the case of sexual assault, are apt to be underreported (Tyler & Johnson, 2006). Kipke and colleagues found that more than 50% of their sample of Hollywood street kids had been beaten up on the streets, 45% had been chased, 26% had been shot at, 9% had been stabbed, and 15% had been sexually assaulted. Their risk was such that they lived in constant fear. More than one half feared being shot or stabbed, and nearly one half feared sexual and physical assault (Kipke, Montgomery, Simon, Unger, & Johnson, 1997). In a four-state Midwest sample, 19.7% reported they had been robbed, 26.8% beaten up, 31.5% threatened with a weapon, and 15.6% assaulted with a weapon. Of the young women, 18% had been sexually assaulted when on the streets (Whitbeck & Hoyt, 1999). Rotherum-Borus and associates reported rates of physical and sexual assault on the streets at 20% of their sample of homeless adolescents in New York City (Rotheram-Borus, Rosario, & Koopman, 1991).

Prevalence of various types of caretaker maltreatment

To our knowledge, there has yet to be a comprehensive breakdown of various types of caretaker maltreatment of homeless and runaway adolescents. Here we present adolescent reported rates of caretaker neglect, emotional abuse, physical abuse, and sexual abuse. Because there is evidence that nonheterosexual runaway and homeless adolescents report higher rates of parental rejection, neglect, and abuse than their heterosexual counterparts (Cochran, Stewart, Ginzler, & Cauce, 2002; Whitbeck, Chen, Hoyt, Tyler, & Johnson, 2004), we provide comparisons of self-reports of victimization by adolescent gender and sexual orientation.

Caretaker neglect

Reports of caretaker neglect ranged from 83.8% who said they were ignored by their parents to 27.7% who reported that their caretakers refused to get them help for emotional and behavioral problems (Table 8.1). Approximately 45% reported that caretakers had threatened to abandon them, and about one half (51.2%) said that their caretakers actually had left them in the care of relatives or friends for an extended period of time. More than one third (33.4%) of the adolescents said that their caretakers had refused them needed medical care. A full 43% of the adolescents said that their caretakers had driven recklessly or when drunk when they were in the car. About one half (54.8%) reported that their caretakers did not monitor their whereabouts, and 46% indicated that caretakers did not attempt to monitor negative behaviors such as alcohol and drug use. More than three fourths said that they had been expected to perform caretaker roles for self and siblings.

Only two of the gender differences on the neglect measure were statistically significant among heterosexuals. Females were more likely than males to say that a caretaker had driven recklessly or while intoxicated when they were in the vehicle. Females were also more likely to report that a caretaker refused to get them help for emotional or behavioral problems. There were six statistically significant differences between heterosexual and nonheterosexual young people. Nonheterosexual young women were more likely than their heterosexual counterparts to report that they had been threatened with abandonment, had been delayed in getting needed medical care, and had been refused or delayed in getting help for emotional or behavioral problems. Nonheterosexual males were less likely than heterosexual males to recount that they had been left with relatives or friends and more likely than heterosexual males to say that they had been refused help for emotional or behavioral problems by caretakers.

The picture of caretaker behaviors that emerges from the neglect measure is one of disengagement, failure to provide for basic needs, lack of monitoring, and an expectation that the adolescents could care for themselves and siblings. For example, one young woman (aged 19 years) told us:

> My dad he used to drink and do drugs, on a daily basis and he used to beat us kids a lot. My mom she's worse. She still drinks she's a very big alcoholic and she's still a drug addict. But before we went into state's custody she used to lock us out of the house for days at a time. And she would leave for like months at a time and go do her thing and then come back and so I mean yeah it's been around. And now it's still a thing. Only difference is that my dad, he still smokes pot and he still drinks but he knows

Table 8.1 Caretaker Neglect at Wave 1 (N = 427)

	Heterosexual (N = 365)			Nonheterosexual (N = 62)		
	Total (%)	Male (%)	Female (%)	Total (%)	Male (%)	Female (%)
Ignored	83.8	81.5	85.8	85.5	83.3	86.4
Threatened to abandon	44.7	47.0	42.6	54.8	44.4	59.1[b]
Refused medical care	33.4	29.2	37.1	45.2	33.3	50.0
Waited for medical care	40.5	39.3	41.6	54.8	38.9	61.4[b]
Left with friends or relatives	51.2	50.0	52.3	43.5	27.8[a]	50.0
Not cared who with, where, or when	54.8	57.1	52.8	59.7	55.6	61.4
Reckless or drunk driving with you	42.6	36.9	47.4*	53.2	38.9	59.1
Not prevented from using alcohol or drugs	46.0	49.4	43.1	46.8	44.4	47.7
Not prevented from skipping school	38.8	37.7	39.8	44.3	44.4	44.2
Not prevented from negative things (e.g. fighting)	49.3	49.4	49.2	48.4	38.9	52.3
Refused get help emotional or behavior problems	27.7	23.4	31.5[†]	50.0	44.4[b]	52.3[c]
Long time for help for emotional behavior problems	31.6	29.9	33.0	53.2	44.4	56.8[c]
Expected you take care of self and siblings	75.3	72.0	78.2	85.2	82.4	86.4

[†] $p \leq .10$ (gender significance test).
[*] $p \leq .05$ (gender significance test).
[a] $p \leq .10$ (sexuality by gender significance test).
[b] $p \leq .05$ (sexuality by gender significance test).
[c] $p \leq .01$ (sexuality by gender significance test).

how to control himself now. And my mom she's still
a drug addict and an alcoholic.

Another young woman (aged 20 years) told us she had essentially
raised herself and her siblings:

> When I was 11 my mom was always working and my
> mom's boyfriend was always off in the bar drinking
> or in jail so from the time I was 11 I started raising
> myself—cooking, cleaning, doing my own laundry.
> I started taking care of my brother from the time I
> moved back to my mom's house when I was 13....
> My brother would have been 3 months old.... I took
> care of my sister from the day she was born when I
> was 16 until I moved out of my house when she was
> turning 2. I just couldn't handle it anymore, I went
> from being at school to being at home taking care of
> two kids, cleaning house, doing dishes, doing laun-
> dry, making sure dinner's done, making sure the
> kids had clean clothes, the baths, the stories, mak-
> ing sure their toys were picked up. I felt like I was
> going from 17 to 37, and I couldn't take it no more.

Caretaker emotional abuse

The adolescents reported high levels of emotionally abusive and rejecting behaviors by caretakers (Table 8.2). In the study, 80% to 90% said that
their caretakers were critical of them and had said hurtful and insulting
things to them. More than 70% of heterosexuals and more than 80% of
nonheterosexuals reported that their caretakers had told them that they
were a bad person. More than one half indicated that their caretakers had
threatened or actually abused another family member in front of them.
For example, one young man (aged 20 years) reported that he had never
been physically abused but:

> Hmmm...no. Other than well mentally abused I
> could say because I watched my dad beat my mom
> when I was really young and that sucked.

Table 8.2 Emotional Abuse at Wave 1 (*N* = 427)

	Heterosexual (*N* = 365)			Nonheterosexual (*N* = 62)		
	Total (%)	Male (%)	Female (%)	Total (%)	Male (%)	Female (%)
Said hurtful and insulting things	84.4	81.0	**87.3†**	87.1	77.8	90.9
Called names or criticized you	90.1	88.1	91.9	88.7	88.9	88.6
Told you, you were bad person	73.2	70.2	75.6	85.5	83.3	86.4
Made you feel unimportant or not special	77.5	73.2	**81.2†**	87.1	83.3	88.6
Threatened to hit/ throw thing at family member	59.7	57.1	61.9	54.8	44.4	59.1
Hit/throw thing at family member	62.9	58.1	**67.0†**	59.7	44.4	65.9

† *p* ≤ .10 (gender significance test).

Physical abuse

The adolescents reported rates of physical abuse very similar to those in our first Midwestern multistate study (Whitbeck & Hoyt, 1999, Table 5.2, p. 59), which lends credence to the findings. More than 70% of the adolescents reported that an adult caretaker had thrown something at them in anger, pushed, shoved, or grabbed them, slapped them in the face or head, or hit them with an object (Table 8.3). There were no statistically significant differences in these caretaker behaviors by gender or sexual orientation of the adolescents. More than 40% of heterosexual adolescents and more than 50% of nonheterosexual adolescents reported that they had been beaten with fists by an adult caretaker. A full 27% of the heterosexual males said that an adult caretaker had threatened them with a weapon compared with 19.3% of their heterosexual female counterparts. The rates were very similar for nonheterosexual males (22.2%) and females (25%). Nonheterosexual females (13.6%) were more likely than heterosexual males (7.7%), heterosexual females (5.6%), or nonheterosexual males (11.1%) to say that a caretaker had assaulted them with a weapon.

Often there were long histories of abuse. One young man (aged 19 years) described physical abuse beginning at age 5 or 6:

Table 8.3 Caretaker Physical and Sexual Abuse at Wave 1 (*N* = 427)

	Heterosexual (N = 365)			Nonheterosexual (N = 62)		
	Total (%)	Male (%)	Female (%)	Total (%)	Male (%)	Female (%)
Locked in closet	23.9	21.0	26.4	**35.5ª**	**38.9ª**	34.1
Tied arms or legs together	12.9	14.9	11.2	19.4	22.2	18.2
Thrown something at in anger	70.7	68.5	72.6	80.6	72.2	84.1
Pushed, shoved, or grabbed	83.8	82.1	85.3	85.5	88.9	84.1
Slapped in the face or head	78.1	74.4	81.2	74.2	66.7	77.3
Hit with an object	74.4	74.1	74.6	77.4	66.7	81.8
Beat with fists	42.3	43.1	41.6	53.2	55.6	52.3
Threatened with weapon	23.0	27.4	**19.3†**	24.2	22.2	25.0
Wounded with weapon	6.6	7.7	5.6	**12.9ª**	11.1	**13.6ª**
Asked for sexual favors	17.0	7.7	**25.0****	**38.3ᵈ**	**29.4ᶜ**	**41.9ᵇ**
Sexually abused	20.3	8.9	**30.1****	**38.3ᶜ**	17.6	**46.5ᵇ***

† *p* ≤ .10 (gender significance test).
* *p* ≤ .05 (gender significance test).
** *p* ≤ .001 (gender significance test).
ª *p* ≤ .10 (sexuality by gender significance test).
ᵇ *p* ≤ .05 (sexuality by gender significance test).
ᶜ *p* ≤ .01 (sexuality by gender significance test).
ᵈ *p* ≤ .001 (sexuality by gender significance test).

It had a lot to do with physical abuse and just starting to get tired of it a little.... I'd tell people and nobody would listen. I mean like my parents would portray me out to be a pathological liar to the police and everybody else. It was like you know, there wasn't anything I could do.... The police would take me back home. I would try to tell them what was going on and they'd talk to my parents and my parents would tell them their story, my mom covering

> up for my stepdad and my stepdad just sitting there
> bluntly lying to them. So the moment the police left
> I left too. I actually ended up with frostbite one time
> because of that.

As the young people became older, the violence was often mutual.
For example, one young woman (aged 20 years) described a fist fight with
her mother:

> She was really upset. She was had probably been
> drinking and on top of that she did crack so you
> know her moods was like wild. And I was stand-
> ing there washing dishes and she came in and she
> chocked me and she started hitting me with her
> fists. I fell down and my first reaction was you know
> to hit her back. When somebody's hitting you, you
> know you gonna hit them back. And I drew back
> on her and she was kind of just like you gonna hit
> me. It became really physical after that she kind of
> pretty much stomped me to the ground.

As we have shown elsewhere, as the young person matures and
begins to fight back, both parents and child will report violence, but each
views himself or herself as the victim (Whitbeck et al., 1997b).

Sexual abuse

The young women were significantly more likely than young men to
report having been asked for sexual favors by a caretaking adult or to
have been sexually abused by a caretaking adult, regardless of sexual orientation (Table 8.3). A total of 30% of heterosexual females and 46.5% of
nonheterosexual females reported that they had been sexually abused.
Nonheterosexual males (17.6%) were about twice as likely to report sexual
abuse than were heterosexual males (8.9%) and more than three times
more likely to report that they had been asked for sexual favors (29.4% vs.
7.7%). In general, the nonheterosexual adolescents were much more likely
to report any kind of sexual maltreatment by caretakers than were their
heterosexual counterparts. Those most likely to have been maltreated sexually were nonheterosexual females.

The average age at first abuse was about 6 1/2 years for heterosexual adolescents and 10 1/2 years for nonheterosexual adolescents.
Nonheterosexual males on average reported the youngest age of first

abuse, 4.7 years (not shown in table). One young woman (aged 19 years) recalled very early abuse:

> I've always been abused. I've been abused ever since I was little; that's one of the reason's why I went into the state's custody was because I was mentally physically emotionally abused sexually abused.

One of the young men (aged 21 years) recalled being sexually abused by his father at age 6 or 7 years:

> My mom and dad was separated, and me and my sister was visiting and I was living with my father for a little while. I really don't remember all the details; I just remember when I was sleeping and he was messing around with me. And when my sister was taking a bath he went in there messing around with her.

Street victimization

Physical victimization

Leaving home proved to be very dangerous. At baseline, about one third (31.5%) of the heterosexual adolescents reported that they had been beaten up, as did 50% of the nonheterosexual adolescents (Table 8.4). Approximately one fourth (26%) of the heterosexual adolescents had been robbed while on the streets. Nonheterosexual males (55.6%) were nearly twice as likely to report having been robbed on the streets than were heterosexual males (26.2%). Heterosexual males (57.1%) and nonheterosexual females (54.5%) were more likely to have been threatened with a weapon when on the streets than their opposite-sex counterparts. Heterosexual males (35.1%) were more than twice as likely to have been assaulted with a weapon when on the streets than were heterosexual females (14.2%). Weapon assault rates for nonheterosexual males (16.7%) were similar to those for heterosexual females, and the rates for nonheterosexual females (29.5%) were similar to those for heterosexual males. One young man (aged 19 years) shared his experience of being threatened with a gun:

> I had I was staying with these people ... and one day these people got robbed, see ... so I came back the next day and they told me they got robbed or whatever. And then all of a sudden these guns started

Table 8.4 Street Victimization at Wave 1 (*N* = 427)

	Heterosexual (N = 365)			Nonheterosexual (N = 62)		
	Total (%)	Male (%)	Female (%)	Total (%)	Male (%)	Female (%)
Beaten up	31.5	35.7	27.9	50.0	44.4	52.3[c]
Robbed	26.0	26.2	25.9	37.1	**55.6**[c]	**29.5**[†]
Threatened with weapon	46.6	57.1	**37.6****	51.6	44.4	**54.5**[b]
Assaulted with weapon	23.8	35.1	**14.2****	25.8	16.7	**29.5**[b]
Sexual advances	31.0	19.2	**41.1****	53.2	**38.9**[b]	**59.1**[b]
Sexual assault	15.7	3.0	**26.4****	33.9	**11.1**[a]	**43.2**[b*]

[†] *p* ≤ .10 (gender significance test).
[*] *p* ≤ .05 (gender significance test).
[**] *p* ≤ .001 (gender significance test).
[a] *p* ≤ .10 (sexuality by gender significance test).
[b] *p* ≤ .05 (sexuality by gender significance test).
[c] *p* ≤ .01 (sexuality by gender significance test).

appearing in the house; they got guns over here, guns behind the clock, and guns in the basement or whatever…. Then one day I came back. Somebody was all up in there eating because they couldn't find no scraps. And somebody told the person that I had took it. So there they drug me down to the basement they put the guns to my stomach and they was like this is where my gun at I'm going to shoot you…. And then from that point I left.

Often the threats or assaults with weapons were connected to some sort of fight or criminal behavior. In this example the young man (aged 20 years) was engaged in a robbery when he was shot at:

And then another time up in Illinois this is the second time I got shot at. Because I was hanging out with my friend…. he decided that he was gonna rob somebody and we went to this apartment and we were in there and next thing you know Jim comes flying out of the bedroom and I hear somebody yelling at him. He has a big old bag under his fucking

arm like a backpack and we take off running out
the apartment and next thing you know I hear *crack
crack crack* behind us. I fucking fell down, fucking fall down in front. Crawl to the car and got in.
Apparently my friend fucking robbed the people of
a quarter pound of marijuana. This is what it sounds
like you know. And that's that's like the second time
I've been shot at.

Sexual victimization

In general, young women were more likely to be subjected to sexual
advances and sexual assault on the streets than were young men. A total
of 41% of heterosexual women and 59.1% of nonheterosexual women
reported unwanted sexual advances when on the streets. This is more
than twice that reported for heterosexual males (19.2%). Rates of unwanted
sexual advances for nonheterosexual males (38.9%) were very similar to
those for heterosexual females. More than one fourth (26.4%) of the heterosexual women and 43.2% of nonheterosexual women had been sexually assaulted while on the streets. This compares with 3% of heterosexual
males and 11.1% of nonheterosexual males.

Women alone in the neighborhoods and "camps" that homeless people frequent are easy prey, as this example illustrates:

I was 19 and hitchhiking and I was in a big city at
the mission for a day and cause I needed to shower
and all that good stuff. My friend Kat who was with
me. He's like well I'll leave you in there. I'll find a
camp so you can come to camp when you're done
with everything and so I went in there and I took
a shower and I ate and I you know got everything
situated and stuff. then I'm walking toward where
he said camp was and a man raped me. It wasn't
physically violent because I'm not stupid. When a
man is trying to get something from you as far as
sexualness and he's trying to rape you to show no
fear and to maybe show a little bit of pleasure in it.
As weird as it sounds he's not going to want to do
it anymore because it's all about control and fear.
That's what I did and it didn't last very long and he
didn't even get a nut or anything. He's like fuck you
bitch and he walked off and so I pulled back on my

pants and went to down to the river where Kat was. (female, aged 22 years)

Most often it was acquaintance rape:

> He seemed really nice and sweet and we'd been talking for, I don't know, a month and a half two months, and I finally let him come to my apartment. I went to go use the restroom and I came back and when I came back into the living room.... He trapped me in the corner and he told me you know pretty much what anybody would tell you. Don't scream don't do nothing, cause I'll hurt you. And then he told me you know he'll be watching me he'll be watching me closely and don't say nothing because if I did then not only would he hurt me he was going to hurt Crystal too because she lived there. And so I didn't say nothing and then right before he was getting his clothes on or whatever and I went to I went to go clean myself off and everything and when I came back he took all my money ... my identification, my social security card, my driver's license—everything, he took everything. And then he left, and I never seen him since then. (female, aged 19 years)

And, when it was acquaintance rape, the young women typically blamed themselves for being in the situation and felt powerless to do anything:

> I actually did think I was pregnant and I ended up going to [agency name] and getting checked out for [sexually transmitted diseases] STDs and stuff like that and it ended up I wasn't pregnant. And that was just like a total relief and I was extremely happy about it. My friends wanted to take me to the hospital that night but I was so incredibly gone I mean I just I drank like a keg of beer on my own literally and I smoked like an ounce of weed on my own. It was just one of those things that if you went to the hospital or something they'd be like this was your own doing. You know your own fault and I figured nothing would be done about it so I didn't take the legal way out. (female, aged 19 years)

Because of the inebriation I didn't feel that there was any way that I could I could press charges. Since then I found out that you can, but still it's like just because I'm drunk doesn't mean that my mind should be altered. And basically I admit half the responsibility for what happened simply because um I shouldn't be getting inebriated around certain people or because whatever reason that it happened something had to be done on my part to let it. To an extent. (female, aged 22 years)

Physical and sexual street victimization across time

We did survival analyses to track physical and sexual street victimization from Wave 2 through Wave 13 of the study. By the final wave only 9% of the men and 15% of the women who had remained in the study had not been physically victimized when on the streets (Figure 8.1). At Wave 1 of the study about 30% of the young women reported they had been sexually assaulted. By Wave 13, of those who had remained in the study, this had increased to 42%, a 40% increase in 3 years. Sexual assault among males tripled in the 3 years of the study—from approximately 3% at Wave 1 to approximately 11% by Wave 13 (Figure 8.2).

Revictimization among homeless and runaways adolescents: the relationship between caretaker maltreatment and subsequent street victimization

Research consistently has shown that correlations between childhood physical and sexual maltreatment and later adolescent and adult physical and sexual victimization are persistent and robust. That caretaker maltreatment has negative development impacts is well established (Kendall-Tackett, Williams, & Finkelhor, 1993 (review); MacMillan et al., 2001; Molnar, Buka, & Kessler, 2001; Rind & Tromovitch, 1997 (review); Silverman, Reinherz, & Giaconia, 1996). However, it remains unclear precisely what outcomes are important risk factors for later revictimization and what specific mechanisms are at work (Messman & Long, 1996 (review); Rich, Combs-Lane, Resnick, & Kilpatrick, 2002 (review). Several prospective studies have linked psychological outcomes attributed to childhood maltreatment to adult risk. For example, Swanston and colleagues identified externalizing and internalizing symptoms that could result in later victimization (Swanston, Plunkett, O'Toole, Shrimpton, Parkinson, & Oates, 2003). Externalizing behaviors put individuals at risk

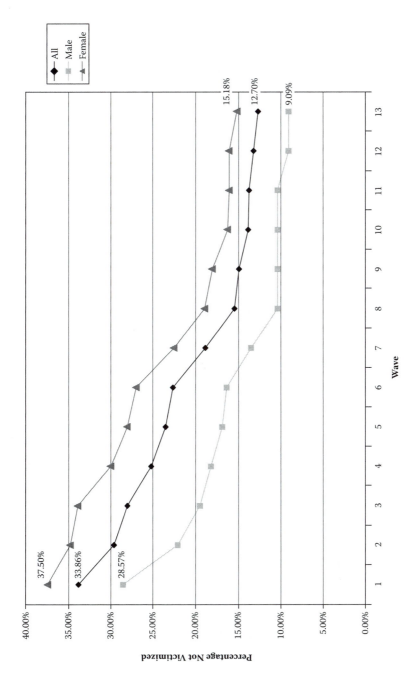

Figure 8.1 Physical victimization survival curve from initial status.

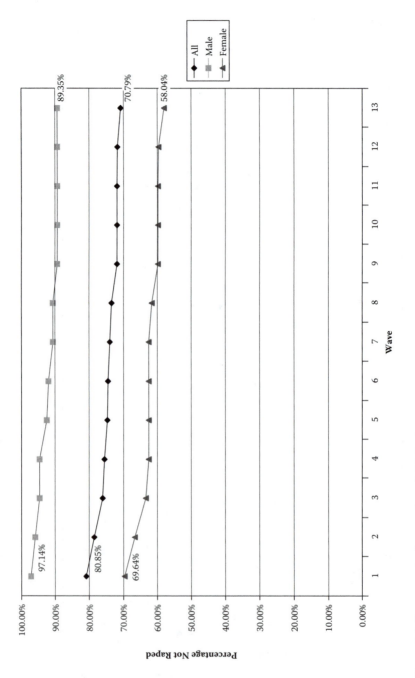

Figure 8.2 Rape survival curve from initial status.

from mutually aggressive behaviors with antisocial peers as well as risk factors associated with alcohol and drug abuse. Internalizing symptoms such as PTSD and depressive and dissociative symptoms may increase tolerance for abuse (Messman-Moore & Long, 2003 (review); Messman-Moore, Long, & Siegfried, 2000) and impair judgments regarding risky situations (Wilson, Calhoun, & Bernat, 1999). Self-medicating substance abuse behaviors may result in a "vicious cycle relationship in which substance use increases risk of future assault and assault increases substance abuse" (Kilpatrick, Acierno, Resnick, Saunders, & Best, 1997, p. 834). Women who were sexually abused as children tend to have more lifetime sexual partners and more one-time partners and to take greater sexual risks than nonabused women (Kendall-Tackett et al., 1993; Koss & Dinero, 1999; Raj, Silverman, & Amaro, 2000; Wyatt, Guthrie, & Notgrass, 1992).

We hypothesized that runaways who had been physically and sexually abused by caretakers would be more likely to experience revictimization when on the streets and that, consistent with the literature just cited, the relationship between caretaker abuse and later street victimization would be mediated by the effects of caretaker abuse on risky street behaviors.

Physical revictimization

Structural equation modeling was used to estimate the effects of caretaker physical abuse on negative street behaviors and street victimization during Waves 2–13 of the study. Lifetime caretaker physical abuse at Wave 1 was significantly correlated ($r = .11$ $p < .05$) with street physical victimization over the course of the 3-year study (Waves 2–13).

Caretaker physical abuse was measured at Wave 1 with a summation of seven variables assessing amount of physical abuse respondents reported. If respondents answered four of the seven questions, they were included in the scale. Questions concerned having objects thrown at them or being hit with objects, being pushed, shoved, or grabbed, being slapped, being beat up with fists, and being threatened or assaulted with a weapon.

Nonsexual deviant behaviors was assessed with a latent construct made up of nonsexual deviant survival strategies, association with deviant peers, and engagement in victimizing behaviors. *Nonsexual deviant survival strategies* was first measured by assessing the number of strategies employed (e.g., panhandled, spare changed, broke into a store, broke into a house, stole/shoplifted, dumpster dived) at each wave. Respondents must have answered four of the six questions to be included in analyses. A final scale was computed by summing scores across Waves 2–13 and dividing by the number of waves respondents had completed. *Deviant peers* was measured at each wave with a sum of 13 variables assessing if respondents' close friends had run away, sold drugs, used drugs, been suspended or expelled from school, dropped out of school, shoplifted, broke into buildings, took money from someone, sold sexual favors, been arrested, threatened or assaulted someone with a weapon, or beaten someone up. Respondents must have answered all 13 questions to be included in the scale. The resulting scales for Waves 2–13 were summed, and respondents must have answered at least one wave to be included in analysis. The final scale was proportioned by the number of waves respondents had completed to weight for number of responses.

Victimizing behaviors was measured at each wave with a summation of four questions about whether the respondent had started a physical fight that could have resulted in injury, tried to injure someone, or hurt or threatened someone with a weapon. The resulting scales for Waves 2–13 were summed, and respondents must have answered at least one wave to be included in analysis. The final scale was proportioned by the number of waves respondents had completed to weight for number of responses.

Physical victimization was assessed with an average at each wave of four items assessing if respondents had been beaten up, robbed, threatened, or assaulted someone with a weapon. Respondents must have answered at least two questions to be included in the individual wave scale. Scales from Waves 2–13 were summed, and respondents must have answered the physical victimization questions during at least one wave to be included in analyses. The final street victimization scale was proportioned by the number of waves respondents had completed to weight for response.

The effects of caretaker abuse were mediated by a latent construct of negative street behaviors made up of measures of nonsexual survival strategies, association with deviant peers, and engaging in victimizing behaviors Waves 2–13 (Figure 8.3). Caretaker physical abuse was significantly associated with negative street behaviors ($\beta = .14, p < .05$), which, in turn, were strongly associated with physical victimization ($\beta = .64, p < .001$) during Waves 2–13. The direct correlation between Wave 1 caretaker abuse and Waves 2–13 street victimization was reduced to nonsignificance.

Sexual revictimization

We investigated a similar structural equation modeling (SEM) mediation model for sexual victimization when on the streets. *Caretaker sexual abuse* was measured at Wave 1 with a summation of two questions that asked respondents if an adult caretaker had ever propositioned them for sexual favors or forced them to engage in sexual activities. The variable was dichotomized before analyses. Respondents must have answered one of the questions to be included in analyses.

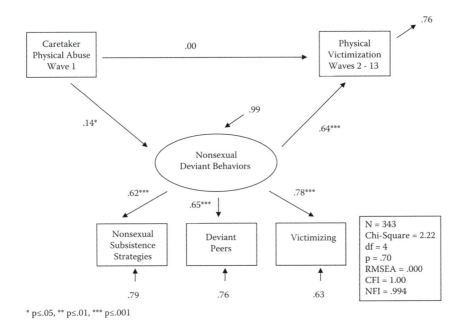

* p≤.05, ** p≤.01, *** p≤.001

Figure 8.3 Physical victimization structural equation modeling (SEM) model.

Sexual deviant behaviors was assessed with a latent construct made up of measures of risky sexual behaviors that included number of lifetime sexual partners, survival sex, and number of one-night stands. *Number of lifetime sexual partners* was a summation of the number of partners respondents reported across Waves 2–13. *Trade sex* measured whether respondents had ever traded sex for food, money, drugs, or shelter during Waves 2–13. This variable was proportioned by the number of waves respondents participated in. *One-night stands* was assessed with a single variable at each wave where respondents reported the number of one-night stands in which they had engaged. The final measure was a dichotomous variable assessing whether respondents had had any one-time partners in their lifetimes.

Sexual victimization was assessed with the average of two items at each wave assessing if respondents had been propositioned for sex or been forced to do something sexual. Respondents must have answered at least one question to be included in the individual wave scale. These items were summed across Waves 2–13 and divided by the number of waves respondents had answered to weight for response.

Caretaker sexual abuse was significantly correlated ($r = .20$, $p < .001$; not shown in table) with sexual victimization in Waves 2–13. However, this association was not mediated by risky sexual behaviors (Figure 8.4).

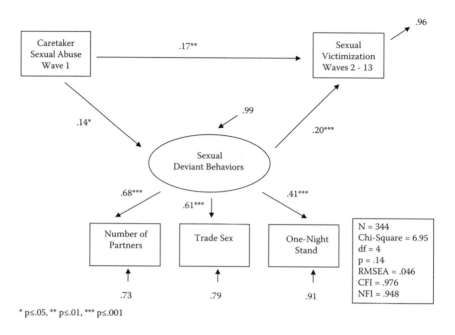

Figure 8.4 Sexual victimization structural equation modeling (SEM) model.

In the SEM, caretaker sexual abuse was positively related to risky sexual behaviors ($\beta = .14$, $p < .05$), which, in turn, was positively associated with sexual victimization during Waves 2–13 ($\beta = .20$, $p < .01$). However, the association between caretaker sexual abuse measured at Wave 1 and sexual victimization at Waves 2–13 was virtually unchanged and remained statistically significant ($\beta = .17$, $p < .01$).

The lack of a mediating effect of street sexual behaviors on revictimization was contrary to our hypothesis. It may be that the variables pertaining to sexual activity when on the streets were so skewed that any effects of sexual behaviors were masked. The runaways report very high levels of sexual activity (see Chapter 10, this volume) compared with other samples where the relationship between sexual activity and revictimization has been found.

Another way to think about revictimization is to compare the frequencies of those who were sexually abused by caretakers with those who later experienced sexual assault when on the streets (Table 8.5). Among young women who were sexually assaulted during Waves 2–13, nearly one half (47.7%) had reported caretaker sexual abuse at Wave 1. All of the young women who experienced sexual assault on the streets during Waves 2–13 had reported caretaker physical abuse at Wave 1. Among the young men

Table 8.5. Street Victimization Waves 2–13 by Caretaker Abuse

| | Street Victimization Ever Wave 2-13 | | | | | |
| | Physical (N = 272) | | | Sexual (N = 107) | | |
	Total (%)	Male (%)	Female (%)	Total (%)	Male (%)	Female (%)
Caretaker sexual abuse Wave 1	25.1	12.5	**37.8***	34.6	14.3	**47.7***
Caretaker physical abuse Wave 1	96.0	94.1	97.8	99.1	97.6	100.0

* $p \le .001$ (gender significance test).

who had been sexually assaulted during Waves 2–13, 14.3% reported caretaker sexual abuse at Wave 1. It is particularly noteworthy that nearly all of the adolescents who reported either physical or sexual assault during Waves 2–13 had reported caretaker physical abuse at Wave 1.

Summary and discussion

The high rates of victimization by caretakers at home and later victimization when on the streets reported here have been widely documented across numerous studies. And, as we have seen in previous chapters, victimization is a strong correlate of mental and substance abuse disorders. Abuse by caretakers is cited as the reason for leaving home by one fifth of the adolescents, exceeded only by conflict with caretakers (Chapter 2, this volume), which itself may denote emotional abuse or physical abuse in some cases. Moreover, multivariate analyses throughout this volume indicate that caretaker abuse and street victimization are associated with conduct disorder (Chapter 3, this volume), major depressive episode (Chapter 4, this volume), dissociative symptoms (Chapter 7, this volume), self-mutilation (Chapter 9, this volume), and suicide attempts and ideation (Chapter 10, this volume). Of those diagnosed with posttraumatic stress disorder, nearly two thirds reported severe caretaker physical abuse, 42% reported caretaker sexual abuse, and approximately one third reported physical or sexual assault when on the streets (Chapter 5, this volume). Risk for revictimization is linked to victimization by caretakers and exacerbates the emotional damage already done.

Theoretical implications

We believe that victimization and revictimization are the most critical factors in the "cumulative continuity" of maladaptive behaviors (Caspi & Bem, 1990; Moffitt, 1997). This succession of traumatic events and violent behaviors shapes the developmental trajectories of runaways and amplify risk of psychopathology (Whitbeck & Hoyt, 1999; Whitbeck, Hoyt, & Yoder, 1999). Caretaker abuse increases the likelihood of high-risk behaviors such as leaving home. And when the adolescents do strike out on their own they find themselves in potentially more dangerous environments where affiliation with delinquent peers and risky survival strategies increase the likelihood of revictimization. The cumulative consequences of these chains of negative events on education, relationships, mental health, substance use, employment, and involvement in the criminal justice system may be so powerful that the adolescents will become entrapped on society's margins as they move into early adulthood.

Policy implications

One of the central messages of this volume is that victimization and revictimization are the most salient factors associated with mental and substance abuse disorders among runaway and homeless young people. If this is true, then the most important intervention is to prevent further victimization and trauma regardless of the adolescents' behaviors or circumstances—this means implementing new policies or extending and refining existing policies to create well-staffed, safe, and inviting shelters. From this point of view, *safe* means protection of their status as runaways, protection from parents until it is certain that they are not dangerous, and protection from the criminal justice system for less than violent offenses (e.g., underage alcohol use, drug use, victimless street survival strategies).

Implementing such policies will be expensive and controversial. Safe, welcoming shelters would have to be professionally staffed, carefully monitored for security, and use highly skilled people to intervene at critical junctures. This approach also would require patience and skills necessary to deal with extremely difficult, often high, and occasionally dangerous people. However, given the social services and health burden we can expect from long-term homelessness, interventions that prevent the amplification of symptoms that led to running away will probably be cost-effective.

Conclusions

Runaway and homeless adolescents are probably the most victimized population in our society, yet our primary response has been through the criminal justice system. Admittedly, these are highly damaged and difficult young people; however, there are numerous opportunities for nonpunitive interventions. The first priority should be to prevent further victimization. This will mean changing how we think about runaway adolescents. First, we have to give up our assumptions that they are still "children" and develop intervention strategies that view their independence as an asset. Second, we need to develop infrastructure that provides early and effective protection from revictimization during periods of independence.

chapter 9

Self-mutilating behaviors from adolescence to young adulthood

With Katherine A. Johnson

Self-mutilating behaviors are severely understudied among adolescents in the general population (Goldston, Daniel, & Mayfield, 2006), and we are aware of only one published article that addresses self-mutilation specifically among homeless and runaway adolescents (Tyler, Whitbeck, Hoyt, & Johnson, 2003). Although definitions and attempts at typology diverge on particulars, the most common conceptualization for *self-mutilation* is "the deliberate, direct destruction or alteration of body tissue without conscious suicidal intent" (Favazza, 1998, p. 260). Self-mutilating behaviors range from very serious injuries such as genital and ocular self-injury to less serious behaviors such as cutting, self-battery, biting, burning, hair pulling, and interfering with wound healing to more passive self-neglect such as stopping or manipulating medication or medical protocols and intentionally putting oneself in harm's way (Skegg, 2005, review).

Estimates of prevalence vary widely by age and type of sample. Epidemiological studies in the United States and England indicate lifetime prevalence rates of about 4% in the general population (Briere & Gil, 1998; Klonsky, Oltmanns, & Turkheimer, 2003). Prevalence estimates are substantially higher among adolescents, and they appear to have increased over the past several decades (Hurry, 2000; Kress, 2003; Olfson, Gameroff, Marcus, Greenburg, & Shaffer, 2005). Nonclinical samples of high school and college students indicate prevalence rates of between 14% and 16% among high school students (Muehlekamp & Gutierrez, 2004; Ross & Heath, 2002) and between 12% and 17% among college students (Favazza, DeRosear, & Conterio, 1989; Whitlock, Eckenrode, & Silverman, 2006). Prevalence rates appear to be curvilinear by age, emerging in early adolescence, peaking in late adolescence and early adulthood, and tapering off among adults (Feldman, 1988 (review); Skegg, 2005 (review)). For example, prevalence for "interview validated nonsuicidal physically self-damaging acts" among younger adolescents aged 12–14 years was only 2.5% for adolescent males and 2.8% for females (Garrison, Addy, McKeown, Cuffe, Jackson, & Waller, 1993, p. 339).

Most of what we know about self-mutilation comes from myriad clinical and institutional studies that date back decades (for a review of early studies see Ross & McKay, 1979). The older studies are typically based on small samples or case studies and are psychoanalytically driven. More recent clinical samples indicate a wide range of estimates of self-injurious behaviors from 4.3% among psychiatric patients to 40% among institutionalized violent and antisocial youth (Feldman, 1988 (review); Skegg, 2005 (review)). Briere and Gil (1998) reported a 21% rate in their clinical sample with no gender differences. Schwartz and colleagues found that 48% of adolescent girls in an inpatient drug and alcohol abuse treatment facility had engaged in "deliberate cutting, without suicide intent" (Schwartz, Cohen, Hoffmann, & Meeks, 1989, p. 340).

Correlates of self-mutilating behaviors among adolescents and young adults

Attempts to explain self-mutilating behaviors go back decades (e.g., Ross & McKay, 1979; Rosenthal, Rinzler, Wallsh, & Klausner, 1972), and over time a constellation of associated risk factors has emerged. Nonclinical prevalence estimates indicate there are no gender differences in self-mutilating behaviors (Briere & Gil, 1998; Klonsky et al., 2003); however, there is evidence of considerable gender variation in some clinical studies. Some researchers report wide gender variation among adolescents (Ross & Heath, 2002; Whitlock et al., 2006), and others find no gender differences (Garrison et al., 1993). There is also some evidence that gay males and lesbians are more at risk for self-injurious behaviors (Skegg, Nada-Raja, Dickson, Paul, & Williams, 2003). Within the clinical research, there tends to be a gender bias where the majority of the studies focus solely on females (e.g., Darche, 1990; MacAniff & Kiselica, 2001; Schwartz et al., 1989; Suyemoto & MacDonald, 1995).

There is general consensus that childhood histories of disruptions of parental care, neglect, physical abuse, and sexual abuse are associated with self-mutilation (Briere & Gil, 1998; Darche, 1990; Joyce et al., 2006; van der Kolk, Perry, & Herman, 1991; Whitlock et al., 2006). Although there is evidence that measures of types of parental abuse are highly collinear (Andover, Pepper, Ryabchenko, Orrico, & Gibb, 2005), the predominant evidence is that among measures of caretaker maltreatment, sexual abuse is the most highly associated with self-mutilating behaviors (Noll, Horowitz, Bonnano, Trickett, & Putnam, 2003).

The *Diagnostic and Statistical Manual of Mental Disorders,* fourth edition, text revision (*DSM IV-TR*; American Psychiatric Association, 2000) treats self-mutilation symptomatically as part of the diagnostic criteria for several psychiatric disorders such as stereotypic movement disorder, trichotillomania, impulse control disorder not otherwise specified, and borderline personality disorder. Self-injurious behaviors are particularly associated with the diagnosis of borderline personality disorder (Kress, 2003; Paris, 2005; Sansone, Songer, & Gaither, 2001). However, there is plentiful evidence that self-mutilating behaviors co-occur with many different types of emotional and behavioral problems, such as depressive symptoms and depressive disorders (Andover et al., 2005; Bennum, 1983; Garrison et al., 1993; Guertin, Lloyd-Richardson, Spirito, Donaldson, & Boergers, 2001; Klonsky et al., 2003; Ross & Heath, 2003; Schwartz et al., 1989), dissociative symptoms (Saxe, Chawla, & Van der Kolk, 2002; Suyemoto & MacDonald, 1995; Van der Kolk et al., 1991; Zlotnick, Shea, Pearlstein, Simpson, Costello, & Begin, 1996), anger and rage (Bennum, 1983; Laye-Gindhu & Schonert-Reichl, 2005; Schwartz et al., 1989), anxiety (Andover et al., 2005; Klonsky et al., 2003; Ross & Heath, 2003), eating disorders (Levitt, Sansone, & Cohn, 2004), and suicidal behavior (Cooper et al., 2005; Darche, 1990; Garrison et al., 1993; Laye-Gindhu & Schonert-Reichl, 2005; Stanley, Gameroff, Michalsen, & Mann, 2001; Whitlock et al., 2006). In a follow-up study of emergency treatment of adolescents who had harmed themselves, self-mutilation more than doubled the rate of completed suicide over a 4-year period (Cooper et al., 2005).

As many as eight theoretical models explaining motivations for self-mutilation have been identified (Suyemoto & MacDonald, 1995), but the research literature has tended to focus on aspects of impulse control and affect regulation as the central explanation of self-mutilating behaviors. Affect regulation includes the need to express anger or to release the pressures of anxiety or depression that cannot be expressed verbally. It also involves responding to dissociation where the self-mutilating behaviors help maintain a sense of self-identity in the face of overwhelming negative emotions (Suyemoto, 1998 (review)). Clinical studies based on interviews with people who self-mutilate provide evidence of need for emotional release after periods of building tension (Favazza, 1998 (review); Huband & Tantum, 2004; Sachsse, Von der Heyde, & Huether, 2002). Questionnaire-based studies have also provided evidence for the affect regulation model, particularly through the expression of hostility and relief from anxiety (Ross & Heath, 2003). The clinical evidence suggests that episodes of self-mutilation, particularly cutting, can result in substantial release of tension resulting in feelings of relief and calm (Raine, 1982 (review); Schwartz et al., 1989; Suyemoto, 1998 (review)).

Self-mutilation among homeless and runaway adolescents and young adults

Based on the correlates described thus far, homeless and runaway adolescents are at particular risk for self-mutilating behaviors. Homeless and runaway adolescents are highly likely to report caretaker physical and sexual maltreatment (see Chapter 8, this volume; Janus, Burgess, & McCormack, 1987; Silbert & Pines, 1981; Kurtz, Kurtz, & Jarvis, 1991; Pennbridge, Yates, David, & MacKenzie, 1990; Tyler, Hoyt, Whitbeck, & Cauce, 2001b) and experience violent victimization and sexual assault when on the streets (Chapter 8, this volume; Hagen & McCarthy, 1997; Kipke, Simon, Montgomery, Unger, & Iverson, 1997; Whitbeck & Hoyt, 1999). And, as we have demonstrated throughout this volume, homeless and runaway adolescents are likely to manifest numerous symptoms of emotional distress including depressive symptoms, dissociation, posttraumatic stress disorder (PTSD), and suicidal ideation. Moreover, they often have minimal support systems and few healthy ways to release pent-up feelings of anxiety, depression, and hostility that are associated with and amplified by their circumstances (Johnson, Whitbeck, & Hoyt, 2005a).

Prevalence and correlates of self-mutilating behaviors

Prevalence of self-mutilating behaviors

More than one half (52.8%) of the homeless and runaway adolescents in our study had engaged in self-mutilating behaviors in the past 12 months at Wave 1 (Table 9.1). This rate is more than 10 times that estimated for the general population and exceeds some of the highest rates reported for clinical samples. Although there were no significant gender differences among those who had ever engaged in self-mutilating behaviors, males employed a greater variety of self-mutilating behaviors than did females. Males were more likely than females to have hit themselves on purpose, picked at a wound, burned themselves, or inserted objects under their skin or nails. Females were more likely than males to have pulled their hair out and erased skin.

In our in-depth interviews, only one young woman (aged 19 years) reported self-mutilating behaviors. This was with another person and in an institutional setting:

> No it's a group home girls and boys co-ed, and I
> stayed there, until like about 1995. Then so I couldn't
> take it there no more because they was acting crazy
> I couldn't, I ain't really like staying there. There was

Table 9.1 12-Month Prevalence of Self-Mutilation Behaviors at Wave 1

| | Total (%) | Gender (N = 428) | | Sexuality (N = 427) | |
		Male (%)	Female (%)	Hetero-sexual (%)	Non-heterosexual (%)
Cutting or carving	18.5	18.2	18.7	15.1	38.7%
Hit self on purpose	8.9	13.9	5.0***	8.2	12.9
Pulled hair out	3.0	1.1	4.6*	2.5	6.5†
Given self tattoo	8.9	9.1	8.7	8.2	12.9
Picked wound	25.5	30.5	21.6*	23.6	37.1*
Burned self	12.6	17.6	8.7**	12.6	12.9
Inserted objects under skin or nails	4.7	7.0	2.9*	4.4	6.5
Bit mouth for blood	13.3	11.8	14.5	12.6	17.7
Picked at body for blood	5.9	6.5	5.4	4.7	12.9**
Scraped skin for blood	8.4	8.0	8.7	6.0	22.6***
Erased skin	1.2	0.0	2.1*	1.1	1.6
Ever self-mutilated	52.8	55.6	50.6	49.6	72.6***

Notes: P-values under "Gender" for differences between males and females and those under "Sexuality" for differences between heterosexuals and nonheterosexuals.

† $p \le .10$.
* $p \le .05$.
** $p \le .01$.
*** $p \le .001$.

this girl that was there. We used to cut each other with. It was I don't know it was crazy. We used to cut each other.... I let her do it. Then she let me do her. Till they found out, then we couldn't, we was the only kids that was using plastic silverware. I mean plastic forks and knives. I don't know because we had a rule like we was sitting there and we'd come out in the kitchen and she'd grab a knife or something and come back and sit in the corner and cut each other.

Nonheterosexuals (72.6%) were much more likely than their hetero-sexual counterparts (49.6%) to have self-mutilated in the past 12 months at Wave 1 with no gender differences. They were twice as likely as hetero-sexuals to have cut or carved on their skin (38.7% vs. 15.1%), three times more likely to have picked at their bodies to draw blood (12.9% vs. 4.7%), and more than three times more likely to have scraped their skin to draw blood (22.6% vs. 6.0%).

Self-mutilation and mental disorders

We grouped self-mutilating behaviors by diagnoses to ascertain whether they were likely to be associated with particular disorders. Self-mutilation was very common across all six diagnoses (Table 9.2, last row). Ever having engaged in self-mutilating behaviors ranged from a low of 80.2% among depressed females to high of 93.9% among depressed males.

When we examined the prevalence of specific types of self-mutilating behaviors by diagnosis, the variation between diagnoses increased. For example, cutting was particularly prevalent among females who met cri-teria for alcohol dependence (64.3%) and males who met criteria for PTSD (65.9%) or major depressive episode (MDE) (67.3%). Of the 24 gender differ-ences in specific self-mutilating behaviors across the six diagnoses, males had higher rates than females for three fourths of the behaviors.

Self-mutilation across time

Self-mutilation is known to peak in late adolescence and decrease as indi-viduals move into adulthood (Feldman, 1988 (review); Skegg, 2005 (review). This was true for the homeless and runaway young people. We assessed 12-month self-mutilating behaviors annually, and rates decreased from Wave 1 to the final Year 3 assessment (Wave 13). As Figure 9.1 indicates, any self-mutilating behavior decreased by nearly one half between the initial and second-year assessments and then leveled off through Year 3. A similar pattern is evident for cutting and carving.

Correlates of self-mutilation among homeless and runaway adolescents

To better understand correlates of self-mutilation, we investigated a logistic regression model where the dependent variable was ever having engaged in any of the 11 self-mutilating behaviors (Table 9.3) 1 year after the baseline interviews. As shown in Figure 9.1, self-mutilating behaviors declined as the adolescents moved toward young adulthood. To capture

Table 9.2 Lifetime Prevalence of Self-Mutilation Behaviors by Diagnoses and Gender

	Alcohol Abuse (N = 187)		Alcohol Dependence (N = 128)		Drug Abuse (N = 173)		Posttraumatic Stress (N = 152)		Major Depression (N = 130)	
	Male (%)	Female (%)	Male (%)	Female (%)	Male (%)	Female (%)	Male (%)	Female (%)	Male (%)	Female (%)
Cut or carved skin	53.3	62.9	56.9	64.3	52.3	62.4	65.9	61.1	67.3	56.8
Hit self on purpose	20.0	17.5	29.3	20.0	33.0	20.0*	34.1	19.4*	34.7	17.3*
Pulled hair out	5.6	18.6**	8.6	18.6	9.1	20.0*	4.5	21.3**	4.1	16.0*
Given self a tattoo	44.4	37.1	41.4	44.3	38.6	35.3	36.4	38.9	42.9	35.8
Picked a wound	55.6	41.2*	62.1	41.4*	53.4	35.3*	54.5	38.9†	63.3	35.8**
Burned with cigarette, match, or other	50.0	35.1*	41.4	41.4	48.9	36.5*	45.5	28.7*	53.1	30.9**
Inserted objects under skin or nails	20.0	11.3†	25.9	15.7	21.6	7.1**	18.2	12.0	20.4	12.3
Bit self on mouth or lip for blood	14.4	26.8*	19.0	25.7	13.6	22.4	9.1	21.3†	16.3	24.7
Picked at body to draw blood	10.1	9.3	6.9	10.0	11.4	12.9	18.2	15.7	18.4	12.3
Scraped skin to draw blood	16.7	19.6	19.0	20.0	20.5	24.7	20.5	21.3	24.5	24.7
Erased skin	16.7	23.7	15.5	27.1	12.5	21.2	13.6	21.3	8.2	23.5*
Ever self-mutilated	88.9	87.6	89.7	88.6	90.9	88.2	86.4	87.0	93.9	80.2*

Note: All p-values denote differences between males and females in self-mutilative behaviors by diagnosis.

† $p \leq .10$.
* $p \leq .05$.
** $p \leq .01$.

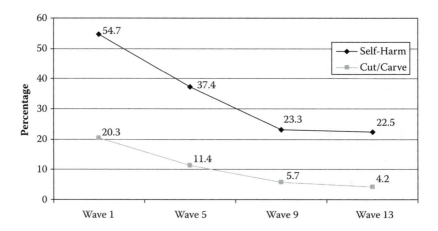

Figure 9.1 Self-mutilation across time.

change, but at a point where the behaviors were still quite prevalent, we regressed baseline variables on Year 2 (Wave 5) 12-month self-mutilating behaviors when controlling for self-mutilation at baseline. All of the independent variables in the regression equations have been discussed in previous chapters.

With only age of adolescent, gender, and sexual orientation in Model 1, being female and of nonheterosexual orientation were statistically significant. When we added lifetime reports of ever having engaged in self-mutilating behaviors in Model 2, age of adolescent also became statistically significant, indicating that younger adolescents were more likely to engage in self-mutilating behaviors. Caretaker sexual abuse at Wave 1 was added to the equation in Model 3 and was nonsignificant. However, caretaker physical abuse at Wave 1 was statistically significant when added to the equation in Model 4. Neither of the Wave 1 street victimization variables (Models 5 and 6) was statistically significant.

With all the variables in the model (Model 6), for each year of age, the likelihood of self-mutilation was reduced by about 40%. Females and nonheterosexuals were more than twice as likely as males and heterosexuals to engage in self-mutilating behaviors. Those with a history of self-mutilation were about 30% more likely to continue to do so 1 year later. The only environmental predictor of self-mutilating behaviors 1 year after baseline assessment was a history of caretaker physical abuse.

Table 9.3 Logistic Regression Model Predicting Self-Mutilation One Year Out (N = 210)

	Model 1		Model 2		Model 3		Model 4		Model 5		Model 6	
	b	Exp(b)	b	Exp(b)	b	Exp(b)	b	Exp(b)	b	Exp(b)	b	Exp(b)
Age	-0.17	0.84	-0.30	0.74*	-0.34	0.71*	-0.38	0.69*	-0.38	0.69*	-0.39	0.68*
Female	-1.01	0.37***	-0.99	0.37**	-1.14	0.32***	-1.15	0.32***	-1.12	0.33**	-1.07	0.35**
Heterosexual	-0.80	0.45†	-0.76	0.47†	-0.72	0.49†	-0.77	0.46†	-0.78	0.46†	-0.79	0.45†
Lifetime self-mutilation Wave 1			0.32	1.38***	0.32	1.37***	0.30	1.35***	0.30	1.35***	0.30	1.34***
Sexual abuse					0.11	1.11	0.07	1.07	0.08	1.08	0.07	1.08
Physical abuse							0.06	1.06†	0.06	1.06†	0.05	1.06†
Sexual victimization									-0.14	0.87	-0.21	0.81
Physical victimization											0.13	1.14
Constant	0.73	2.08†	-0.17	0.84	-0.24	0.79	-0.64	0.53	-0.63	0.53	-0.66	0.52
Nagelkerke		0.08		0.22		0.23		0.25		0.25		0.25
Cox & Snell		0.06		0.16		0.17		0.18		0.18		0.18

† p ≤ .10.
* p ≤ .05.
** p ≤ .01.
*** p ≤ .001.

Summary and discussion

The rates of ever having engaged in self-mutilation among the homeless and runaway adolescents were higher than or commensurate with those of clinical samples. Briere and Gil (1998) reported a 21% rate in a clinical sample. Our rate of 54.7% was more than twice that but was much closer to the rate of 48% reported by Schwartz and colleagues (1989) for adolescent girls in an inpatient alcohol and drug treatment facility. Though much higher than the rate reported by Schwartz and colleagues, our rate of 88.6% self-mutilation among alcohol-dependent homeless and runaway young women supports their findings of high self-injury rates among alcohol and drug abusing women.

Self-mutilating behaviors were ubiquitous among the young people regardless of psychiatric diagnosis. There was only one gender difference by diagnosis: Males who met criteria for MDE were more likely to self-mutilate than were females. There were no gender differences across the diagnostic categories in the propensity to cut or carve on oneself. However, other mutilating behaviors did vary by gender. For example, males were more likely than females to hit oneself on purpose, pick a wound, or burn oneself. One of our more striking findings was the large difference in self-mutilating behaviors between heterosexual and nonheterosexual homeless and runaway young people. Almost three fourths of the nonheterosexual young people had at some point engaged in self-mutilating behaviors compared with about one half of heterosexuals. Because self-mutilation is associated with more serious psychiatric distress, nonheterosexuals who meet diagnostic criteria for any of the disorders and who also self-mutilate should be considered a particularly high-risk group.

The use of 1-year prospective data for the self-mutilation analyses allowed us to address issues of causality. Only age, gender, sexual orientation, and caretaker physical abuse predicted self-mutilating behaviors 1 year later when controlling for lifetime self-mutilating behaviors at Wave 1. This is an interesting finding in that our measures of recent street victimization were nonsignificant. It suggests that a history of caretaker abuse is more salient for self-mutilating behaviors than more proximal experiences of victimization.

Theoretical implications

The rates of self-mutilating behaviors among this population of young people were higher than we anticipated. They appear to represent severe distress within psychiatric diagnoses and probably, along with dissociative symptoms (Chapter 7), indicate overlooked diagnostic categories such as dissociative disorders and borderline personality disorder. Self-mutilating behaviors are indicative of high-risk adolescents within each diagnostic category.

One of the complications of responding to self-mutilating behaviors is the degree to which some forms are acceptable and fashionable. We removed tattooing from our measure for the multivariate analyses because it is so commonplace. However, other body art fads are harder to differentiate. For example, when does piercing become a symptom rather than a fashion statement? What about genital piercing or burning or branding? There is much measurement work to be done to distinguish what is and what is not symptomatic mutilation.

Self-mutilation as we measured it diminished across time. Indeed, in the multivariate analyses, each year of age nearly halved the odds of the behavior. However, it remains unclear how self-mutilating behaviors interact with psychiatric diagnoses (or represent unscreened diagnoses) to affect the transition to adulthood. To our knowledge this is the only study of homeless young people to have assessed it. We need much more research to understand its origins and its short- and long-term consequences among this population of young people.

Policy implications

It is very likely that most service providers who work with homeless and runaway adolescents screen for self-mutilating behaviors. If they are not doing such screenings, these findings suggest they should be doing so. There is plentiful evidence that the behaviors are very difficult to treat (Goldston et al., 2006), and it is likely they will interfere with treatment of co-occurring diagnoses. Working with self-mutilating runaways on an outpatient basis will be particularly challenging because there is no way to control the environment as the staff in the inpatient setting attempted to do with the young woman in our in-depth interview. It may be that evidence of self-mutilation should serve as a marker for referral for inpatient treatment, particularly in light of its strong correlation with suicidal behaviors (Cooper et al., 2005).

Conclusions

Self-mutilating behavior is understudied among adolescents in general and almost ignored in studies of homeless and runaway adolescents. It may be that these behaviors mark the more severe end of the continuum of psychiatric distress among homeless and runaway adolescents and that these adolescents will be among those most difficult to treat and those most at risk for other, more lethal forms of self-harm. Our investigation of self-injury will continue in the next chapter, where we address suicidal ideation and behaviors.

chapter 10

Suicide ideation and attempts

With Katherine A. Johnson

A recent review of 128 population studies of adolescent suicidal behaviors reports an average prevalence of lifetime suicide attempts among North American adolescents of 12.6%, with an average 1-year prevalence of 7.7% (Evans, Hawton, Rodham, & Deeks, 2005, p. 243). In the United States, suicide is the third leading cause of death among children, adolescents, and young adults (Spirito & Esposito-Smythers, 2006 (review)). According to the 2003 Youth Behavior Risk Surveillance (YBRS) survey, 16.9% of U.S. adolescents reported suicidal ideation in the past year, and 8.5% had made an attempt (Grunbaum et al., 2004). The attempt rates are much higher among homeless and runaway adolescents than in the general population, ranging from 20% to 40% for lifetime attempts (Adlaf & Zdanowicz, 1999; Greene & Ringwalt, 1996; Molnar, Shade, Kral, Booth, & Watters, 1998; Stiffman, 1989; Yoder, 1999). Rates of suicidal ideation among homeless and runaway adolescents range from 14% (Kingree, Braithwaite, & Woodring, 2001) to the mid-50% range (Molnar et al., 1998; Yoder, Hoyt, & Whitbeck, 1998). These broad ranges of suicide attempts and ideation are the result of widely diverse measures and sampling procedures (Evans et al., 2005; Goldston, 2003; O'Carrol, Berman, Maris, Moscicki, Tanney, & Silverman, 1996). Because these are difficult populations to access, many samples have focused on a single city or even a single shelter, resulting in very specific estimates. In this chapter we address suicidal behaviors by psychiatric diagnosis and other risk factors among homeless and runaway adolescents in a variety of settings across four Midwestern states.

Risk and protective factors for suicidal behaviors among runaway and homeless adolescents

Homeless and runaway adolescents are subject to all of the known risk factors for suicidal behaviors with very few of the protective factors. Suicide attempts have been linked to being female (Leslie, Stein, & Rotheram-Borus, 2002), problems in family of origin (Ringwalt, Greene, & Robertson, 1998; Stiffman, 1989), caretaker physical and sexual abuse

(Feitel, Margetson, Chamas, & Lipman, 1992; Kurtz, Kurtz, & Jarvis, 1991; Molnar et al., 1998; Yoder et al., 1998), length of time on the street (Leslie et al., 2002; McCarthy & Hagen, 1992; Milburn, Rotheram-Borus, Rice, Mallet, & Rosenthal, 2006), physical and sexual assault when on the streets (Molnar et al., 1998; Yoder, 1999), being nonheterosexual (Leslie et al., 2002; McDaniel, Purcell, & D'Augelli, 2001 (review); Whitbeck, Chen, Hoyt, Tyler, & Johnson, 2004), prostitution (Kidd & Kral, 2002; Leslie et al., 2002; Yates, MacKenzie, Pennbridge, & Cohen, 1988), having substance abuse problems (Greene & Ringwalt, 1996; Stiffman, 1989; Yoder et al., 1998), conduct problems (Booth & Zhang, 1996; Stiffman, 1989), depressed affect (Rohde, Noell, Ochs, & Seeley, 2001; Rotheram-Borus, 1993), and hopelessness (Kidd, 2004; Rohde et al., 2001).

In population studies (Spirito & Esposito-Smythers, 2006; Evans et al., 2005) and in the very few diagnostic studies of suicide among homeless and runaway adolescents, meeting criteria for a psychiatric disorder is strongly associated with suicidal behaviors (Booth & Zhang, 1996; Rohde et al., 2001; Unger, Simon, Newman, Montgomery, Kipke, & Albornoz, 1998). Evidence from the New Zealand longitudinal study indicates that adolescents who met criteria for conduct/oppositional disorders were more than 13 times more likely to attempt suicide than those who did not meet criteria for those disorders (Fergusson & Lynskey, 1995). Similarly, Beautrais and colleagues reported that conduct disordered or antisocial personality youth aged 13–24 years were more than four times more likely to have made a suicide attempt, than those without the disorders (Beautrais, Joyce, & Mulder, 1996).

Comorbidity increases the risk of suicide attempts among adolescents (Gould, King, Greenwald, Fisher, & Schwab-Stone, 1998) with comorbid substance abuse and depression a particularly lethal combination (Brent, 1987; Reinherz, Giaconia, Silverman, Friedman, & Pakiz, 1995). Comorbid conduct and depressive disorders also heighten risk, particularly among young males (Lewinsohn, Rohde, & Seeley, 1995; Rohde, Mace, & Seeley, 1997). Recall that two thirds (67.3%) of the adolescents in the present study met criteria for two or more disorders at Wave 1 and that by Wave 13, nearly all of the youth who met criteria for major depressive disorder (MDE) also met criteria for antisocial personality disorder (87.5%) and approximately one half also met criteria for alcohol or drug abuse (see Chapter 4, this volume). Along with the myriad other risk factors for suicidal ideation, these high rates of co-occurring mental disorders place homeless and runaway adolescents at particular risk for suicidal behaviors.

The prevalence and correlates of suicide behaviors and suicidal ideation among homeless and runaway adolescents

Suicide attempts

At Wave 1, about one third of the adolescents had attempted suicide at some point in their lives. Young women (41.9%) were more likely to have made an attempt than young men (31%), and nonheterosexuals (58.1%) were more likely to have attempted than heterosexuals (33.7%). During the 3-year course of the study, the rates of suicide attempts increased so that by Wave 13, nearly one half (45.2%) of the young women and more than one third (33.2%) of the young men who remained in the study had attempted suicide.

Based on the lethality scale (Smith, Conroy, & Ehler, 1984), well over one half (59.7%) of the attempts by the runaway and homeless adolescents were life threatening, with a 50% or greater possibility of death from the attempt. For 28.9% of the attempts, death was highly probable. Potential lethality among nonheterosexual young people was even higher. More than three fourths (77.8%) of attempts by nonheterosexual runaway and homeless youth had a 50% or greater likelihood of resulting in death; for more than one third (36.1%) of the attempts, death was highly probable.

Suicidal ideation

Suicidal ideation was very common among the adolescents. At Wave 1, about two thirds reported that at least "some of the time" they had thoughts about hurting themselves (60.7%), felt they would be better off dead (64.7%), or felt life wasn't worth living (69.1%) (Table 10.1). Of those who reported suicidal ideation at Wave 1, 60% had made plans at some point, and 51.3% believed their lives would end in suicide. Nonheterosexuals (16.1%) were more than twice as likely as heterosexual adolescents (7.1%) to have thoughts of hurting themselves "all of the time," approximately three times more likely to think "all of the time" about killing themselves (14.5% vs. 4.7%), more than twice as likely to believe "all of the time" that their lives would end with suicide (15.2% vs. 5.7%), and to believe that there was no solution but to take one's own life (12.9% vs. 4.7%).

During the 3 years of the study, thoughts of killing oneself increased nearly nine percentage points among the young women and seven percentage points for young men. Suicidal thoughts were often expressed obliquely and in the past; for example, one young woman (aged 19 years) discussed having felt suicidal in a very off-handed manner:

Table 10.1 Lifetime Measures of Suicidal Ideation by Gender and Sexual Orientation

	All (N = 428)	Gender (N = 428)		Sexuality (N = 427)	
	Total (%)	Male (%)	Female (%)	Hetero-sexual (%)	Non-heterosexual (%)
Thought about hurting self					
Some time	52.3	50.3	53.9*	51.0c	61.3
All time	8.4	5.3	10.8	7.1	16.1
Felt better off dead					
Some time	53.3	51.3	54.8*	52.6	58.1
All time	11.4	8.6	13.7	11.0	14.5
Thought about killing self					
Some time	50.0	48.7	51.0†	48.5d	59.7
All time	6.1	3.7	7.9	4.7	14.5
Had plans to kill self (N = 240)					
Some time	54.2	56.1	52.8	52.6	60.9
All time	5.8	3.1	7.7	5.7	6.5
Felt life would end in suicide (N = 240)					
Some time	43.8	39.8	46.5	42.3b	50.0
All time	7.5	6.1	8.5	5.7	15.2
Felt life is not worth living					
Some time	56.5	59.4	54.4†	56.4c	58.1
All time	12.6	8.0	16.2	11.0	22.6
Felt like giving up because life is bad					
Some time	55.1	56.7	53.9***	55.3a	54.8
All time	18.0	11.2	23.2	16.7	25.8
Wished life would end					
Some time	49.1	47.6	50.2**	48.2a	54.8
All time	8.2	4.3	11.2	7.1	14.5
No solution but to take own life					
Some time	31.1	24.7	36.1***	29.9b	38.7
All time	5.9	2.7	8.3	4.7	12.9

Note: Independent t-tests to assess significant differences are indicated in "some time" rows.

† p ≤ .10 (gender significance test).
* p ≤ .05 (gender significance test).
** p ≤ .01 (gender significance test).
*** p ≤ .001 (gender significance test).
a p ≤ .05 (sexuality significance test).
b p ≤ .01 (sexuality significance test).
c p ≤ .001 (sexuality significance test).

> I don't know it just I didn't feel like anybody under-
> stood me or even cared about me or whatever and
> it was just like a really rough time with my par-
> ents and everything and I just got depressed and
> suicidal.

Suicide attempts and mental disorders

Meeting criteria for any of the five psychiatric disorders placed the young people at significant risk for suicide attempts. The majority of attempters (86.3%) met criteria for conduct disorder (CD) with male attempters (95.2%) more likely than female attempters (80.6%) to meet criteria for CD (Table 10.2). In the study, 40% of attempters met criteria for major depressive disorder (MDE), and 49.4% met criteria for post-traumatic stress disorder (PTSD). Female attempters (59.2%) were more likely to meet criteria for PTSD than male attempters (33.9%). Of attempt-ers, 65% met criteria for one of the substance abuse disorders (SUDs). More than 80% of attempters met criteria for two or more disorders. The

Table 10.2 Suicide Attempts by Wave 1 Diagnoses and Gender ($N = 160$)

	Total (%)	Males (%)	Females (%)
One diagnosis	13.1	11.3	14.3
Conduct disorder (CD)	86.3	95.2	80.6**
Major depressive disorder (MDE)	40.0	40.3	39.8
Posttraumatic stress disorder (PTSD)	49.4	33.9	59.2**
Substance abuse disorder (SUD)	65.0	67.7	63.3
Two or more diagnoses	81.3	85.5	78.6
CD and MDE	36.3	38.7	34.7
CD and PTSD	43.1	32.3	50.0*
CD and SUD	62.5	67.7	59.2
MDE and PTSD	26.3	21.0	29.6
MDE and SUD	28.1	27.4	28.6
PTSD and SUD	33.1	22.6	39.8*

* $p \leq .05$.
** $p \leq .01$.

most prevalent comorbid disorders among the attempters were CD and SUD (62.5%).

The worrisome arbitrariness of adolescent suicide behaviors was nicely summed up by a young woman (aged 19 years):

> It's when you're stressed out and you're depressed that you sometimes you have good days, most times you have bad days, you cry all the time either you just like eat and get fat like me or you just don't eat at all or you think about killing yourself and you sometimes you act upon it. And sometimes you don't.

Given the impulsivity, substance abuse, and lack of supportive, monitoring adults, it is very difficult to ascertain when a young person like this one will act.

Another young woman (aged 20 years) told us about her suicide attempt and subsequent hospitalization:

> I had gone through this like really, really bad depression. Like, I wouldn't go anywhere; I was always in my room. I wouldn't talk unless somebody talked to me and that was just like, yes, no, whatever, you know? I wasn't like making conversation. I would walk and stare at the ground. I didn't look at anybody. I didn't even realize really what was going on myself, but I was in my own world. Something happened one night that I totally went psycho. And I sliced up my arms and everything, and they were just like "Ok, we're taking you to the hospital." So, I ended up there for 2 weeks.

Although this attempt in a group home setting does not appear to be high on lethality, it provides insight in the impulsive nature of the behaviors (e.g., "something happened one night"). Think of this without nearby supervision and with the added disinhibiting effect of alcohol or drugs.

Correlates of suicidal ideation

We assessed correlates of lifetime suicidal ideation at Wave 1 using ordinary least squares regression (Table 10.3). Suicidal ideation was measured with the mean of nine items pertaining to thoughts of death and harming oneself (all of the items are listed in Table 10.1). To be included in the analysis the respondents must have answered at least five of the questions.

Table 10.3 Ordinary Least Squares Regression Model of Correlates of Suicide Ideation at Wave 1 (N = 423)

	Model 1		Model 2		Model 3		Model 4		Model 5		Model 6		Model 7	
	b	Standard Error	b	Standard Error	b	Standard Error	b	Standard Error	b	Standard Error	b	Standard Error	b	Standard Error
Age	0.09***	0.02	0.06**	0.02	0.05*	0.02	0.04†	0.02	0.04†	0.02	0.04*	0.02	0.04*	0.02
Female	0.17***	0.05	0.12**	0.05	0.10*	0.05	0.09†	0.05	0.07	0.05	0.09†	0.05	0.09†	0.05
Heterosexual	-0.17**	0.07	-0.12†	0.07	-0.09	0.06	-0.08	0.06	-0.08	0.06	-0.09	0.06	-0.08	0.06
Age on own	0.02*	0.01	-0.00	0.01	-0.00	0.01	-0.00	0.01	-0.00	0.01	-0.00	0.01	-0.00	0.01
Sexual abuse			0.04**	0.01	0.03*	0.01	0.03*	0.01	0.02†	0.01	0.02†	0.01	0.02†	0.01
Physical abuse			0.02***	0.00	0.02***	0.00	0.02***	0.00	0.02***	0.00	0.02***	0.00	0.02***	0.00
Physical victimization					0.06	0.04	0.05	0.04	0.04	0.04	0.03	0.04	0.02	0.04
Sexual victimization					0.07*	0.03	0.07*	0.03	0.07*	0.03	0.06*	0.04	0.06*	0.03
Major depressive disorder							0.19***	0.05	0.16***	0.05	0.16***	0.05	0.15***	0.05
Posttraumatic stress disorder									0.12**	0.05	0.12*	0.05	0.11*	0.05
Conduct disorder											0.12*	0.05	0.11*	0.05
Substance use													0.03	0.05
Constant	-0.59		-0.60		-0.40		-0.26		-0.27		-0.44		-0.42	
Adjusted R²	0.08		0.17		0.19		0.22		0.23		0.23		0.23	

† p ≤ .10.
* p ≤ .05.
** p ≤ .01.
*** p ≤ .001.

"Age on own" is the first age of first reported runaway episode. All of the other measures used in the regression equations have been discussed in previous chapters.

In Model 1, age of adolescent, being female, having a nonheterosexual sexual orientation, and running away at an early age were significantly associated with lifetime suicidal ideation. In Model 2, caretaker physical and sexual abuse were added to the regression equation, and both were statistically significant. In Model 3, subsequent street physical and sexual victimization were added to the equation. Sexual victimization when on the street was significantly associated with lifetime suicidal ideation. In Model 4, meeting lifetime criteria for MDE was added to the equation and was significantly associated with suicidal ideation. Similarly, the addition of lifetime PTSD and CD, respectively, in Models 5 and 6 significantly positively affected suicidal ideation. With the other diagnoses in the model, meeting lifetime criteria for SUD was nonsignificant in Model 7. There were no statistically significant interactions. Also significant in the final Model (Model 7) were age of adolescent, being female ($p < .10$), and caretaker sexual abuse ($p < .10$) and physical abuse, sexual victimization when on the street, and meeting lifetime criteria for MDE, PTSD, and CD. The final model explained 23% of the variance of lifetime suicidal ideation.

Correlates of suicide attempts

We investigated correlates of lifetime suicide attempts at Wave 1 using logistic regression (Table 10.4). All of the independent variables were those used in the previous analysis. In Model 1, age, gender, sexual orientation, and age of first runaway episode were all statistically significant. Older adolescents, females, nonheterosexuals, and those who ran away at an earlier age were more at risk for suicide attempts. These variables remained statistically significant when the caretaker physical and sexual abuse measures were added to the equation in Model 2. Both caretaker sexual abuse and physical abuse were associated with suicide attempts. The street victimization variables were added in Model 3. Only sexual victimization when on the streets was statistically significant. With the street victimization variables in the equation, gender of adolescent lost statistical significance. Meeting lifetime criteria for MDE was added to the equation in Model 4 and was statistically significant, as was CD in Model 5. Neither PTSD nor SUD (Models 6 and 7) were statistically significant.

In the final model (Model 7), age, nonheterosexual sexual orientation, age of first runaway episode ($p < .10$), caretaker sexual abuse ($p < .10$) and physical abuse, MDE ($p < .10$), and CD remained statistically significant with all of the variables taken into account. Meeting lifetime diagnostic criteria for MDE and CD were the strongest predictors of a suicide attempt.

Table 10.4 Logistic Regression Model of Correlates of Suicide Attempts at Wave 1 (N = 423)

	Model 1		Model 2		Model 3		Model 4		Model 5		Model 6		Model 7		Model 8		Model 9	
	b	Exp(b)	b	Exp(b)	b	Exp(b)	b	Exp(b)	b	Exp(b)	b	Exp(b)	b	Exp(b)	b	Exp(b)	b	Exp(b)
Age	0.32**	1.38	0.23**	1.26	0.21†	1.23	0.18	1.20	0.23*	1.26	0.23*	1.26	0.22*	1.25	0.24*	1.27	0.23*	1.26
Female	0.61**	1.84	0.43†	1.54	0.29	1.33	0.24	1.27	0.40	1.49	0.37	1.44	0.37	1.45	0.38	1.47	0.37	1.44
Heterosexual	-0.84**	0.43	-0.70*	0.50	-0.64*	0.53	-0.59†	0.55	-0.70*	0.50	-0.70*	0.50	-0.69*	0.50	-1.77**	0.17	-1.15**	0.32
Age on own	-0.12***	0.89	-0.07†	0.93	-0.07†	0.94	-0.07†	0.94	-0.07†	0.94	-0.06†	0.94	-0.06†	0.94	-0.06	0.94	-0.06	0.94
Sexual abuse			0.16**	1.17	0.12†	1.13	0.12†	1.13	0.12*	1.13	0.12†	1.12	0.12†	1.13	0.13*	1.14	0.12†	1.13
Physical abuse			0.09***	1.10	0.09***	1.09	0.08***	1.09	0.08***	1.08	0.08***	1.08	0.08***	1.08	-0.01	0.99	0.08***	1.08
Physical victimization					0.01	1.01	-0.02	0.98	-0.12	0.89	-0.13	0.88	-0.15	0.87	-0.15	0.86	-0.15	0.87
Sexual victimization					0.32*	1.38	0.34*	1.40	0.28†	1.32	0.28†	1.32	0.28	1.32	0.27	1.31	0.26	1.30
Major depression							0.54*	1.72	0.52*	1.67	0.47†	1.61	0.47†	1.60	0.46†	1.59	-0.48	0.62
Conduct disorder									1.06***	2.88	1.05***	2.86	1.01**	2.74	1.11***	3.04	1.05***†	2.87
Posttraumatic stress disorder											0.18	1.20	0.17	1.19	0.17	1.18	0.17	1.18
Substance use													0.12	1.13	0.10	1.11	0.10	1.11
Sexuality × physical abuse															0.11†	1.12		
Sexuality × major depression																	1.12†	3.07
Constant	-4.15		-4.35		-3.97		-3.60		-5.25		-5.24		-5.20		-4.61		-4.93	
Nagelkerke	0.11		0.20		0.21		0.23		0.26		0.26		0.26		0.27		0.27	
Cox & Snell	0.08		0.15		0.16		0.17		0.19		0.19		0.19		0.20		0.20	

† p ≤ .10.
* p ≤ .05.
** p ≤ .01.
*** p ≤ .001.

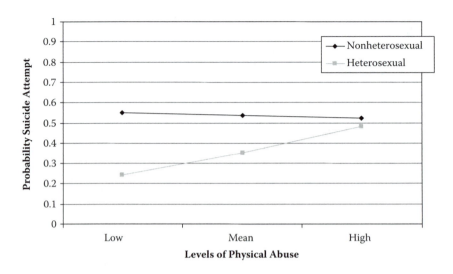

Figure 10.1 Suicide attempt by sexuality and physical abuse.

Lifetime MDE increased the odds of a suicide attempt 60% and meeting lifetime criteria for CD nearly tripled the odds of a lifetime suicide attempt ($Exp(b) = 2.74$). The final model included two statistically significant multiplicative interactions: (1) sexual orientation by caretaker physical abuse (Model 8); and (2) sexual orientation by meeting lifetime criteria for MDE (Model 9). Figure 10.1 illustrates the interaction between caretaker physical abuse and sexual orientation, indicating that the effects of caretaker physical abuse are greater for nonheterosexuals but that the effects converge for heterosexuals and nonheterosexuals at one standard deviation above the mean. High levels of physical abuse have similar effects on suicide attempts for heterosexual and nonheterosexual adolescents. Figure 10.2 depicts the interaction between sexual orientation and meeting lifetime criteria for MDE. MDE affects the likelihood of lifetime suicide attempts equally among nonheterosexuals and heterosexuals. However, nonheterosexuals who do not meet criteria for MDE are more likely than heterosexuals to have attempted suicide at some point in their lives.

Summary and discussion

Discussion: the high cost of being homeless during adolescence

In previous chapters we have documented the emotional costs of being homeless during adolescence in terms of distress and psychiatric disorders. Here it is apparent that the consequences may be life-threatening. The risk for suicide is in some part attributable to the degree to which the

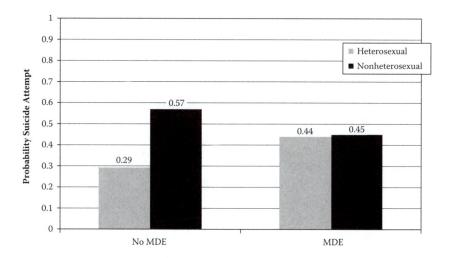

Figure 10.2 Suicide attempt by major depressive episode and sexuality.

adolescents had been victimized thus far. Lifetime suicide attempts were associated with a history of caretaker physical or sexual maltreatment and more proximal sexual victimization on the streets. The emotional consequences of maltreatment and victimization denoted by psychiatric diagnoses also reflect risk. Meeting lifetime criteria for MDE increased the odds of a lifetime suicide attempt by nearly two thirds, and meeting criteria for CD nearly tripled the odds of an attempt. Externalization was more predictive of an attempt than was depression. As noted previously, more than two thirds (67.3%) of our sample met lifetime criteria for two or more psychiatric disorders at Wave 1, and, consonant with research on nonrunaway adolescents (Gould et al., 1998), the majority of suicide attempters (81.3%) met criteria for two or more disorders. To place this in context, it is important to recall that these attempts were not trivial. The majority of the attempts (59.7%) were life-threatening, and 28.9% had a very high probability of death.

Theoretical implications

Aside from the very high rates of attempts and ideation, the results are congruent with our research team's recent work on the dimensionality of suicidal ideation. A three-factor confirmatory factor analysis (CFA) based on these data indicated that sucidality (ideation and attempts) was associated with meeting diagnostic criteria for both internalizing and externalizing psychiatric disorders (Yoder, Longley, Whitbeck, & Hoyt, 2008). The CFA results are consistent with the work of Krueger and others (Krueger, 1999;

Krueger & Markon, 2006; Lahey, Applegate, Waldman, Loft, Hankin, & Rick, 2004) regarding co-occurring internalizing and externalizing symptoms and suicidality. Moreover, the finding that suicidality, internalizing disorders, and externalizing disorders loaded on a single factor lends credence to the concept of a suicide spectrum, a separate clinical syndrome that occurs across a range of psychiatric disorders (Ahrens & Linden, 1996; Leboyer, Slama, Siever, & Bellivier, 2005). These findings indicate that it is important to view externalizing young people as potential suicide risks even in the absence of internalizing symptoms and that those who manifest symptoms of both should be considered a heightened risk.

In addition, our work from these data suggests that current screenings for suicide risk may not be sufficiently sensitive. Thoughts of death as well as specific suicidal ideation may be predictive of suicide attempts and should be taken very seriously (Yoder, Whitbeck, & Hoyt, 2008). It is possible that our traditional approaches to assessing suicidality are underestimating risk.

Policy implications

These findings have very serious intervention implications for those who work with homeless and runaway adolescents. First points of contact personnel such as free clinic staff, shelter personnel, hospital emergency department staff, and law enforcement officers should be aware of the extremely high rates of attempts among runaways. Externalizing adolescents should be viewed as potential risks, particularly in the presence of internalizing symptoms and substance abuse. Moreover, we may want to consider revising adolescent suicide screeners to put more emphasis on thoughts of death and dying as well as suicide-specific ideation. Runaway adolescents who present with trauma may be particularly at risk: More than one half (59.2%) of the female attempters met criteria for PTSD.

Clinicians also should be aware of the increased risk of psychiatric comorbidity among this population of young people. These findings add to already substantial evidence that co-occurring externalizing and internalizing disorders increase risk (Lewinsohn et al., 1995; Rohde et al., 1997; Yoder, Longley, et al., 2008). Although the self-reported lethality scale we used may be an imperfect measure, it indicated that well over one half of the suicide attempts among this population could have been fatal. At the very minimum, the young people view their attempts as serious. This means treating suicidal ideation and "gestures" involving self-harm very seriously. The high rates of self-mutilating behaviors among the younger runaways (see Chapter 9, this volume) further complicate assessment of suicide risk.

Conclusions

On several levels our findings suggest that the belief that suicidal gestures are a "cry for help" by homeless and runaway adolescents is outdated and dangerous. Pervasive lack of support, hopelessness, adolescent impulsivity, abuse history, and the threat of harm or actual harm when on the streets combined with severe psychiatric problems and substance abuse form a potentially lethal mix among homeless and runaway adolescents. Whatever risks existed prior to running away are exacerbated by the environments and sense of hopelessness that the adolescent encounter on the streets. These high rates of suicide attempts add yet another dimension to an already dangerous developmental context.

chapter 11

Health and services utilization

With Devan M. Crawford

The costs of living on the streets are not all emotional and psychological. Hunger and malnutrition coupled with stress, lack of rest, and substance abuse weaken immune systems and exacerbate risk for infectious diseases. High levels of sexual activity increase risks of pregnancy, sexually transmitted infections (STIs), sexual assault, and gynecological problems (Barkin, Balkrishnan, Manuel, Anderson, & Gelberg, 2003). And, as we have seen in previous chapters, unintentional and intentional injuries may result in serious physical injuries that require medical attention.

These health risks are not trivial. Studies from the United States and Canada indicate that mortality rates are much higher among homeless people compared with those who are housed (see O'Connell, 2004 (review)). This is particularly true for younger homeless women (18–44 years), whose mortality rates in seven cities in the United States, Canada, and Europe were 5–30 times greater than those for similarly aged women in the general population (Cheung & Hwang, 2004). In Boston, mortality rates for homeless people of similar ages to the participants in our study (18–24 years) are 5.9 times higher than the general population (Hwang, Orav, O'Connell, Lebow, & Brennan, 1997), and in Toronto they are 8.3 times higher (Hwang, 2000). Homicide was the leading cause of death among homeless men aged 18–24 years in Boston (Hwang et al., 1997). Other studies of homeless adults in the United States and Canada indicate high rates of deaths due to suicide, HIV/AIDs, chronic medical conditions (e.g., renal failure, hepatitis, heart disease), and heavy substance use (Cheung & Hwang, 2004; Hwang, 2000; Roy, Haley, Leclerc, Boudreau, & Boivin, 2004).

We have thus far examined multiple health risks among the adolescents in the study. In this chapter we investigate the adolescents' reports about their mental and physical health-care utilization with particular attention to their perceptions about their health-care providers and barriers to use of services.

Health and health-care utilization among runaway and homeless adolescents

Homeless individuals are at once the most vulnerable and least served population in the United States. The lifestyles of runaways and young adult homeless individuals place them at risk for all kinds of maladies, including injury, serious infectious diseases such as HIV/AIDS, STIs, hepatitis and tuberculosis, and intentional injury from suicide attempts (Farrow, Deisher, Brown, Kulig, & Kipke, 1992 (review)). Ensign's (1998) rich qualitative studies illustrate the difficulties of feeling ill when homeless and on your own. When you are feeling bad, everything is more difficult: finding a place to go for care, riding public transportation, and waiting for long periods of time in public clinics. Indeed, basic hygiene is difficult on the street even when adolescents feel good (Ensign, 2000), but when ill, everyday activities such as finding something to eat and staying warm become much more difficult. There are few places to rest or to go to recover when illness strikes (Ensign & Bell, 2004; Ensign & Panke, 2002).

Being independent and under age creates numerous health-care barriers. There is the fear that the provider will contact child protective services, issues of permission to treat, having no identification, and no way to pay (DeRosa, Montgomery, Kipke, Iverson, Ma, & Unger, 1999; Padgett, Struening, & Andrews, 1990). There is embarrassment at the questions asked, nervousness about filling out forms properly, and self-consciousness about unconventional appearance and hygiene (Ensign & Bell, 2004; Ensign & Panke, 2002). Fear of discrimination and potential embarrassment may be even greater among nonheterosexuals (Van Leeuwen et al., 2006).

In addition to barriers of fear and embarrassment, there are problems knowing where to go for treatment, for transportation issues, and for meeting the costs of services. Very few of the adolescents are insured (Padgett, Struening, & Andrews, 1990), and even among those who are there may be problems with copayment. Indeed, the most cited barrier to health care among homeless adolescents and adults is the ability to pay. Most homeless people have no health insurance (O'Toole, Gibbon, Hanusa, & Fine, 1999), although being on Medicaid or Medicare is an enabling factor for health-care utilization (Padgett et al., 1990). The emphasis in many hospital emergency departments to find a responsible party for payment increases fear of ending up in child protective custody and results in avoidance among underage runaways. The humiliation of not being able to pay and the perceived services discrimination that accompanies this also result in avoidance of services (Darbyshire, Muir-Cochrane, Fereday, Jureidini, & Drummond, 2006; Shiner, 1995). Often, the adolescents feel that clinic or emergency department staff members are rude or uncaring and that they see a different provider each time they present for services (Ensign, 2004). Adolescents who are already socially inept may have difficulty with authority figures and may be especially sensitive to how they are treated. As part of the economic equation, Gelberg and colleagues make the case that competing priorities based on subsistence strategies are an often overlooked barrier to medical care among homeless people (Gelberg, Gallagher, Andersen, & Koegel, 1997). Not only can they not afford health care, but also finding something to eat and a place to stay may consume all of their time and energy.

Oral health is an often overlooked health-care component among homeless people. A Toronto study reported that homeless adolescents were three times less likely to have had a dental examination in the past 5 years than those in the general population. The average time since last dental checkup was 2.8 years. When asked about dental problems in the past month, 40.2% reported pain when chewing, and 44.8% reported bleeding gums. Nearly 13% had pain that kept them awake at night (Lee, Gaetz, & Goettler, 1994). In a Montreal study of homeless adults, 85% of those seen during the course of the study were in need of dental treatment (Pizem, Massicotte, Vincent, & Barolet, 1994).

Frequently homeless individuals seek out health care only when the problem has become so acute it can no longer be ignored (Ensign, 1998). This and issues of access result in the overuse of emergency departments at hospitals (Klein, Woods, Wilson, Prospero, Greene, & Ringwalt, 2000). Schnazer and colleagues found that more than one third of their sample of homeless adults used hospital emergency departments as a primary source of health care. This compared with less than 1% in the general population (Schnazer, Dominguez, Shrout, & Caton, 2007). Preferred points of service tend to be those that are viewed as easily accessible, accepting, listening, and nonjudgmental (Darbyshire et al., 2006).

Mental health and substance abuse needs

Although homeless and runaway adolescents are at great risk for physical injury and illnesses, because of age and life circumstances their predominant health needs revolve around mental health and substance use concerns (Farrow et al., 1992). Many have had contact with mental health or substance abuse services either prior to running away or during runaway episodes. In an earlier sample of Midwestern homeless and runaway adolescents we found that 80% of the adolescents had seen a mental health professional, about one half of these prior to their first runaway episode (Berdahl, Hoyt, & Whitbeck, 2005). In a Los Angeles-based study, 45% of runaway adolescents had used mental health services since running away. The most mentioned barrier to mental health services use among the Los Angeles runaways was not knowing where to go. The majority of those who sought help went to crisis centers (Solorio, Milburn, Andersen, Trifskin, & Rodriguez, 2006). Among homeless adults in Los Angeles who met criteria for a serious mental illness or substance use disorder, only one fifth reported receiving treatment in the past 60 days. Only one half of those with recent substance abuse dependence had ever received treatment (Koegel, Sullivan, Burnam, Morton, & Wenzel, 1999). In a San Francisco study, 39% of adolescents had used drug-related services (Carlson, Sugano, Millstein, & Auerswald, 2006).

Health status and services utilization

The majority of the adolescents we talked to viewed themselves as basically in good health. The young women (6%) were less likely than the young men (17.1%) to say they were in "excellent" health. About one fourth of the young people told us they were in "fair" or "poor" health with no gender differences. Most (64.7%) felt they were in "very good" or "good" health. By the third year of the study, 17.4% felt their health had changed for the worse, with women (20.4%) more likely than men (13%) to believe their health had deteriorated over time. The majority (65.8%) felt their health had remained unchanged during the course of the study.

Women (73.2%) at Wave 2 (the first time the question was asked) were much more likely than men (42.6%) to have seen a physician since the last interview. Almost equal percentages of women (24%) and men (20%) had seen a dentist since last interview at Wave 2. These percentages changed very little over the remaining waves of data collection, with females more likely than males to seek medical attention at each wave (Figure 11.1). At Wave 1, 41.1% of the young women and 37.4% of the young men had been to a hospital "because something was wrong." Of these, about one half had been to the hospital on two or more occasions.

Approximately one fourth (26.6%) of the young women and 17.6% of the young men at first interview told us they would like to see a doctor. There were a range of complaints. Some wanted a physical examination (e.g., "to find out what my bulimia has done to me"); others listed mental health problems, most often depression. Many knew their diagnosis from previous mental health contacts (e.g., borderline personality disorder, depression, eating disorder). Several were worried about serious infectious illnesses (e.g., hepatitis C) and chronic diseases (e.g., asthma, sickle cell anemia). A number had chronic conditions that either were being marginally treated or were going untreated altogether. One young man (aged 21 years) told us he was having trouble stabilizing his living situation because of epilepsy:

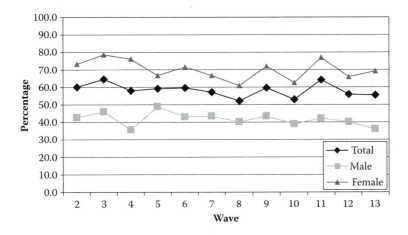

Figure 11.1 Seen a medical doctor since our last interview?

> There's always going to be negatives. My epilepsy for one. I still have uh epileptic seizures. And I still go on…. I don't have a job yet. I don't have an income to where I can put food on the table every week or every other week.

A young woman (aged 19 years) had debilitating respiratory problems:

> Bronchitis mostly. That almost killed me when I was actually on the street. Sleeping on the street. That almost killed me because it was so cold outside. And I was dying, I ended up at my parent's house and my mom actually took me to the doctor. And I stayed over there and slept and my little sister fed me cause I hadn't eaten in like 3 days. I was literally like dying because of that….

Another young woman (aged 19 years) had chronic heart disease:

> Right now my whole program there is kind of at a standstill because of medical issues. Heart problems…. I have a really low heart rate, like it's in the 40's basically, it means that the blood pools in the lower half of my body and it causes me to pass out a lot. So currently I am going through a whole bunch of tests and stuff trying to figure out. The electrical

> pulse in my heart don't go properly. Also so they are trying to figure out … what they can do to help that. So I might end up in a pacemaker so I'm not allowed to work or exercise or anything like that right now.

Still another young woman (aged 20 years) complained of "chronic pneumonia":

> Well I was really susceptible to pneumonia cause I got it when I was really little and like once you've had pneumonia you can get it really easy over and over. Being outside all day or being in skywalks and then going outside and stuff like that. Getting sick with pneumonia and really bad coughing and stuff like that and I was like. I mean that just little stuff, you know like it's just a cold or a fever or whatever and then have to go outside all day and make it worse.

For some, health needs revolved around injuries chronic and acute:

> I have knee problems from getting hit in my knees a lot. A lot of times when I get taken down being jumped and stuff I've always gotten hit in this knee I've been to the doctor quite a few times cause of my knee. I've had water torn behind my kneecap and all this kind of stuff. I've had that problem since I've left. I think I've actually blacked out twice…Whenever weather starts changing and I'll know it because my knee will start aching or it'll swell up or something. Usually I try to hold my knee or I try to I usually suffer with it until it either gets really bad like I can't even walk or I can't even hardly move without bursting into tears. I just suffer with it. (female, aged 19 years)

> I went to the hospital a few more times for an ex-boyfriend who used to physically assault me. It's kind of hard for them to refuse you when you got blood gushing out or your jaw feels broken or something like that. (female, aged 22 years)

A few mentioned dental issues such as wisdom teeth hurting or toothache:

> Like teeth I'm always wanting to go to the dentist. I never go to the dentist but I always want to go to the dentist. My dad, my parents got a dentist and last year I got two of my cavities filled but now I have wisdom teeth growing in. When you first met me and I got it pulled out then and it made my teeth crooked and now I got another one coming in. It hurts like hell; eating hurts. (female, aged 19 years)

Many of the young women were worried about whether they were pregnant, about missed periods, and about other gynecological issues (e.g., cysts on ovaries, sick from an abortion, needing a checkup for STIs). Most of those who sought treatment at the end of Year 2 of the study had gone to a public hospital (25.3% males; 16.2% females), followed by private and public clinics. Women (14.1%) were much more likely to use public clinics than were men (2.7%) and more likely to be on Medicaid (22% vs. 11.8%).

We asked the adolescents if they had ever received inpatient services for substance abuse or mental health needs; 23% of the young men and 15.4% of the young women had been in inpatient treatment for substance abuse. Of those that had been in treatment, 48.6% of the women and 58.5% of the men had been hospitalized two or more times. Of those who had ever been in treatment, 11.5% were first in treatment at age 12 years or less, 35.6% at ages 13–15 years, and 52.6% at age 16 years or older. Nearly one half (48.8%) had been in treatment a month or more.

The rate for inpatient hospitalization for mental health reasons was substantially higher than that for substance use. About one third (36.2%) had been in inpatient treatment for a mental health problem with no gender difference. Of those who experienced inpatient treatment, more than one half (55.6%) had been hospitalized two or more times. More than one fourth (28.6%) had been first hospitalized at age 12 years or younger, 42.2% between ages 13 and 15 years, and 29.2% at age 16 or older. The 45% of adolescents who had been in inpatient treatment estimated their total number of hospitalized days as 1 month or more. One young man (aged 20 years) said he was hospitalized:

> They said I was paranoid schizophrenic. But then my dad paid for a second opinion and the doctor said I just had mood problems, I had mood swings. I'm a typical human being.

One of the young women (aged 19 years) had been hospitalized for bipolar disorder:

> I have manic depression so it's kind of like. Things can put me in a good mood. Like the littlest things. Like sugar wafers. Oh you know those little sugar wafer things? I'm over at Kevin's house and his dad always has sugar wafers. Give me a sugar wafer and I will be happy for the whole night. I will start bouncing off the walls. I would be the happiest person in the world. All over sugar wafers. Oh yeah, I'm a weirdo what can I say.

A young man (aged 21 years) told us he was in and out of inpatient treatment punctuated with periods of homelessness:

> I was there for about a month probably and then I left and I ended up I was homeless. I was staying in the shelter. And all this homeless off and on. And then I got my next place, which was in an apartment complex. And then it got burned down so then I became homeless again. And then I went to psych ward a couple of times; I don't remember how long I was there. And then went to a couple of shelters and I was back into psych ward, don't know how long. And this is where it gets confusing because I don't remember the time frames.

About 10% of the adolescents were taking medicine for psychiatric problems at the time of their first interview, and the number remained quite consistent across all 3 years of the study. Of those on psychiatric medications at Wave 1, the vast majority were on antidepressants (77.3%). About one fourth (22.7%) were taking antipsychotic medication. Although three fourths (77.3%) of the adolescents at Wave 1 told us they took their prescribed dosage the day before the interview, 59.1% said they had missed their dosage at least one time in the past week. The number reporting missing dosages in the past week increased to 76.5% by Year 3 of the study.

As one would expect, the majority of the adolescents had been seen in various outpatient settings. More than 80% had seen a school counselor, 71.7% a mental health therapist, and 38.3% a substance abuse counselor. Slightly more than 40% had met with a probation officer. The young women (77.6%) were more likely than the young men (58.3%) to have talked to a welfare worker, probably due to their pregnancies. About one third (29.9%) of the adolescents had spoken with a minister, priest, or someone from a religious organization.

Their assessments of their outpatient contacts varied. Although there was little variation in the adolescents' assessment on how easy their outpatient contacts were to talk with, welfare workers were scored lowest on interest and helpfulness at Year 1 of the study, and runaway agencies scored highest on interest and helpfulness. Staff from runaway agencies were also rated the highest on our question of whether they would return to that person for services. Mental health workers were also viewed very positively regarding interest and helpfulness and whether the adolescent would return for services.

Barriers to services

At Years 2 and 3 of the study we assessed reasons that the young people did not get needed health care. At both points in time, the young men were significantly more likely than the young women to say they could not afford healthcare and that they had no insurance. The men were also more likely than the women to say that transportation was a barrier and to say at Year 3 that they didn't know where to go for services. There was little concern about confidentiality, treatment, or trust of health-care providers. At Year 2, the young men were more likely than the young women to believe that health care was not available, but by Year 3 there was little gender difference. The barrier mentioned most frequently was money. One young man (aged 19 years) had worked out a scam to deal with payment:

> I get sick all the time. Like, I'm always sick. Like I'm always coughing and hacking up some kind of weird phlegm. I haven't puked in like a year and a half now, which is amazing for as much as I drink and uh not really that many other like broken bones here from like squatting or anything that's just like everyday falling while walking down the sidewalk. If they're bad enough I'll walk into the emergency room and if they're way bad and I know it's gonna be really expensive I just tell them a different name and completely lie about my address and no I don't have any ID I'm hurting. (Laughs) It usually works.

Others nursed themselves due to cost of a checkup:

> I know that I had strep throat but beings that I don't
> have no insurance I just kind of had to pump myself
> full of Benadryl and things like that and it went
> away after a few weeks. (female, aged 20 years)

For some, both cost and transportation to a free clinic was a problem:

> Ended up get lice in the Freemont Jail. That really
> sucked I had to go and steal lice shampoo because
> none of the organizations would provide it for me
> and I didn't I couldn't go way up to the Health
> Department because I didn't have a vehicle or any-
> thing. (female, aged 22 years)

Being on Medicaid was a definite benefit for those who qualified:

> I had to go to the emergency room for a severe sinus
> infection. The doctor told me if I had waited more
> about a week more my sinuses would have exploded
> and that wouldn't have been good because I would
> have been croaked I would have been dead. I was
> still on Medicaid so I had no problem getting help
> and getting prescriptions to get the infection gone.
> (female, aged 22 years)

Multivariate analysis

We used logistic regression to further investigate barriers to health care (Table 11.1). The dependent variable in the regression equation was whether at Wave 13, the final wave of the study, the adolescent had seen a medical doctor since last interview. We chose this time frame because we believed it provided the best indicator of health adaptation of the young people who had remained in the study over time. The only other new variable in the regression models was a dichotomous variable indicating whether the adolescent felt he or she could afford health care. All of the other variables have been described in previous chapters.

In Model 1, with only age of adolescent, gender, and sexual orientation in the equation, being female and heterosexual were positively associated with seeing a doctor since last interview. Women were more than four times ($Exp(b) = 4.10$) more likely than men to have seen a doctor and heterosexuals ($p < .10$) were more than two times ($Exp(b) = 2.06$) more likely to have seen a doctor than nonheterosexuals. In Model 2 we entered street experience variables into the model and both were statistically significant.

Table 11.1 Logistic Regression Predicting Seeing Medical Doctor (*N* = 175)

	Model 1		Model 2		Model 3		Model 4	
	b	*Exp(b)*	*b*	*Exp(b)*	*b*	*Exp(b)*	*b*	*Exp(b)*
Age	−0.10	0.91	−0.05	0.95	0.01	1.01	0.07	1.07
Female	1.41	4.10**	1.07	2.92**	0.97	2.65**	1.76	5.80***
Heterosexual	0.72	2.06†	0.45	1.57	0.49	1.63	0.53	1.70
Ever on street			−0.78	0.46*	−0.91	0.40*	−0.90	0.41*
Deviant subsistence strategies			−0.88	0.41*	−0.72	0.49*	−0.72	0.49*
Afford health care					−0.81	0.45*	0.16	1.18
Female * afford							−1.91	0.15**
Constant	0.46	1.59	1.03	2.80	0.31	1.37	−1.26	0.28
Nagelkerke		0.12		0.18		0.21		0.24
Cox & Snell		0.16		0.25		0.28		0.32

† *p* ≤ .10.
* *p* ≤ .05.
** *p* ≤ .01.
*** *p* ≤ .001.

Having ever spent time directly on the streets reduced the likelihood of seeing a physician since last interview by 54% (*Exp(b)* = .46), and engaging in deviant subsistence strategies when on the streets reduced the likelihood by 59% (*Exp(b)* = .41). Sexual orientation became nonsignificant and remained so in subsequent models.

In Model 3, being unable to afford health care reduced the likelihood of seeing a physician by 55% (*Exp(b)* = .45). This finding is refined in Model 4, which includes a statistically significant multiplicative interaction between female gender and affording health care (Figure 11.2). Men were much less able to afford health care than women. In this final model with all of the variables in the equation, women were nearly six times (*Exp(b)* = 5.8) more likely than men to have seen a doctor since the last interview. The other statistically significant variables in Model 4 were ever having spent time on the streets (*Exp(b)* = .41) and engaging in deviant subsistence strategies (*Exp(b)* = .49): Each reduced the likelihood by 50% or more.

We did a second logistic regression analysis to investigate barriers to dental care with the dependent variable of having seen a dentist since last interview (not shown). The only statistically significant variable in the

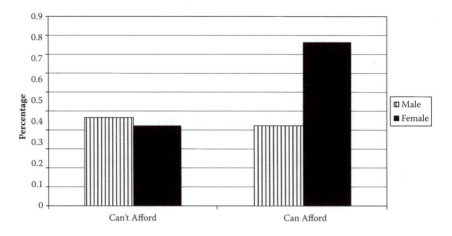

Figure 11.2 Medical care by gender and affordability.

model was affordability, which reduced the likelihood of seeking dental care by 59% (*Exp(b)* = .41).

Summary and discussion

The vast majority of the adolescents reported they were either in excellent or good health. Only about one fourth told us their health was "fair" or "poor." Women were much more likely than men to view their health as deteriorating over the course of the study, and they were nearly twice as likely as men to have seen a physician since their last interview. These gender differences may be due to disparities in real and perceived accessibility of health services. The young men were more likely than the young women to say they didn't know where to go for services and that transportation was a barrier for services. They also were more likely to tell us that they had no insurance or could not afford health care. Young women, as a function of Medicaid rules, were more likely to have health insurance and to be more certain about the availability of health care. This gender difference was particularly apparent in our multivariate analyses where in the final model women were nearly six times more likely than men to have seen a physician since last interview. The interaction term indicates that this was largely due to affordability, which, in turn, is probably attributable to Medicaid eligibility.

Our results are congruent with many other studies that report affordability as a major barrier to services among runaway and homeless adolescents. We did not find the levels of concern about confidentiality that others have reported; however, the subjects in our sample were older and were making the transition into adulthood, which probably reduced concerns about child protective intervention and other confidentiality worries. Of particular concern in this long-term study is the number of young women who believe their health has deteriorated across time. In fact, this may be just the tip of the iceberg for later health complaints.

Theoretical implications

The participants in our study are still very young, and the physical tolls of homelessness may not yet be apparent. Lifestyle-related illnesses associated with smoking, drug use, poor nutrition, and poor preventive health care typically appear later in life. With this in mind, the adolescents' perceived health seems optimistic particularly given the rates of mental and substance abuse disorders and personal victimization they have reported. This speaks to the resiliency of the adolescents but also to their being at an age where chronic physical illnesses are less likely to be present. For example, substance use disorders and impairment associated with early substance use disorders may not manifest themselves until the early or mid-twenties. Similarly, lack of regular dental care is bound to result in needed oral health care later in life. Lack of prenatal care and untreated or recurring STIs may lead to future gynecological problems among the young women. And we have no way of predicting the long-term health effects of alcohol and drug use, exposure to infectious diseases such as hepatitis, tuberculosis (Barnes et al., 1996), and poor nutrition during this developmental period.

Policy implications

Almost all of the adolescents had received some sort of services. About one third had been treated in an inpatient setting for a mental health problem, and about one fifth had been in an inpatient substance abuse program. Given the number of adolescents in the study who met criteria for a mental or substance use disorder, the level of treatment of substance disorders seems somewhat low. It is likely that more of these young people will require inpatient substance use treatment at some point in the future.

Upward of 80% had been seen on an outpatient basis of some kind. Most of the young people viewed their outpatient services providers positively. As one would expect, they viewed welfare workers and probation officers the most negatively. Runaway agencies, those who worked directly on the streets, were viewed most positively. This suggests that street agencies are natural services centers and that health-services providers should work closely with those who already know the street culture and have the trust of the young people.

When Medicaid was available, the young people used it. This speaks to the urgency of health-care coverage for this very vulnerable population. Many of the young people were not getting the health care they needed until the problem become acute. Also, those with chronic illnesses were not receiving regular care. Young women who become pregnant and thus eligible for Medicaid had distinct health advantages. For many of the young women, having a baby meant help with housing and medical expenses, an important pathway off the streets.

Homeless people are last in line for health care in our country. The current system simply ignores them until they are so sick that they require attention. Even when acute care is provided, there are media reports of hospitals "dumping" homeless people on the streets or at the doors of shelters; sometimes news videos show them still in hospital gowns. Accessible health care would be used by these adolescents if available, and preventive health measures could further reduce service burden immediately by shrinking emergency room use and by diminishing lifestyle-related health problems that may emerge later in life.

Conclusions

Just as the presence of mental and substance abuse disorders among young people of these ages portend problems in later adulthood, unmet health needs will take a toll as well. Indeed, the interaction between mental and substance use disorders and physical health among this population is an important area for future research. If histories of caretaker abuse and neglect, the stress of living on their own, and their experiences of street victimization have mental health consequences, it is very likely that they also have stress-related physical consequences. Yet there is a paucity of research regarding the long-term physical health effects of periods of homelessness during adolescence and young adulthood. Common sense tells us there will be health consequences, but we simply do not have good information on which to develop health policy strategies.

Adult roles: social networks, intimate relationships, economic adjustment, and emerging adulthood

chapter 12

Social networks

Friends and families at home and on the streets

With Trina Rose and Kurt D. Johnson

One of the major developmental tasks of adolescence is the expansion of social spheres from predominantly family members to same-aged friends and adults outside the family such as teachers, coaches, and friends' parents. Running away accelerates this process and amplifies the influence of peers and adults outside the home (Whitbeck & Hoyt, 1999). However, the composition and effects of runaway adolescent social networks are not as straightforward as once thought. A rapidly developing literature is changing the way we think of the characteristics and influences of the social networks of runaway and homeless adolescents. Several major findings have emerged in recent years. First, running away does not mean social isolation. New combinations of social networks quickly emerge that include old and new contacts (Ennett, Bailey, & Federman, 1999; Johnson, Whitbeck, & Hoyt, 2005a; Rice, Milburn, & Rotheram-Borus, 2007). Second, ties to home and family are not necessarily severed. Parents and relatives continue to provide tangible and emotional support, particularly among young women and those who have recently left home (Johnson et al., 2005a; Milburn, Rotheram-Borus, Batterham, Brumback, Rosenthal, & Mallett, 2005). Third, peer affiliations are associated with positive as well as negative behaviors. While delinquent social networks increase negative behaviors such as petty crimes and drug use among runaway and homeless young people (Johnson, Whitbeck & Hoyt, 2005b; Kipke, Unger, O'Conner, Palmer, & LaFrance, 1997; Rice, Milburn, Rotheram-Borus, Mallett, & Rosenthal, 2005; Whitbeck & Hoyt, 1999), positive social networks often linked to ties from home and the old neighborhood are associated with fewer risky behaviors (Johnson et al., 2005a; Rice et al., 2005). Fourth, there is growing interest in the ways social networks change across time (Rice et al., 2005; Whitbeck & Hoyt, 1999). We still have much to learn about how social networks change in size, composition, and influence among adolescents who remain homeless for long periods. In this chapter we revisit social network composition and take some first steps in investigating social network change across time among runaway and homeless adolescents.

Adolescent social networks

Peer social networks become increasingly important during adolescence. Associations with prosocial peers are protective and contribute to the development of important social skills (Bierman, 2004), and affiliations with antisocial peers increase risk of negative behaviors such as delinquent behavior, early sexual debut, and substance abuse (Dishion, Andrews, & Crosby, 1995; Kupersmidt, Burchinal, & Patters, 1995; Patterson, 1986). Highly aggressive adolescents, who manifest behavioral problems such as those associated with attention deficit hyperactivity disorder, oppositional defiance disorder, and conduct disorder (CD), are likely to have trouble getting along with others and to experience peer rejection (Dodge, 1989). These adolescents often lack social skills and, rejected by their conventional counterparts, drift into relationships with adolescents who also are inept socially. These low-quality relationships involve more conflict and less stability than relationships between conventional adolescents (Cairns, Neckerman, & Cairns, 1989; Hartup, 1989; Parker & Asher, 1993). Although the friendships provide companionship, they do not offer the opportunity to learn and rehearse behaviors that develop conventional social skills; rather, they reinforce aggressive interaction patterns (Cairns et al., 1989; Cairns, Cairns, Neckerman, Gest, & Gariepy, 1988; Espelage, Holt, & Henkel, 2003) and can be stress producing and demoralizing (Connolly, Geller, Marton, & Kutcher, 1992).

As we have shown throughout this volume, the majority of the adolescents we interviewed (88.6%) met criteria for one or more mental or substance use disorders including conduct disorder, major depressive episode (MDE), posttraumatic stress disorder (PTSD), or a substance use disorder (SUD). Even by our most conservative estimates, two thirds of the adolescents met criteria for CD, and of these we classified roughly one half as highly aggressive. This bodes ill for healthy peer and family relationships. In particular, such children tend to be disliked and rejected by their peers (Hinshaw & Lee, 2003) and to have aggressive, even violent relationships with their parents (Whitbeck, Hoyt, & Ackley, 1997b). Moreover, conduct-disordered adolescents are more likely to be victimized by peers, which reinforces their negative perceptions about others' motives and their expectations of coercive/aggressive behaviors from others.

As evidence begins to emerge regarding the heterogeneity of runaway and homeless adolescents and the potential for social support and protective influences, it is important to consider the ways that the individual characteristics of the adolescents will influence their perceptions of the quality, composition, and stability of their social networks. Aggressive children tend to overestimate the extent to which they are liked and accepted by peers (Cillessen, van IJzendoorn, van Lieshout, & Hartup, 1992; Hughes, Cavell, & Grossman, 1997). It is possible that they also will overestimate the availability and depth of social support available to them. Indeed, the loneliness and vulnerability of homelessness together may lead runaway adolescents to misperceive levels of closeness, intimacy, and trustworthiness and to form new "instant best friendships" that may result in disappointment or even exploitation and victimization. Conversely, among those who are on their own for the first time, this sense of vulnerability may result in turning back to familiar friends and family (Rice et al., 2007).

In our earlier sample of runaway and homeless adolescents we found that adolescents' perceptions of parental warmth were positively associated with maintaining continued family support and that time on the streets was negatively associated with continued family support (Whitbeck & Hoyt, 1999). The less time on their own, the more likely family ties were maintained. Among first-time runaways who have salvageable family ties, continued family support is very likely.

There also is evidence that positive social support from street or peer networks reduces symptoms of depression and reports of poor health among runaway and homeless adolescents (Unger, Simon, Newman, Montgomery, Kipke, & Albornoz, 1998). Bao and colleagues found that positive social support reduced depressive symptoms, whereas affiliation with delinquent peers increased depressive symptoms (Bao, Whitbeck, & Hoyt, 2000). Negative social support such as that from delinquent peers may socialize runaway adolescents into the street economy and lead them away from family ties toward early independence (Hagen & McCarthy, 1997).

Social networks among adolescents are constantly in flux, and this is even more evident among those who have run away from home. Understanding the influence of social networks on homeless and runaway adolescents involves understanding how they change. For example, is there a shift from predominantly home and neighborhood networks to predominantly street networks? If so, how rapid is it, and what factors influence this shift? Does movement from home to street networks vary by support domain (e.g., instrumental vs. emotional support networks)? Also, we have little information regarding the stability of social networks among runaways. Is rapid turnover a consequence of the "revolving door" of living situations we have discussed in other chapters? Finally, is there a turning back to home networks as the adolescents mature and become independent? We address all of these issues in the next sections.

Social networks among homeless and runaway adolescents

Social network composition and type of support

After being asked to nominate up to three people they could count on for emotional or instrumental needs, the adolescents were asked to respond to an open-ended question regarding their relationship to the person nominated. For the purpose of this analysis, the responses were recoded into seven major categories, including biological parents, nonbiological parents, family, significant others, friends, nonrelatives, and professionals.

Emotional support networks

At the Wave 1 interviews, about one fourth (23.4%) of the adolescents viewed their biological parents "the first person you would turn to" for emotional support (e.g., "someone who cares about/accepts you/concerned about you, and to whom you can turn when you are upset"; Table 12.1). Other relatives (21.1%) were about as likely as parents to be viewed as emotionally supportive. The adolescents were most likely to turn first to same-aged friends (33.3%) and significant others (12.6%) for emotional support. For example, many told us about surrogate street families:

> Street families like, street mother's 23 now, she just gives me money, makes sure no one messes with me, takes care of me. I got three brothers, which are people that took care of me before or if I ever get in a fight with someone a little bit bigger than me. But if you don't have anybody, don't beat up somebody. that's the way it works on the streets. The street people are really the only people I'll really accept charity from because I don't really consider it charity I help them out as much as they me out so it's pretty much more like friends helping friends. They help me out. They give me food, clothes, advice. If they can't do something, they'll tell me where to go to get it, they never leave me high and dry. (male, aged 18 years)

> Like I said that was really close-knit. It was you know everybody watched out for everybody else you know. If one of us was going to get in trouble and somebody else knew about it we'd say something .

Table 12.1 Summary Report of Social Networks (First Person Would Turn to for Social Support)

Relationship	Care About You (Accept You/ When Upset/Concerned)			Count on for Help and Aid (Money/Food/Place to Stay)		
	Total (%)	Male (%)	Female (%)	Total (%)	Male (%)	Female (%)
	($N = 372$)	($N = 157$)	($N = 215$)	($N = 346$)	($N = 143$)	($N = 203$)
Biological parents	23.4	23.6	23.3	7.2	5.6	8.4
Nonbiological parents	2.4	1.3	3.3	1.7	1.4	2.0
Other relatives	23.1	22.3	23.7	18.8	20.3	17.7
Significant others	12.6	12.7	12.6	10.7	8.4	12.3
Friends	33.3	33.4	32.6	50.9	52.4	49.8
Professionals	2.7	1.9	3.3	5.2	7.7	3.4
Others	2.4	3.8	1.4	5.5	4.2	6.4

Be like, hey watch out you know. I don't know, it's hard to remember a lot of that stuff cause like 90% of the time I was high. (male, aged 19 years)

Yeah I've got street brothers and street sisters. Matter of fact most of my sisters and brothers have gotten off the streets thank God. Those are the people basically it's the people who are still on the streets after years and years and years and who are doing nothing to save themselves nothing to get themselves off the street. I'll say hi to them I'll hang out with them a bit but I'm not going to go out of my way to see them. (female, aged 22 years)

All my friends, we're all like brothers and sisters. We have a small circle of friends like I said even smaller circle is the bubbas and sissies, but they're part of the circle of friends. It's like kind of like ranking in a club: You reach bubba or sissy status you're one of the prime members of the friends. I've now reached bubba status. (male, aged 20 years)

It is noteworthy that 3.8% of the males named professional helpers their primary source of emotional support. These were largely isolates such as these young men:

> Most of the time I was alone. I don't really I don't really trust people to be honest with you. I'm not a I'm not big on trust you know. Just got to be smart you know. Because because if you're dealing with ruthless people then expect ruthless shit to happen. (male, aged 20 years)

> I keep everything quiet. I don't talk in crowds. I don't like crowds. If I have something of mine with me it's in my hand in my pocket or it's where I can see it at all times. I've since I was 14 years old I've never been without a weapon on me. Now I carry a 1-10 Buck on my hip. Buck Knife, it's a legal weapon it wasn't a legal weapon when I was going to school with it but I'd usually keep it hidden hide in my backpack for self-protection. Most people normally didn't mess with me because I projected the attitude that I was somebody not to be messed with. And it worked pretty well. (male, aged 21 years)

Instrumental support

Fewer adolescents (7.2%) designated their biological parents as first sources of instrumental support (e.g., sources of food, money, a place to stay) than we expected. This may be attributed the older age of the adolescents or that many have burned their bridges to home or have been kicked out. Similarly, fewer designated other relatives as sources of instrumental than emotional support. Clearly, the adolescents were most likely to rely on friendship networks (50.9%) for help in getting by day to day. They tend to gravitate to cities and situations where they know someone. As one young man (aged 20 years) put it:

> Most of the towns I've been to I know people there. That's my purpose for going there, because I know at least one person there.

Correlates of predominantly street social networks at Wave 1

We used ordinary least squares regression analyses to investigate correlates of emotional support predominantly from street social networks
at Wave 1. *Emotional support* for street social networks was measured by
a series of questions that began by asking the adolescents if there was
anyone they could count on that cared for them, was concerned about
them, and to whom they could go when they were sad or upset. If they
responded affirmatively, they were also asked to give us names of up to
three such people. After giving the names, the adolescents were asked
. whether each person they had designated was known "mostly from the
street or from home." The extent to which their emotional social networks
were predominantly from the street networks was then assessed by cal-
culating the proportion of their social networks named at Wave 1 who
were "mostly from the street." The other variables in the regression models were described in earlier chapters of this volume.

In Model 1, with only gender, sexual orientation, and age of adolescent in the regression equation, self-identifying as nonheterosexual and
age of adolescent increased the likelihood of gaining emotional support from street social networks (Table 12.2). Our measures of caretaker
physical and sexual abuse prior to running away were added in Model
2 and experiencing caretaker physical abuse was positively associated
with emotional support from street social networks. In Model 4, being
barred from or kicked out of their home was added to the model and was
nonsignificant. Neither adolescent substance use (Model 4) nor affiliation
with deviant peers (Model 5) increased the likelihood of emotional support from street networks. However, street survival strategies, both sexual
and nonsexual, were positively associated with emotional support from
street social networks (Model 6). Sexual orientation and age of adolescent
remained statistically significant in Model 6; however, caretaker physical
abuse lost statistical significance ($p \leq .10$) in the final model.

We used the same independent variables to investigate instrumental support predominantly from street social networks (Table 12.3). Our
measure for *instrumental support* followed the same steps as that for emotional support networks. The adolescents were asked if there were people that they could count on to give them help and aid, such as money,
food, and a place to stay, without being asked for anything in return. If
they responded affirmatively, they were asked to give us names of three
of these people and whether each of the three nominations was known
"mostly from the street or from home." Instrumental social networks
predominantly from the street were then calculated as the proportion of
networks named at Wave 1 who the participants said they knew "mostly
from the street."

Table 12.2 Ordinary Least Squares Regression of Correlates of Emotional Street Networks (N = 428)

	Model 1			Model 2			Model 3			Model 4			Model 5			Model 6		
	b	Standard Error	Beta	b	Standard Error	Beta	b	Standard Error	Beta	b	Standard Error	Beta	b	Standard Error	Beta	b	Standard Error	Beta
Female	0.00	0.04	0.00	-0.02	0.04	-0.03	-0.02	0.04	-0.02	-0.01	0.04	-0.02	-0.01	0.04	-0.01	0.01	0.04	0.02
Heterosexual	-0.16	0.05	-0.16*	-0.15	0.05	-0.14**	-0.15	0.05	-0.14**	-0.14	0.05	-0.14**	-0.14	0.05	-0.14**	-0.12	0.05	-0.12*
Age	0.07	0.02	0.20*	0.06	0.02	0.18**	0.06	0.02	0.17**	0.06	0.02	0.17**	0.06	0.02	0.17**	0.05	0.02	0.14*
Caretaker physical abuse				0.06	0.03	0.13*	0.06	0.03	0.12*	0.05	0.03	0.12*	0.05	0.03	0.11*	0.05	0.03	0.09†
Caretaker sexual abuse				0.05	0.05	0.05	0.05	0.05	0.05	0.05	0.05	0.05	0.04	0.05	0.04	0.01	0.05	0.02
Barred from home							0.06	0.04	0.07	0.06	0.04	0.07	0.04	0.04	0.07	0.04	0.04	0.05
Substance use										0.02	0.02	0.04	0.01	0.02	0.02	-0.01	0.02	-0.03
Deviant peers													0.00	0.01	0.06	0.00	0.01	0.00
Survival strategies (sexual)													0.08	0.04	0.12*	0.08	0.04	0.12*
Survival strategies (nonsexual)																0.04	0.02	0.16*
Constant	-0.83			-0.85			-0.83			-0.83			-0.84			-0.64		
Model adjusted R²	0.06			0.08			0.08			0.08			0.08			0.10		

† p ≤ .10.
* p ≤ .05.
** p ≤ .01.
*** p ≤ .001.

Table 12.3 Ordinary Least Squares Regression of Correlates of Instrumental Street Networks (N = 428)

	Model 1			Model 2			Model 3			Model 4			Model 5			Model 6		
	b	Standard Error	Beta	b	Standard Error	Beta	b	Standard Error	Beta	b	Standard Error	Beta	b	Standard Error	Beta	b	Standard Error	Beta
Female	-0.06	0.04	-0.07	-0.09	0.04	-0.12*	-0.09	0.04	-0.11*	-0.06	0.04	-0.08	-0.06	0.04	-0.07	-0.03	0.05	-0.04
Heterosexual	-0.13	0.06	-0.12*	-0.10	0.06	-0.10†	-0.10	0.06	-0.10†	-0.09	0.06	-0.08	-0.08	0.06	-0.08	-0.06	0.06	-0.05
Age	0.04	0.02	0.11*	0.03	0.02	0.08	0.03	0.02	0.08	0.02	0.02	0.06	0.02	0.02	0.05	0.01	0.02	0.02
Caretaker physical abuse				0.09	0.03	0.18**	0.08	0.03	0.16**	0.08	0.03	0.15**	0.07	0.03	0.13*	0.06	0.03	0.11*
Caretaker sexual abuse				0.14	0.06	0.14*	0.14	0.06	0.14*	0.13	0.06	0.13*	0.12	0.06	0.12*	0.09	0.06	0.09
Barred from home							0.09	0.05	0.11**	0.10	0.05	0.11*	0.10	0.05	0.11*	0.08	0.04	0.09†
Substance use										0.05	0.02	0.14*	0.03	0.02	0.08	0.01	0.02	0.03
Deviant peers													0.02	0.01	0.15**	0.01	0.01	0.09
Survival strategies (sexual)																0.11	0.04	0.16**
Survival strategies (nonsexual)																0.04	0.02	0.13*
Constant	-0.28			-0.31			-0.30			-0.25			-0.29			-0.07		
Model adjusted R²	0.03			0.08			0.09			0.10			0.12			0.15		

† p ≤ .10.
* p ≤ .05.
** p ≤ .01.
*** p ≤ .001.

In Model 1 of the regression analyses for correlates of predominantly street instrumental networks, self-identifying as nonheterosexual, and age of adolescent were associated with instrumental support from street networks (Table 12.3). Both physical and sexual abuse prior to running away were related to instrumental support from street networks (Model 2) as was being barred from or kicked out of the house (Model 3). In Model 4, substance use by the adolescents was positively associated with instrumental support from street networks but lost significance in Model 5 when affiliation with deviant peers was added to the equation. Age of adolescent and self-identifying as nonheterosexual lost statistical significance when substance use was added to the equation and remained so in Models 5 and 6. In the final model (Model 6) with all of the independent variables in the regression equation, caretaker physical abuse and street survival strategies (sexual and nonsexual) were statistically significant. Being barred from home was significant at the .10 level.

Social network turnover across time

Although the social networks served important support functions for the adolescents, they were highly unstable across time. For example, 15.7% of the adolescents' emotional social networks and 16.6% of their instrumental social networks turned over completely during the 3 years of the study. That is, none of those nominated at Year 1 were still part of their network at Year 3. The median turnover rate was 63% of nominees for emotional networks and 54% for instrumental networks.

We used logistic regression to investigate correlates of high social network turnover. At each interview, adolescents could renominate all three of the people designated 3 months earlier in the previous wave of data collection, or they could nominate up to three new people to whom they go to for emotional or instrumental support. Our measure of *network turnover* was calculated by dividing the total number of new network nominations by the total number of network members nominated over all waves. This generated a variable with more than 100 categories, which ranged from 0 to 1 where 1 equaled complete turnover. A dichotomous variable was then created to identify those with high turnover. This variable designates the top quartile of the proportion of new nominations as 1 and all others as the reference category 0.

The first logistic regression focused on correlates of high turnover (the top quartile) in the emotional social networks of the adolescents (Table 12.4, columns 1 and 2). Age of adolescent was negatively associated with inclusion in the high network turnover group. Each year of age decreased the likelihood of inclusion in the top turnover quartile by 29% ($Exp(b) = .71$). Participating in deviant subsistence strategies while on the streets increased the odds of inclusion in the top turnover quartile nearly four times (*Exp(b)* = 3.93). None of the other variables introduced into the regression equation significantly affected the likelihood of high turnover in emotional networks.

For instrumental networks, the likelihood of inclusion in the top quartile for network turnover was negatively associated with average network size (Table 12.4, columns 3 and 4). The smaller the instrumental social network the greater the likelihood of turnover. For each person reduction in network size, the likelihood of inclusion in the top turnover quartile nearly doubled (*Exp(b)* = .52). Having ever spent time directly on the streets more than doubled the odds of inclusion in the top turnover quartile (*Exp(b)* = 2.13), and meeting criteria for CD more than tripled the odds of inclusion in the high-turnover quartile (*Exp(b)* = 3.21).

Social network composition across time

Network composition not only was highly unstable; it also changed qualitatively during the 3 years of the study. For example, the percentage of adolescents designating friends as their primary sources of emotional support declined, whereas the percentage designating biological parents increased (Figure 12.1). Also, as the adolescents grew older, they were more likely to name a significant other as their primary source of emotional support. The number designating other family members was essentially the same across time.

The same general trends held for instrumental support networks across time (Figure 12.2). The adolescents were less likely to designate friends and more likely to designate family members as their primary sources of money, food, and shelter by Wave 13 of the study. The increase in naming biological parents as sources of instrumental support was particularly sharp (4.8% to 20.2%). There was little change in the rest of the instrumental support networks across time. Both of these figures suggest a rapprochement with family as the adolescents aged.

Summary and discussion

These findings are congruent with a long tradition of research on the instability of social networks among adolescents with behavioral problems. The study adolescents' social networks were highly unstable over time and were most unstable among those who engaged in delinquent behaviors. Indeed, meeting criteria for CD and spending time on the streets were highly predictive of being within the top quartile for instrumental network instability. Engaging in street survival strategies was predictive of being in the top quartile for emotional network instability. Moreover,

Table 12.4 Logistic Regressions of Correlates of High Social Network Turnover (*N* = 308)

	Emotional		Instrumental	
	b	*Exp(b)*	*b*	*Exp(b)*
Age	−0.34	0.71*	−0.18	0.83
Female	−0.25	0.78	−0.18	0.84
Heterosexual	0.04	1.04	−0.04	0.96
Average network size	−0.02	0.98	−0.66	0.52***
Ever on street	−0.07	0.93	0.76	2.13**
Deviant subsistence strategies	1.37	3.93***	−0.54	1.72
Violence	0.06	1.06	−0.14	0.87
Conduct disorder	0.59	1.82	1.17	3.21**
Major depression	−0.08	0.92	−0.49	0.62
Alcohol abuse/ dependence	−0.37	0.69	−0.34	0.71
Marijuana use	−0.10	0.91	−0.36	0.70
Hard drug use	−0.42	0.66	−0.03	0.97
Constant	3.85	46.83	2.37	10.66
Nagerlkerke		0.14		0.21
Cox & Snell		0.10		0.14

* $p \le .05$.
** $p \le .01$.
*** $p \le .001$.

there was little evidence of strong emotional or instrumental ties to biological parents at Wave 1, although there was a trend toward rapprochement over the 3 years of the study. Nonheterosexual adolescents were even more estranged from their biological parents than heterosexual adolescents (see Whitbeck, Chen, Hoyt, Tyler, & Johnson, 2004). As the adolescents moved into young adulthood they were more likely to depend on significant others for emotional and instrumental support. Though nominations decreased across time, friendship networks remained the adolescents' strongest source of instrumental and emotional support.

As the number of studies on the social networks of runaway and homeless adolescents proliferates, it is important to consider several important factors that will affect adolescents' social network composition and the ways social networks, in turn, will influence the adolescents'

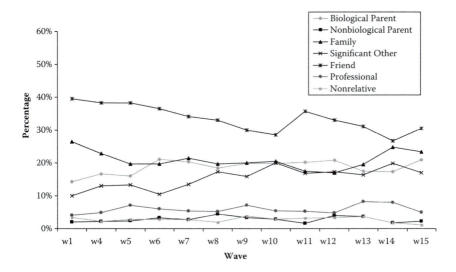

Figure 12.1 Emotional networks by relationship across time.

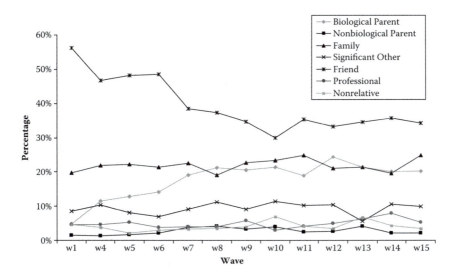

Figure 12.2 Instrumental networks by relationship across time.

behaviors. Our findings suggest that the most salient factor is whether the adolescent meets criteria for CD and the extent to which he or she engages in delinquent street behaviors such as involvement in the street economy. These are the adolescents who are likely to have low-quality, high-turnover social networks that will likely contribute to poor adjustment and fewer ties to home. Adolescents with fewer antisocial behaviors and who are less engaged in the street economy are likely to have more ties to home, school, and the old neighborhood.

With this in mind, the trend toward rapprochement with parents over the 3 years of our study is interesting and warrants more investigation. A minority of the adolescents appear to "age out" of their troubled family relationships. We need to better understand what influences reestablishing family ties. A second potentially positive social relationship is with significant others. Establishing stable intimate relationships is associated with a decrease in antisocial behaviors (Sampson, Laub, & Wimer, 2006); however, assortive mating with antisocial partners diminishes or eliminates this effect (Rutter, Quinton, & Hill, 1990; Sakai et al., 2004). We know almost nothing about mate selection among runaway and homeless young people.

Theoretical implications

Social networks during adolescence are in flux and incredibly powerful. It is evident from our findings that street networks tend to socialize and encourage participation in the street economy and to substitute street networks for failed family networks. The adolescents resourcefully create their own supportive networks, and some even begin to think of them as surrogate families. These provide a sense of safety and teach the new arrivals the skills they need to get by. They model sharing resources and providing mutual protection. They know what agencies to contact for help. However, many of these "families" may encourage drug and alcohol use or even be engaged in illegal activities such as drug dealing.

The transition from home social networks to street networks is an important link in the chain of self-reinforcing negative events. For some young people, street networks are proof of what they have already begun to believe: that nonconventional peers are more receptive to them and understand them better than conventional peers. Moreover, nonconventional peers, although "ruthless," are easy to understand. You know what to expect. You aren't disappointed. Nonconventional networks confirm how the world works. The next step in the chain is the punitive societal response from the criminal justice system: The societal evidence that the most powerful, and the most aggressive "win."

Policy implications

As evidence increases concerning potential protective effects of prosocial networks with ties to home and school (Rice et al., 2007; Johnson et al., 2005a), we need to better understand the ways networks change, how rapidly they change, and what factors affect the shift in networks from predominantly home, school, and neighborhood to predominantly street networks. There may well be two trajectories: one for highly aggressive adolescents who may rapidly engage in street networks and one for less aggressive, less delinquent adolescents who may never make a complete transition to street life, gravitate toward home and the old neighborhood, and eventually reestablish ties there. Social network influence also may be a function of how long the adolescent has been on the street. For those new to the street, interventions that emphasize ties to school, the old neighborhood, and prosocial (or at least housed) friends may prove to be effective (Rice et al., 2007). Again, as we have pointed out in almost every chapter, the more rapid the intervention, the more effective it will be.

For runaways, ties to stable, caring adults are tenuous, and maintaining and establishing such network members may be very important. Ties to caring adults may persist and be an important source of perceived support. For example, someone you call anytime:

> Like Ms. [Name]. She used to be my teacher and I'm really close to her and if I'm in like a bad situation or whatever and I need to get out then I just call her and she'll come get me or whatever. Or like if I just need somebody to talk to I can just like call her like 6 o'clock in the morning, 2 o'clock in the morning whenever and she'll just like talk to me on the phone or whatever. (female, aged 19 years)

Often professional therapist relationships maintain strict boundaries (e.g., "Call me at the office," or "Talk to the person who is on call") that discourage this sense of personal caring and availability. An important intervention may involve establishing ties with a caring conventional adult who is considered to be immediately available.

Conclusions

Social network analysis with runaway adolescents is really measurement of emersion in the street culture. The deeper into street networks, the more difficult it will be to reestablish conventional ties to education, family, and employment. The more ties to family, school, and the old neighborhood, the easier it will be to return. Because of this, interventions that emphasize ties to home social networks and perhaps involve conventional peers and caring adults from home social networks may prove to be effective. This is a promising area for prevention research and program development.

chapter 13

Sexuality, romantic relationships, and pregnancy

With Devan M. Crawford

Forming and rehearsing intimate relationships are fundamental developmental tasks of mid- and late adolescence (Furman & Shaffer, 2003). These early romantic relationships are intensely emotionally charged and a major focus of adolescents' interest and communication (Thompson, 1994). As adolescents branch out beyond the sphere of family relationships, romantic relationships with peers provide important sources of emotional support, especially for those who are experiencing conflicts with parents (Pawlby, Mills, & Quinton, 1997). For example, there is evidence that among adolescent girls, poor relationships with parents are associated with depressive symptoms, which, in turn, are related to early sexual activity. This suggests that depressed girls may compensate for poor parental relationships through alternative supportive relationships with peers and romantic partners (Whitbeck, Conger, & Kao, 1993; Whitbeck, Hoyt, Miller, & Kao, 1992). The supportive aspects of early romantic relationships are thought to be more important to adolescents then sexual experimentation (Furman & Shaffer, 2003); indeed, the most mentioned motivation adolescents cite for first intercourse is attempting to get their partner to love them more (Rodgers, 1996).

Among homeless and runaway adolescents, multiple runaway episodes erode ties to potentially supportive conventional adults in the extended family system, schools, and social services agencies. This serves to enhance the importance of peer support and to focus it on more proximal peers who tend to be runaways as well. Over time, adult influence is substituted for peer influence. We believe that at least three things in the runaway process intensify the importance of romantic attachments. First, separation from primary adult support systems has occurred early and sometimes abruptly. Second, runaway adolescents' social world tends to be predominantly people of the same age and in similar circumstances. Third, the adolescents are often in critical need of nurturance, support, and approval. Regardless of whether the adolescents "drift" out of disorganized families over time or leave home more abruptly, the result is the loss of primary family relationships. Their vulnerability in this new environment creates the need for supportive alliances. Although the young men may respond by joining formal or informal street gangs for protection and mutual support (Yoder, Whitbeck, & Hoyt, 2003), for young women this may mean attaching themselves to a male for protection and support.

Adolescent romantic and sexual relationships

Experimentation with romantic attachments begins soon after puberty and continues throughout adolescence. By age 12 years, approximately one fourth of adolescents report a romantic relationship in the past 18 months. This increases to one half of adolescents at age 15 years, and by 18 years two thirds of males and three fourths of females have been in a romantic relationship in the past 18 months (Carver, Joyner, & Udry, 2003). Early sexual experimentation is most likely in the context of a steady romantic relationship (Thornton, 1990), and national estimates of sexual experimentation closely resemble rates of romantic involvement. In the Wave 2 National Longitudinal Study of Adolescent Health, only 8% of males and 7% of the females under the age of 14 years had experienced sexual intercourse. This increases to 35% of males and 40% of females by age 16 years and to 51% of males and 66% of females by age 18 years (Carver et al.).

Most studies of homeless and runaway adolescents indicate their lives have been sexualized beyond their years. They are more likely to have experienced early involuntary sexual activity with adults or adult caretakers than are nonrunaways. They are highly sexually active, likely to have had multiple sexual partners, likely to have had a sexually transmitted infection (STI), and more likely than nonrunaways to have engaged in survival sex (Cauce et al., 1998; Kufeldt & Nimmo, 1987; Rotheram-Borus, Koopman, & Ehrhardt, 1991; Silbert & Pines, 1981; Whitbeck & Hoyt, 1999).

Nearly all homeless and runaway adolescents are sexually active. In both the four-state Midwest study and Rotherum-Borus' New York City sample more than 80% of the adolescents were sexually experienced (Rotheram-Borus, Meyer-Bahlburg, Koopman, Rosario, Exner, Henderson, Matthieu, & Gruen, 1992; Whitbeck & Hoyt, 1999). Many have had numerous sexual partners and a smaller number have engaged in sexual exchanges for food, shelter, drugs, or money. About one fourth of Los Angeles runaway adolescents that were seen in a street medical clinic reported engaging in survival sex compared to 0.2% of nonrunaways (Yates, MacKenzie, Pennbridge, & Cohen, 1988). Rotheram-Borus and colleagues reported that 13% of males and 7% of females in their New York City study had engaged in survival sex (Rotheram-Borus, Meyer-Bahlburg, Koopman, Rosario, Exner, Henderson, Matthieu, & Gruen, 1992). The four-state Midwest study, reported lower rates of survival sex (i.e., 6.4% females; 7.1% males); however, it is highly likely that at least some of the survival sexual activity was coerced or thought of in terms of spontaneous or short-term romantic relationships that did not work out (Tyler & Johnson, 2006; Whitbeck & Hoyt, 1999). Although much has been written about their prolific sexual activity, the contexts of intimate relationships among homeless and runaway adolescents largely have been ignored. In this chapter we will investigate the spectrum of the adolescents' relationships from survival sex to romantic relationships, marriages, pregnancies, and parenthood.

Sexual behaviors and sexual risk

More than 85% of the adolescents in our study reported they were hetero-sexual. Young women (18.3%) were about twice as likely as young men (9.7%) to say they were nonheterosexual (i.e., gay, lesbian, bisexual, or unsure of sexual orientation). About 90% of the adolescents said they were sexually experienced (Table 13.1) at Wave 1 of the study with no gender differences except that nonheterosexual women (97.7%) were more likely to report they were sexually experienced than nonheterosexual young men (83.3%). Sexual experience increased with age of adolescents so that by age 19 years, 92.9% of heterosexual males and 100% of heterosexual females were sexually experienced.

The average age of first intercourse was about 14 years. When taking into account very early sexual experience, the mean age of adolescents who said they had first intercourse at 11 years or younger was around 8.9 years, and the mean age of those who experienced first intercourse at age 12 years or older was 14.3 years.

The range for lifetime sexual partners was 0–100 for the heterosexual young people with a mean of 8.6 sexual partners. For nonheterosexual young people, the range for lifetime partners was 0–56 with a mean of 11.8 sexual partners. Nonheterosexual young men had a mean of 14.3 life-time sexual partners; the average number reported by heterosexual young men was nine partners. The range for sexual partners during the last 12 months was 0–23 for heterosexuals and 0–56 for non-heterosexuals. The mean number of sexual partners for the last 12 months was 2.5 for hetero-sexual young people and 4.5 for nonheterosexuals, with nonheterosexual young men having about two times the average number of sexual part-ners as heterosexual young men (5.4 vs. 2.8).

Table 13.1 Sexual Behavior Descriptives at Wave 1

| | | Heterosexual (N = 329) | | | Nonheterosexual (N = 58) | | |
		Total (%)	Male (%)	Female (%)	Total (%)	Male (%)	Female (%)
Sexual orientation		85.5	90.3	81.7	14.5	9.7	18.3
Ever had sex		90.1	89.2	90.9	93.5	83.3	**97.7***
Age 16		85.1	87.1	84.3	75.0	50.0	83.3
Age 17		87.5	81.8	91.7	95.5	75.0	100.0
Age 18		94.8	94.0	95.7	94.7	83.3	100.0
Age 19		95.2	92.9	100.0	100.0	100.0	100.0
Age at first sex	Range	3–19	3–19	3–18	5–17	8–17	5–17
All	Mean	13.9	13.8	14.0	14.1	14.3	14.0
≤ 11	Mean	8.9	9.2	8.3	9.1	8.0	9.3
> 12	Mean	14.3	14.4	14.3	15.0	14.8	15.1

* $p \le .05$ (gender significance test).

Condom use and sexually transmitted infections (STIs)

The majority of the young people reported they had used condoms the last time they had vaginal sex (Table 13.2). Heterosexual youth (50%) were less likely to report condom use at last anal intercourse than were non-heterosexual youth (75%). Less than one fourth of the adolescents had used condoms at last oral sex.

Rates of STIs among runaway and homeless adolescents have been of serious concern, particularly in terms of potential HIV infections (e.g., Kipke, Montgomery, Simon, Unger, & Johnson, 1997; Rotheram-Borus et al., 1991; Tyler, Whitbeck, Hoyt, & Yoder, 2000). Of the 386 adolescents who reported having sex, approximately one fifth of the adolescents reported ever having an STI. Young women (28.5%) were nearly three times more likely to have had an STI than were young men (9.8%). The most often reported STIs were chlamydia (41.0%), gonorrhea (21.8%), and pubic lice (11.6%). It is noteworthy that 6.3% of the males and 3.4% of the females had been diagnosed with syphilis. Given the high levels of sexual contact, low levels of condom use among heterosexuals at last anal intercourse, and prevalence of STIs, the adolescents' self-reported concern about HIV infection was quite low. Less than one half (44.5%) of the adolescents were "very concerned" about contracting HIV. There were no significant differences in HIV concern by gender or sexual orientation.

Table 13.2 Condom Use at Wave 1 (N = 427)

	Vaginal Sex			Anal Sex			Oral Sex		
	Total (%)	Male (%)	Female (%)	Total (%)	Male (%)	Female (%)	Total (%)	Male (%)	Female (%)
Heterosexual (N = 365)	79.0	81.3	76.9	50.0	48.0	52.9	21.5	17.2	26.2
Nonheterosexual (N = 62)	78.3	66.7	81.1	75.0	71.4	77.8	24.4	25.0	24.2

Note: N's differ slightly based on missing patterns within type of sex (e.g., vaginal, anal, oral).

Involuntary early sexual experiences

Early sexual experience among the runaways was not always voluntary. As indicated in Table 13.1, among those whose first sexual experience occurred at 11 years or younger, the average age of first intercourse was around 8 years. Sexual intercourse at this early age is by definition sexual abuse. When we examined the prevalence of caretaker sexual abuse (see Chapter 8, Table 8.3, this volume), 30% of heterosexual females and 46.5% of nonheterosexual females reported that they had been sexually abused. Nonheterosexual males (17.6%) were about twice as likely to report sexual abuse than were heterosexual males (8.9%). In general, the nonheterosexual adolescents, particularly nonheterosexual females, were much more likely to report any kind of sexual maltreatment by caretakers then were heterosexual adolescents.

Current sexual contexts

Regardless of their early histories, most of the young people were optimistic about their romantic relationships. Often sex was in pursuit of closeness and intimacy. As one young woman (aged 20 years) put it:

> I always thought that if you have sex with somebody that they were a part of you. Because that's how I feel about it. And I mean I would sleep with a lot of people but I mean I was trying to find something and I never found it. So I kept trying but I don't know, and they were cute. And then I wanted to tell people hey I had sex with him. I don't know that's probably a bad way to think though.

The current contexts of sexual relationships of most of the runaway adolescents were similar to those of nonrunaways. The vast majority of heterosexual (86.8%) and nonheterosexual (88.5%) youth indicated they were sexually active in steady relationships. Heterosexual young women (92.6%) were more likely than heterosexual young men (80%) to tell us they were sexually active with a steady partner. However, the adolescents indicated they had been sexually active with several steady partners. About one half (58.0% heterosexuals; 47.8% nonheterosexuals) said they had had one steady partner; about one fourth (24.8%) of heterosexuals and one fifth (19.6%) of nonheterosexuals had had two steady partners. Nonheterosexual young people (32.6%) were about two times more likely than heterosexual young people (17.2%) to have had three or more steady sexual partners.

Survival sex

In this sample, survival sex was relatively rare compared with that reported in large city samples such as Los Angeles or New York (e.g., Yates, MacKenzie, Pennbridge, & Cohen, 1988; Rotheram-Borus et al., 1992). Many more of the adolescents had thought about engaging in survival sex when in desperate straits than to have actually gone through with it (Table 13.3). Nonheterosexual males (33.3%) were more than twice as likely as the other young people to have thought about trading sex for money, food, or drugs. Between 7% and 9% of the young women had traded sex for money. Approximately 5% of heterosexual males had traded sex for money compared with 11.1% of nonheterosexual males. Nonheterosexual young men (16.7%) were about three times more likely than heterosexual young men to have traded sex for drugs or food.

The opportunity for trading sex was always present. One young woman (aged 19 years) told us she never had engaged in survival sex, but "I had a guy try to pay me $50 to give him a blow job, though." Young men and women on the streets are constantly getting offers:

> They would slow down their car and say come here and so I would come over there. Like you know what's your name? I'd tell them and then he's like what are you doing? I'd be like nothing what are you doin? And then he was like want to come with me and I said all right. I get in the car then they ask you to do stuff with them. Like when they're driving the car, like perform oral sex on them. (male, aged 19 years)

> I've been approached many times. People will drive up or walk up to me and just offer money for this, that, and this. Want to have sex, fuck me … and some guys I don't know … people that offer me the money. (female, aged 19 years)

We are not certain that our numbers reflect the extent to which sexual exchanges actually take place. Many exchanges occurred when sharing alcohol and drugs and may not be viewed as outright exchanges. Others viewed sexual exchanges as one way to get what they wanted:

> As long as you get what you want you're going to do whatever you can to get it, regardless of it's by going and asking people for it or stealing it or stealing

Table 13.3 Survival Sex

	All (N = 427)			Heterosexual (N = 365)			Nonheterosexual (N = 62)		
	Total (%)	Male (%)	Female (%)	Total (%)	Male (%)	Female (%)	Total (%)	Male (%)	Female (%)
Thought about trading sex for ...									
Money	15.9	17.7	14.5	15.6	16.1	15.2	17.7	33.3[a]	11.4
Drugs	6.1	5.9	6.2	5.2	4.8	5.6	11.3	16.7[b]	9.1
Food	9.6	9.7	9.5	9.0	8.3	9.6	12.9	22.2[a]	9.1
Traded sex for ...									
Money	6.6	5.4	7.5	6.0	4.8	7.1	9.7	11.1	9.1
Drugs	5.2	5.4	5.0	4.4	4.2	4.6	9.7	16.7[b]	6.8
Food	6.3	4.9	7.5	5.2	3.6	6.6	12.9	16.7[c]	11.4
Age first survival sex Range	8–19	12–18	8–19	8–19	13–18	8–19	12–18	12–18	14–18
Mean	15.3	15.9	14.8	15.2	15.9	14.7	15.5	15.8	15.2
Median	15	16	15	15.5	16	15	15	16	15

[a] $p \leq .10$ (sexuality significance test).
[b] $p \leq .05$ (sexuality significance test).
[c] $p \leq .01$ (sexuality significance test).

> money to get it or exchanging food or money or sex
> for it whatever. (male, aged 21 years)

> I would stay in motels if people would buy it for me.
> But other than that I would just I would wait out-
> side and wait for a guy to drive by or something and
> hope that they'd take me home with them. (female,
> aged 19 years)

Some were coerced to trade sex by friends or boyfriends. One drug-using young woman (aged 19 years) was pimped by her boyfriend:

> He would try to sell me for crack. Literally, tried
> to, tried to sell me, because several people offered.
> They'd stand on the corner and say, "Hey, you know,
> how much for this?" and I'm like, "Excuse me?" And
> he'd just be like, "Well, let me talk to her about it."
> And we'd walk around the corner, and I'd never, you
> know, I wouldn't do it. But he would really, really
> try and threaten and hit and everything to get me
> to do that.

Another young woman (aged 20 years) felt pressured into trading sex by her girlfriend:

> Just like my friend would need a pack of cigarettes or
> whatever and then I'd want a pack of cigarettes, too.
> She'd be like just go sleep with this guy for a pack of
> cigarettes or whatever. And I'd be like no and then
> I'd just keep on saying no and then she just wouldn't
> she wouldn't quit bugging me. I'd end up getting in
> a fight with her so finally I just gave in. Like we were
> just at this party or whatever and everybody was
> pretty much toasted or whatnot. And girls wanted
> a cigarette and instead of just going and asking for
> one she asked me to go have sex with a guy so we
> could get cigarettes.

Others who do not admit to trading sex may engage in one-night stands or transitory "romantic" relationships that carry with them the advantage of shelter, food, or drugs.

It is well known that many adolescent relationships are short-lived and that those of delinquent young people are particularly so. Delinquent young people tend to overinvest in short-term relationships and, based on peer reports, tend to view relationships as more intimate then they actually are (Cotterell, 1994). This certainly appears to be the case among these vulnerable young people.

Pregnancy and child outcomes

Nearly one half (46.8%) of the young women had become pregnant by Wave 1, and over the 3 years of the study, this increased to 77%. Nearly one third (30.4%) of the young men reported that they had impregnated a partner by Wave 1, and this nearly doubled (58.8%) by the end of the study (Figure 13.1). At Wave 1, about one half (44.7%) of the young women who had been pregnant had been so on more than one occasion, 31.1% had been pregnant twice, 8.7% three times, and 4.8% four or more times. A total of 28% reported their first pregnancy at age 14 years or younger.

The majority of the pregnancies reported at Wave 1 were not carried to term. Among young women in the study, 41% of pregnancies ended in miscarriage, and 11% were ended by abortion. Of those carried to term, about 7% of the babies had been placed for adoption, 21.3% had been kept by the mother or a family member, and almost 4% had been kept by their partner or partner's family. Among mothers (4.9%) who had kept their children, nearly all (81.8%) were in contact with their child, although only 18% had daily contact. More than one third (36.4%) had contact with their child less than once a month.

Two thirds of the Wave 1 young women who had been pregnant said that they had left home because of their pregnancy. The decision to leave was almost evenly split between the young woman deciding to leave on her own (57.1%) and her parent/caretaker making the decision that she should leave (42.9%).

The young fathers were much less likely to be currently involved with their children than were the mothers. Of those who had fathered births carried to term, only 6.3% of the young men and their partners kept the child. At the time of the Wave 1 interview, almost one half (46.2%) of the young fathers reported that they never saw their child.

Summary and discussion

For the most part, the early sexual socialization of the runaway and homeless people was very different from that of other adolescents. Nearly one third of the young women had been sexually abused by caretakers, and, by the end of the study, 42% of the women with whom we had maintained contact had been sexually assaulted when on their own compared with a lifetime sexual assault rate of 17.6% among women in the general population (Tjaden &

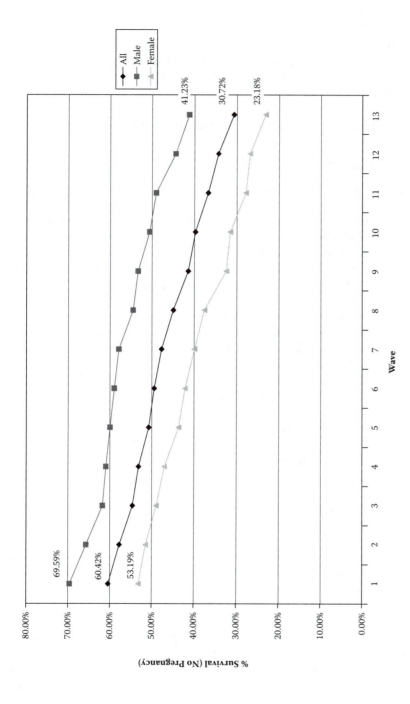

Figure 13.1 Pregnancies over time by gender

Thoennes, 2000). The young people reported early ages of first sexual experience, multiple sexual partners, and high rates of STIs. By age 18 years, 94% of the homeless and runaway young men and 95.7% of the young women were sexually experienced compared with 51% of males and 66% of females at age 18 years in the Longitudinal Study of Adolescent Health (Carver et al., 2003). By the end of the study, the pregnancy rate for young women with whom we maintained contact was 77%, six times the U.S. pregnancy rate of 12.6% for 18–19-year-old women (Guttmacher Institute, 2006).

Theoretical implications

These early sexual histories almost certainly will have relationship consequences as the young people move into early adulthood. As we have shown in previous chapters, caretaker sexual abuse and assault when on the streets were associated with meeting lifetime criteria for conduct disorder (Chapter 3, this volume), depression (Chapter 4, this volume), posttraumatic stress disorder (Chapter 5, this volume), and dissociative symptoms (Chapter 7, this volume). These mental disorders, in turn, affect the stability and quality of intimate relationships. We also know that substance abuse increases the likelihood of risky sexual behaviors and of making poor sexual choices (Kipke, O'Conner, Palmer, & MacKenzie, 1995; Kipke, Montgomery, et al., 1997; Koopman, Rosario, & Rotheram-Borus, 1994; Rotheram-Borus, Luna, Marotta, & Kelly, 1994).

Based on these characteristics, it would be easy to surmise that sex was viewed casually and recreationally by the runaway and homeless adolescents, but this does not appear to be the case. Although there was tremendous variation in early sexual experiences, nearly all of the young people had been sexually active within steady relationships, and nearly one half had experienced a "marriage-like" relationship at some point in their lives. This suggests to us that sex was very much part of a quest for intimacy, affection, and support.

As the runaways move through the critical developmental stage of rehearsing and forming adult intimate relationships, they aspire to the same ideal of a stable intimate relationship as nonrunaways. However, their sexual histories may complicate this quest on several levels. Finkelhor (1984; Finkelhor & Browne, 1986) and others would argue that the immense differences in early sexual socialization between these and "normal" adolescents will create a sense of stigmatization or "spoiled sexual identity." Intimate relationships may be highly "sexualized" and relatively unstable because of early sexual misuse. Given high rates of traumatic sexual experiences, the ability to establish and maintain stable intimate relationships may be impeded by symptoms of depression, PTSD, and dissociation (Beitchman, Zucker, Hood, daCosta, Akman, &

Cassavia, 1992 (review); Noll, Trickett, & Putnam, 2003; Paolucci, Genuis, & Violato, 2001 (review)).

Although there is evidence that entering into stable intimate relationships may moderate antisocial behaviors (Sampson, Laub, & Wimer, 2006), there is also evidence that assortive mating processes may increase the risk of romantic alliances between substance abusers and antisocial young people and may exacerbate antisocial behaviors (Rutter, Quinton, & Hill, 1990; Sakai et al., 2004). The degree to which the sexual histories and experiences of runaway and homeless adolescents affect their ability to achieve a stable, nurturing intimate relationship will be a critical factor that influences the course of their adult lives.

Policy implications

As noted in Chapter 1, many of these young people do not know what healthy intimate relationships are like. They were raised in coercive/aggressive family environments and developed interaction styles based on these early experiences. These can be purposely "unlearned" (Rutter et al., 1990) if there is the opportunity and motivation to do so. Unfortunately, very few are likely to have the chance for long-term therapy to explore and change negative interaction styles. Given all the challenges we have documented in this chapter and throughout this volume, it is likely that many will experience difficulties in establishing and maintaining long-term intimate relationships.

Not only will there be difficulties with intimate relationships; there may well also be problems in parenting their children as well. More than three fourths of the young women who remained in the study had become pregnant. This represents a huge challenge in preparing these young women and their partners for parenthood. Parenting classes exist in most transitional living programs, and social services agencies also provide this kind of help; however, often the situations are so complex and resources are so few that the young women lose custody of their children. When this happens they often do not have the resources to make the necessary changes to regain custody. For example, one young woman (aged 21 years) lost custody of her children more than a year ago and seemed at a loss about what to do:

> Because some guy I was dating I'd say about a little over a year ago, a year and a half ago. I was working one night and he stayed at my house and he was watching my kids and I got a call from my brother's girlfriend saying that my son was hurt and had to go home and get him and take him to the hospital

> and found out he broke my son's arm. And the next
> day they took my two kids away. And they've been
> gone ever since.

Dealing with situations like these often means starting from scratch: no permanent housing, either no employment or low-wage employment, no child care, no transportation, and no way to pay health costs. There are few resources on which to build, and, in addition, there may be seriously behavioral and psychological issues to overcome.

Successful interventions will take time and be expensive. Traditional social services due to high volume of case loads and high costs may not provide the intensive case management necessary to stabilize these young parents. This is a relatively "silent" population of the most marginal parents, yet writing them off may mean writing off the next generation as well.

Conclusions

Most of these young people aspire to future marriage and parenthood. Given backgrounds of abuse, victimization, and street survival strategies, many are ill-prepared for this stage of life. Yet some relationships will temper antisocial behaviors and provide much needed support:

> I've got a girl that loves me. She cares about me, I've
> got friends that care about me and watch out for me.
> There's people that help me. And I have the ability
> to make my life better. (male, aged 20 years)

> But I don't really care. I'm happy, I got a great boy-
> friend, my family is great, I'm living in a great place.
> I'm happy. (female, aged 19 years)

Other relationships will intensify maladaptive behaviors such as engaging in mutual drug abuse or criminal activities. Coercive/aggressive interaction styles may increase the risk for relationship violence. Indeed, many have already experienced this:

> And then he reached back and punched me in the
> face. And I mean, we would, we got to the point
> where we couldn't go to a friend's house together.
> We could, one at a time, go. But we couldn't go
> together, because we'd get drunk, but we'd start
> beating the crap out of each other, physically. You
> know, he'd hit me, I'd hit him, he'd pull my hair,

I'd pull his, he'd grab me by the throat, I'd grab him by the throat. You know, he'd kick, I'd kick…. I mean he never really actually hurt me, he never really even scared me. I wasn't really scared, sometimes I was shocked. You know, cause I didn't think he would do it. But after I got over being shocked that he did it, I just got mad and I'd hit him back. And I mean, there was no way I was just going to sit there, and let him hit me and think that he could just do that and I'll do what he wants. I mean, I was like determined to have my way with something, you know? And that's all I could do. So I defended myself, but he didn't stop hitting me or anything, or kicking me, you know? Yeah, we put each other through a lot of pain. (female, aged 20 years)

That he was a psycho. I mean that's about all there was to it. It wasn't even like we were arguing or something. There'd be times we're sitting some-where and he'd all of a sudden get really mad. Because we were just sitting there talking and if I said the wrong word at the wrong time. And you know something like that he was all backhand me or something like that. I wound up with bruises and had to wear makeup to cover it and you know dif-ferent stuff like that. Eventually he broke my arm. I mean he would always tell me I'm stupid or I'm nothing but a whore. I've been called every name in the book and the worst things I've ever had said to me in my whole entire life was from him. You know I would rather have him hit me than emotionally abuse, because bruises fade you know emotional pain scars. (female, aged 20 years)

The ability to form stable intimate relationships is a critical develop-mental task for emerging adulthood. Thus far, these young people have had poor training and a poor track record of accomplishing this. Yet, like other young adults, they have time to learn and experiment, and, like oth-ers, over time they may just get it right.

chapter 14

Survival strategies, hunger, education, and housing

With Devan M. Crawford and Katherine A. Johnson

Resilience among runaway and homeless adolescents can mean at least two things. It may denote successful conventional adjustment despite early independence. This means successfully navigating through disadvantages and risks of growing up with few or no adult caretakers to provide protection, emotional, and economic support. Resilience also may mean successfully adapting to the vagaries of street life with its succession of revolving living situations that range from living on the streets, doubling up, staying with friends or relatives until their welcome runs out, transitional living programs, and group homes, all of which may be viewed as temporary. Runaway and homeless adolescents learn survival skills that are very different from those learned by nonrunaway adolescents. These may include being highly vigilant about one's safety and security, a streetwise suspicion of other's motives, the ability to defend oneself and one's property, knowing how to find safe places to stay, and ways of procuring food when there is little or no money. This skill set, while requiring great acuity and innovation, represents the antithesis of most of the skills we typically associate with resilient adolescents.

Traditionally, resilience has referred to maintaining competence in fundamental areas of adjustment in the face of adversity (Luthar, Cicchetti, & Becker, 2000). These basic competencies are usually thought to include academic success, social skills that foster affiliations with prosocial friends and positive interactions with caretakers and other mentoring adults, being able to conform to rules of conduct that allow productive work with others (Masten & Powell, 2003), and being able to competently plan for one's future (Clausen, 1991). The dilemma of early independence is that often the skills learned to survive in the context of adolescent homelessness conflict with those needed to succeed as a competent adult. Early independence typically interrupts educational progress, often takes place in the context of conflict with adults, may involve separation from prosocial adult mentors and peers, and can erode socialization for cooperative work with others. Most often early independence occurs without planning or interrupts whatever plans for the future the adolescent may have had in place. In this chapter we review the different types of competencies demonstrated by homeless and runaway adolescents and discuss how these various skills may influence their futures.

Survival strategies

Runaway minors have very few legitimate means of independent economic support. Even if they are able to secure a job, these are often part-time, minimum wage positions that do not provide enough income to pay for a place to live (McAnally, 1989). More than one half of those we interviewed listed employment (e.g., chores, odd jobs) as a source of income (Table 14.1). A smaller proportion—mostly young women—received public assistance. The modal category for young men was receiving money "for doing things for someone." This was a very diverse category that may include getting tips, doing errands and odd jobs, and even shoplifting for someone. Many of the runaways "borrowed" money from relatives and friends. Sharing is common in the free-wheeling street economy in that generosity may come back around when they are in need.

Table 14.1 Ways to Get Money at Wave 1 (N = 428)

	Total (%)	Male (%)	Female (%)
Ask parents or caretakers for money	43.9	42.2	45.2
Allowance	18.2	11.8	**23.2****
Borrow money	45.6	43.9	46.9
Chores or odd jobs	53.3	55.6	51.5
Sell blood, plasma, or bone marrow	4.9	7.5	**2.9***
Public assistance	19.6	15.5	**22.8†**
State vouchers	15.9	13.9	17.4
Social security	12.4	13.4	11.6
Get money for doing things for someone	55.1	63.6	**48.5****
Prostitution	3.3	3.2	3.3

† $p \leq .10$ (gender significance test).
* $p \leq .05$ (gender significance test).
** $p \leq .01$ (gender significance test).

Money from home

We found those who listed money from caretakers or allowances as a source of income very intriguing. The young person had left home and supposedly was seeking independence but was still tied economically to home. Often parents and relatives would provide help but would not allow the young person to live with them. For example, one young woman (aged 19 years) told us that her mother would help her out financially but would not let her stay at home:

> Give me money, she won't give me a place to stay. Because she doesn't like my lifestyle, doesn't want that around her home and I'll bring it there.

Another (aged 20 years) told us that her parents would help with showers or laundry:

> Well when we were living in the cars it was even harder but like once in awhile my parents would let us shower there like our friends, you know, if we would go to a friend's house and be like hey can we just shower and hang out with you guys. And they were like yeah whatever. And like doing laundry that was really bad cause we never had clean clothes.

To better understand the characteristics of these young people with economic ties to home, we collapsed the categories "Ask parents or caretakers for money" and "Allowances" into a single dichotomous variable and used logistic regression to investigate the correlates of receiving assistance from home. One independent variable pertaining to social support networks not used so far in this volume was included in the regression equations. Respondents were asked if they had anyone they could count on for help and aid or go to for emotional needs (e.g. acceptance, go to when you are upset, concerned about feelings and welfare). If respondents answered yes, they were then asked to nominate three people to whom they would go for emotional needs. Respondents were then asked if they had anyone they could count on for help and aid or go to for instrumental needs (e.g., lend money, give food or place to stay). If respondents answered yes, they were then asked to nominate three people to whom they would go for instrumental needs. To gauge whether their core networks were primarily from the street or home, we then asked, "Do you know (nomination) mostly from being on the street or mostly from back home?" A variable was then created identifying the proportion of their network that they knew from the street. This variable is a dichotomous measure that allowed us to note the consequences of having personal network ties from the street.

Only two variables were associated with receiving money from home at Wave 1. For each increase in year of age, the adolescents were about 25% less likely to receive money from home, and for each unit increase in the adolescents' instrumental street network the likelihood of receiving money from home decreased by nearly one half.

Employment

When we asked more specifically about employment, about one third (34.0%) of the adolescents said they had a job at Wave 1 with no differences by gender or sexual orientation. Nearly one half (47.9%) of those who were employed worked in food services. Among those we were able to track to Wave 13, 55% were employed at least part time, 60.3% of the young men and 51.3% of the young women.

The problem with employment was low pay, often much less than they could earn in the street economy:

> You know I need to get a job that pays more than 5 fucking dollars an hour. That's the reason I do a lot of things I do. Why should I work making $5.60 an hour 8 hours a day? That's like what 40 bucks. But then with 3 to 4 hours I can make $400. It doesn't make any sense. (male, aged 20 years)

Many could find only part-time employment so they worked more than one part-time job:

> My other job I work 2 days out of the week—Wednes-days and Sundays. And I clean an office building for this real cool chick named Renee who has her own little cleaning business. (female, aged 22 years)

And without education or work experience, jobs can be hard to come by:

> The hardest is about job finding. It's like you're homeless you don't have that much of an education you're not going to college and you don't have a lot of previous work experience. Basically you're screwed. People are going to hire a college student

over a homeless kid any day of the week. (female, aged 22 years)

Beause I'm tired of looking at the damn newspaper classified ads for jobs and seeing you know experience. Well everybody wants experience everybody wants experience. What the hell am I supposed to do. I ain't got no experience in anything except for telemarketing and you know general labor. (male, aged 19 years)

I put applications in at two or three places. And then I've done like a ton of them online but haven't heard anything back and I've called back on them and called back on them and emailed back on them. Um I really want childcare, but a lot of the places you have to have a degree and everything and I think that's why. But eventually I want to go back to school and get all that done too. I really want to be a teacher. That's what I really want to do. But right now I'll take just anything. Any job. (female, aged 20 years)

There also were seasonal employment issues:

Winter. Period. Winter. It's cold, it's windy, there's less work um everything just goes it dies basically. The work situation dies. It's just this cold bitter thing where you can't get anywhere because you can't work. A lot of people depend on day labor to get regular jobs and get into where they need to be and that doesn't happen in winter so if you get homeless in the winter. You're screwed. (female, aged 22 years)

But the economic bottom line was that employment often did not provide enough income to house and feed themselves. This led to other strategies of self-support.

Street survival strategies

Many of the study cohort adolescents were highly involved in the street economy (Table 14.2). Young men and nonheterosexual young people were

Table 14.2 Subsistence Strategies at Wave 1 (*N* = 428)

	Heterosexual			Nonheterosexual		
	Total (%)	Male (%)	Female (%)	Total (%)	Male (%)	Female (%)
Money						
Panhandle or spare change	14.0	19.0	9.7*	29.0	33.3	27.3[c]
Broken in and taken things	23.0	38.7	9.6**	19.4	16.7[a]	20.5[b]
Sold drugs for money	42.2	60.1	26.9**	48.4	50.0	47.7[c]
Food						
Panhandle or spare change	12.1	19.0	6.1**	30.6	38.9[b]	27.3[d]
Stealing or shoplifting	16.2	22.0	11.2*	17.7	16.7	18.2
Dumpsters	3.3	6.0	1.0*	12.9	11.1	13.6[d]
Trade sex	11.5	10.1	12.7	16.1	22.2	13.6

* *p* ≤ .01 (gender significance test).
** *p* ≤ .001 (gender significance test).
[a] *p* ≤ .10 (sexuality significance test).
[b] *p* ≤ .05 (sexuality significance test).
[c] *p* ≤ .01 (sexuality significance test).
[d] *p* ≤ .001 (sexuality significance test).

more apt to be active in the street economy than were the young women. For example, 60.1% of the young heterosexual men, 50% of the nonheterosexual men, and 47.7% of nonheterosexual women had sold drugs at Wave 1 of the study compared with 26.9% of the heterosexual young women. This ranged from providing for friends to serious drug dealing:

> I used to deal drugs just about half the drugs out there I've dealt. Marijuana, hash, heroin, angel dust, cocaine, meth, although I never did make the meth. I just got it and then I sold it but [it is] too dangerous to make it. I had a gun back then, kept my house protected. There was one time where someone shot out my house windows Drug dealer got me mistaken for somebody else. (male, aged 21 years)

> Be in the drug business for a month and you'll understand. (Laughs) Drug business is a fast way to make money but it's also a fast way to lose your life, you know what I'm saying? (male, aged 20 years)

Some started dealing at a very young age:

> You know, basically it was like I was always the man handling the dope, you know out there on the block making the money. They made sure I was high, they made sure I was never hungry, they made sure I had money. That's what it's supposed to do make sure I was cool every day. I was young 13, 12, 11, when I first started. (male, aged 19 years)

In a pinch adolescents could always panhandle. Nonheterosexuals were more likely to report panhandling for money than were heterosexuals, and young heterosexual males were more likely to have panhandled than heterosexual females:

> Panhandling for food pretty much that's about all you know. It was just like either I had to sleep on the streets or go to a shelter and at that point in time there was no openings in the area that I was in for shelter so I was pretty much stuck. (female, aged 20 years)

> I had to go to the department City Hall. I had to go to City Hall to get a permit because I had to have a permit for standing out there collecting money for the homeless. I lied and said I was from [the university] and I was collecting money for the homeless. I'm serious you gotta have stories. People just ain't going to give you money you got to have a story. So I had a good story but they wound up calling the police on me. Right, and I was collecting money for the homeless. That was my gimmick I had to I had to have something because unless then I sound like a regular bum. I need a dollar. You got a dollar you got a quarter? So I'd be like collecting money for the homeless do you want to give a donation? And you'd be surprised how many people would give you money for that. (female, aged 20 years)

> So panhandling is really not good cause they deal with a lot of people asking for a lot of different things from quarters to dollars. When you out there trying to get money people look at you like get a job. So I just pretty much didn't eat. (female, aged 20 years)

The more venturesome were involved in shoplifting, theft, and burglary. Heterosexual males (38.7%) were about four times more likely to have burglarized for money than were heterosexual females (9.6%) and twice as likely to have done so as nonheterosexual males (16.7%):

> Because I was with this guy who burglarized my grandmother's home and he was already on probation so I told my grandma I did it. So I ended up in prison. And now he's not around. (female, aged 19 years)

> I'm a little klepto—I used to be a little kleptomaniac. I actually got fired from working at Target for stealing. They only caught me like with $400 worth of stuff. I had like $6,000 worth of stuff. But they only caught me with like $400. (female, aged 19 years)

> The most that I've ever stolen and I don't really steal it I kind of helped some people steal it, car seats. People go to local hospitals and people leave their doors unlocked and they got these expensive car seats you know and you take them. You take them to like a baby store, you can get $80–$100 for a car seat. (female, aged 20 years)

> I'm a thief from way back. I steal anything, anything under the sun you name it I could probably steal it and get away with it. (Laughs) You know there's no end to the list of things I can steal. (male, aged 20 years)

> I live with a whole bunch of thieves. They don't care what they do and I'm taking a big chance of getting busted all the time, for drugs and stolen cars, stolen stereo systems, fighting, getting beat up or beating up people. My big one is definitely living with

a whole bunch of thieves and my drug problem. (female, aged 19 years)

Heterosexual males (22%) were about twice as likely to have shop-lifted for food as were heterosexual females (11.2%):

> I was currently on the run, and I got caught shoplift-ing. I lied to police and told them I was I was skip-ping school hoping they would take me back to the school. I told them I was going to and I could just turn around and leave again. But it didn't work out that way. They ended up taking me to jail. (male, aged 18 years)

> When I was on the run I stole, I used to steal from grocery stores and stuff to get food for me. I'd lie to people to get money from them, just lie about any-thing, anything that I knew would make them give me money. And I'd do it continuously until they knew what the truth was. Once they started know-ing the truth. I would ease up and go to somebody else and try and get money off them. (female, aged 19 years)

> I've stolen from stores, corporations, stuff like that I don't believe in stealing from everyday people though. Like K-Mart, there's a pretty big franchise they can afford to lose some stuff here and there. Like K-Mart, Kohl's, Gordman's all those places. The little hole-in-the-wall family-owned stuff, I'm not gonna steal from them cause they're probably barely making it by to start with. I probably steal a good like two things a month. (male, aged 19 years)

> Just go into Wal-Mart and steal something for under 10 bucks and just keep doing that and returning it. And get money back, you know? As long as it's under 10 dollars, they didn't ask for a receipt. And you just got your money back for it. (female, aged 20 years)

Very few of the adolescents engaged in dumpster diving. Nonheterosexuals were more likely to have resorted to this than were heterosexuals:

> Whoppers coming out of the dumpster within half an hour after they close up are hunky dory, but when it comes to dumpsters you have to be very safe you have to smell it—you have to look at it and you have to make sure that it's not old. Like basically if you go into a dumpster that's full of bags don't dig too deep just keep on like the top layer. Make sure everything's fairly fresh. Of course there's so many preservatives it probably doesn't really matter that much. (female, aged 22 years)

About 10% of the heterosexual adolescents (10.7% males; 12.7% females) had been involved in survival sex (i.e., trading sex for food, money, drugs, or a place to stay). Male nonheterosexuals (22.2%) were about twice as likely as the other adolescents to have done so (see Chapter 13, this volume, for a complete discussion of survival sex).

Hunger

As the previous quotes indicate, street survival strategies don't always work well, and sometimes the adolescents went hungry. However, there has been very little research about how often this occurs or for how long. We were able to locate only three studies dealing with food insecurity among runaway and homeless adolescents, and all of these were based on Canadian samples (Antonaides & Tarasuk, 1998; Dachner & Tarasuk, 2002; McCarthy & Hagen, 1992). These studies document the precariousness of obtaining food regularly and the necessity of turning to street survival strategies to obtain it. The nutritional value of the food consumed, a concern for all adolescents (Grunbaum et al., 2004), has never been addressed for a population of homeless adolescents. Based on current estimates of 500,000 homeless and runaway adolescents on the streets or in shelters in the United States (Finkelhor, Hotaling, & Sedlak, 1990), we have projected elsewhere that approximately one third or 165,000 homeless young people went hungry in the past 30 days (Whitbeck, Chen, & Johnson, 2006). We believe that this is a very conservative estimate of hunger among homeless and runaway adolescents.

Our measure of food insecurity indicated that the adolescents in our study had often gone hungry. In the past 30 days, more than one third (36.5%) said that "many times" they had gone a whole day without eating, and nearly one half (48.4%) reported that "a few times" they had gone a whole day without eating (Table 14.3). Although skipping meals is not unusual among adolescents, well over one half of the study cohort had cut the size or skipped meals "many times" in the past 30 days because they could not get food, and 41.1% had gone hungry in the past 30 days because they couldn't afford to buy food.

Many of the adolescents were not eating regularly, and even when they did eat they were probably not getting proper nutrition. For example, one young woman told us:

> Let's just say crackheads, number one, they don't eat. Crackheads don't eat at all. It's like they just want their fix and that's it. So going to a crackhead for food would really not be that good. In all honesty I just didn't eat you know what I'm saying? I mean either I would like go to the corner store and get me some chips and a soda and they would like pass me over all day long. (female, aged 20 years)

Table 14.3 Food Insecurity at Wave 1

	Total (%)	Male (%)	Female (%)
Cut the size of meals or skipped meals (*N = 153*)			
Once	3.3	3.8	2.7
A few times	37.3	33.8	41.1
Many times	59.5	62.5	56.2
Not eat for whole day (*N = 126*)			
Once	15.1	12.7	17.5
A few times	48.4	54.0	42.9
Many times	36.5	33.3	39.7
Hungry because couldn't afford food (*N = 146*)			
Once	8.2	5.5	11.0
A few times	50.7	47.9	53.4
Many times	41.1	46.6	35.6
Lose weight because did not have money for food (*N = 93*)			
Once	8.6	3.9	14.3
A few times	54.8	60.8	47.6
Many times	36.6	35.3	38.1

> I was living with people who bought food but they
> bought food for themselves and their kids so it would
> be wrong of me to eat with him. They only had enough
> to feed their family so I was basically like I'd eat or I
> didn't eat, or when I did eat you know what I'm say-
> ing it was very very little. (female, aged 20 years)

> When I was on the run it was what am I going to
> eat you know today or tomorrow whatever. (female,
> aged 19 years)

Even in late adolescence, brains and bodies are still growing. When
you couple poor eating patterns with pervasive drug and alcohol use (see
Chapter 6, this volume), stress, and lack of rest, the health and developmental consequences may be enormous.

Education

Because of "revolving door" living arrangements it is hard to get an accu-
rate picture of educational progress. Adolescents in shelters or any institutional placements were likely to be in some sort of educational program,
although these were often interrupted during times on their own or by
moves. Most of the adolescents in the study had a difficult time adjusting
to school. Approximately one half of the young women (52.5%) and three
fourths of the young men (76.9%) had been suspended from school two
or more times. Nearly one half of the young men (46.8%) and one fifth of
the young women (21%) had been expelled from school at least once, and
nearly one half of the adolescents (51.1% males; 56.3% females) at Wave 1
told us they had dropped out of school at some point in their lives. Over
the course of the study, 21.1% of the males and 29.7% females had dropped
out on one or more than one occasion (total unduplicated count Waves
2–13). As one young man (aged 19 years) put it:

> I was 16 when I dropped out. I dropped out as soon
> as I turned 16. I just kind of you know said screw
> school cause I'm tired of going through the same
> thing that I went through when I was in first grade.
> Just relearning the stuff over and over they keep
> putting me in the same classes. I'm not learning
> anything, it's not doing me any good. Might as well
> leave a spot open for somebody else for the taxpay-
> ers' money to go to instead of wasting my time and
> their money.

We have only self-report for learning problems, and, therefore, we can only speculate about their effects on school leaving; however, more than one third (37.7%) told us they had a learning disability. The young men (44.1%) were more apt to report a learning disability than were the young women (32.8%). One half of the young men and 29% of the young women had had special education classes. Of those who had been in special education, 74.2% of the males and 81.2% of the females had been in special education classes on two or more occasions.

Regardless of academic problems and school leaving, at Wave 13, 86.5% of the young people remaining in the study told us that their future plans included going back to school. When asked how far in school they would go in school if they could attend as long as they wanted nearly 79.6% said a college degree or further, and most thought that this was a reasonable expectation. In answer to the question, "How far do you think you will actually go in school?" 65.4% responded, "A college degree or more." Many were looking for ways to continue their education:

> I'm not satisfied with my life. I'm not because I dropped out of school. True I got my GED but I want to make something more of myself. Not just because I want to but because I want to show my son that I'm somebody I can do something for myself and I don't need nobody's help. (female, aged 19 years)

> That was one of those things though that I realized when I was on the streets I had to get was a GED. That's one thing I realized you're always going to be a nobody unless you have a high school diploma or GED. That's just the way our life is, it's the way our world works. You know you're going to be making $5.60 for the rest of your life if you don't have a GED or high school diploma. (male, aged 20 years)

Housing

One way to measure the housing status of the cohort across time is to track where they were located for interviews every 3 months. For example, at Wave 2 of the study, 3 months after the baseline interviews, 37.6% of the young people were located directly on the street at the time of the interview and only 16% were located at home (Figure 14.1). The number of street intercepts increased from 37.6% at Wave 2 to 46.1% at Wave 13, whereas the number of interviews at the home the adolescents had originally left decreased from 16% at Wave 2 to 11% at Wave 13. The decrease in

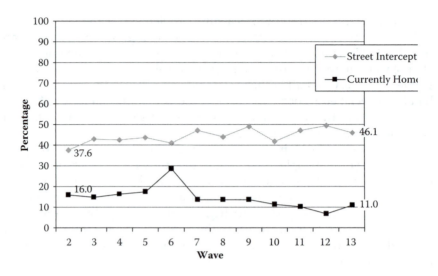

Figure 14.1 Housing patterns across time (in percentages)

home intercepts could be indicative of several things. The cohort has aged into young adulthood, and it is now developmentally appropriate to be living independently. The increase in street intercepts, however, is more ominous. After 3 years nearly one half of the remaining study cohort was on the street at the time of the last interview.

Summary and discussion

It is in the areas of education, survival strategies, and housing that the cumulative consequences of early independence become apparent. "Street-resilient" adolescents are acquiring survival skills that lead them further and further away from conventional adjustment and that over time may make such adjustment difficult. The percentages of those who have gone hungry suggest that survival strategies are not working very well. Yet conventional education and opportunity have been interrupted for those who need it most: those with special education needs and learning disabilities. Because they are now "off time" in the educational sequence, there will be fewer opportunities to address these special needs outside the traditional education system. Finally, as we address in more depth in subsequent chapters, there does not appear to be a noticeable increase in secure housing across time. On almost every indicator of resilience, the young people appear to be losing ground.

Theoretical implications

This chapter illustrates our theoretical premise of cumulative continuity more directly than any of the others. Recall from Chapter 1 (this volume) that *cumulative continuity* refers to the progressive accumulation of behavioral consequences (Caspi, Bem, & Elder, 1989). Many of these young people are becoming deeply mired by bad choices. Because of interrupted education they can't get the jobs they need, yet it is hard at this point to catch up. It is difficult, if not impossible, to establish independent housing with part-time or minimum wage jobs so they turn to the street economy. The most lucrative opportunities in the street economies may eventually bring them into contact with the criminal justice system. Involvement in drug use and the drug economy may dramatically change priorities so that obtaining and using becomes more important than other aspects of life—even nutrition.

Note also that there are very few examples of traditional resilience. Many have adapted well to street life. Although they aspire to traditional markers of resilience such as education and housing, few show improving social or employment skills. They also are laboring under the challenges of serious externalizing and internalizing mental disorders that continue to affect their judgment and responses to others.

Policy implications

The primary policy message is that we must develop strategies that break the chains of negative consequences that accumulate over time and that block opportunities. Although everyone agrees about the necessity of early prevention measures, the current system is clearly failing these young people. Promising work by the research team led by Milburn and Rotheram-Borus indicates that young people new to the streets are much more malleable than those who have spent more time there. Adolescents who are new to the streets have more ties to home, family, and school and have more housed, prosocial friends (Milburn, Rotheram-Borus, Batterham, Brumback, Rosenthal, & Mallett, 2005; Rice, Milburn, & Rotheram-Borus, 2007). This research provides empirical support for interventions that engage runaways early before the processes of cumulative continuity of their behaviors begin to close doors. Such early interventions also would serve to reduce the devastating psychological effects of revictimization on the streets.

Conclusions

The empirical ground work is being laid to support new approaches to runaway and homeless adolescents that involve protection and early intervention rather than a criminal justice approach. These new approaches will be controversial, challenging to implement, and more expensive than current policies of denial and benign neglect. To make the case, we need cost–benefit analyses that will compare the expense of early intervention to life long marginality and involvement in the social services, health, and criminal justice systems. We believe that early intervention will reduce service burden in the long run.

section 5

Lost opportunities— new opportunities

chapter 15

Continuities of mental disorders and problem behaviors

Most of what we know from studies of adult homeless populations suggests that the young people we interviewed are at considerable risk of homelessness and marginality as adults. Several researchers have reported that mental and substance abuse disorders typically precede onset of homelessness (Castaneda, Lifshutz, Galanter, & Franco, 1993; Koegel & Burnam, 1987; North, Pollio, Thompson, Spitznagel, & Smith, 1998; Sullivan, Burnam, & Koegel, 2000). Others have linked childhood histories of economic disadvantage, childhood residential instability, running away, spending time in foster care or institutions, family conflict, and sexual and physical abuse to adult homelessness (Koegel, Burnam, & Farr, 1988; Koegel, Melamid, & Burnam, 1995; Simons & Whitbeck, 1991; Sullivan et al., 2000). As the previous chapters attest, the majority of the young people in this study fit nearly every risk factor for homeless episodes as adults. Indeed, the prevalence of early mental and substance abuse disorders, early runaway episodes, and troubled family backgrounds combine for a particularly bleak prognosis.

Several factors, however, may mitigate potential negative outcomes. It is possible that situational characteristics inflate our estimates of mental disorders and thus produce more discouraging projections than are warranted. As noted throughout this volume, the vulnerability of homelessness at an early age induces enormous stress and changes behaviors. Homelessness may result in various situational adaptations such as petty theft, sexual exchanges, and self-medicating drug use that could inflate estimates of externalizing disorders. Normal emotional responses to the stress associated with homelessness may increase the likelihood of meeting criteria for internalizing disorders. Also, those who do not meet criteria for any mental disorder or those who meet criteria for internalizing disorders such as major depressive disorder (MDE) or posttraumatic stress disorder (PTSD) associated with situational factors may prove to be more resilient than those with externalizing or substance use disorders (SUDs) or comorbid internalizing and externalizing disorders.

In this chapter we consider factors that will potentially affect the adult life trajectories of these young people. We review the continuity of mental and substance abuse disorders as the young people move into adulthood. Also, we investigate the possibility that situational factors related to homelessness affect our diagnostic estimates. Finally, we consider resiliency factors, taking into account the most resilient—those who did not meet criteria for any mental disorder.

Continuities of mental disorder across the 3 years of the study

To investigate the possibility that the adolescents will "age out" of diagnostic categories as they become young adults, we matched the Wave 1 and Wave 13 samples across diagnostic categories. Rates of mental and substance use disorders decreased slightly over time (Table 15.1). For example, the percentage of adolescents who met criteria for drug abuse declined over the 3 years of the study from 27.3% to 20.1% ($p \leq .10$). Rates of drug abuse disorder among males dropped more than 10% from 35.9% at Wave 1 to 25.6% at Wave 13, and rates for female drug abuse declined from 21.6% to 16.4%. Similarly, rates for male alcohol abuse decreased from 42.3% to 34.6% and for females 31% to 25%, though the changes were not statistically significant. The rates of PTSD decreased from 17% to 10.3% ($p < .10$), and rates of major depressive episodes declined from 25.8% to 22.2% (nonsignificant). The percentage of those who met criteria for any single disorder

Table 15.1 Matched Sample Diagnostic Criteria From Wave 1 to Wave 13
(*N* = 194)

Matched *N* = 194	Wave 1: 12-Month Diagnoses			Wave 13: 12-Month Diagnoses		
	Total (%)	Male (%)	Female (%)	Total (%)	Male (%)	Female (%)
Alcohol abuse	35.6	42.3	31.0	28.9	34.6	25.0
Drug abuse	27.3	35.9	21.6	20.1[†]	25.6	16.4
Posttraumatic stress disorder	17.0	11.5	20.7	10.3[†]	5.1	13.8
Major depression	25.8	19.2	30.2	22.2	14.1	27.6
Any diagnosis	33.5	35.9	31.9	24.2[**]	29.5[*]	20.7[*]
Comorbidity	30.4	32.1	29.3	25.7	23.1	27.6

[†] .10 significance across waves.
[*] .05 significance across waves.
[**] .01 significance across waves.

among the matched sampled decreased from 33.5% to 24.2% ($p < .01$). Rates for comorbid disorders also declined from 30.4% to 25.7% (nonsignificant).

There are several explanations for this general trend across time. Those with serious diagnoses may have been more likely to leave the study; however, attrition analyses (Chapter 2, this volume) indicate there were essentially no differences in completion rates between those who met diagnostic criteria and those who did not. It is more likely that the adolescents are aging out of some behaviors such as drug abuse and that trauma symptoms are abating across time. However, at the level of individual diagnosis, there was little change. Changes for drug abuse and PTSD were only marginally statistically significant ($p < .10$). The general decline in the overall rate of single diagnoses appears to derive from cumulative small decreases in the rates of individual diagnoses.

In summary, there are two trends in the data. At the level of individual diagnosis, the matched Wave 1 to Wave 13 samples indicate that the rates for individual diagnoses were quite stable across the 3 years of the study. None of the diagnoses reached the .05 level for change across time. However, the general rate of decline across diagnoses was highly significant, suggesting a progression toward slightly less psychopathology as the adolescents mature. This improvement was primarily in decreased drug abuse and trauma symptoms. It is also important to note that though there was a declining trend for single diagnoses across the 3 years, one half of young people still met criteria for a single diagnosis at Wave 13.

The effects of runaway episodes and homelessness on adolescent psychiatric disorders: are we overdiagnosing?

Some years ago, North and colleagues wrote a seminal article regarding the validity of diagnosing antisocial personality disorder (APD) among homeless adults (North, Smith, & Spitznagel, 1993). The authors questioned the extent to which situational characteristics biased diagnostic criteria thus overestimating the prevalence of APD among homeless people. For example, homelessness is one of the diagnostic criteria for APD. Another criterion, employment difficulties, is highly related to homelessness, as is engaging in illegal activities. Vagrancy, petty theft, and public intoxication may all be associated with homelessness, and all are criteria for APD. North and colleagues also point out that carrying a weapon such as a gun or knife for self-protection may be more likely among homeless adults and that alcohol and drugs may be a form of self-medication to cope with the stress and discomforts of homelessness (North et al., p. 578). They systematically deleted diagnostic criteria associated with homelessness to see if this reduced the prevalence rates among homeless adults. However, when the criteria were deleted, "The differences in rates between diagnoses made with and without the identified potentially situation-dependent diagnoses were not significant" (North et al., p. 581). They concluded that APD is a valid diagnosis among adult homeless people.

North et al.'s (1993) work raises some intriguing questions pertaining to the validity of several internalizing and externalizing diagnoses among runaway and homeless adolescents. For adolescents, stress leading up to and following a runaway episode may be greater than for adults in that their developmental stage is predicated on dependence on adult caretakers. This may result in a wide range of symptomatic behaviors associated with their asserting independent status and the environments in which they find themselves. We decided to replicate North et al.'s method to investigate whether potential situational responses overlap with diagnostic symptoms. For example, it is possible that participation in street life and the street economy may lead to overdiagnosing conduct disorder (CD) and major depressive disorder at Wave 1 and antisocial personality disorder at Wave 13.

Conduct disorder

We chose six CD criteria at Wave 1 that might be associated with running away. Three of the criteria clearly pertained to runaway episodes: running away, staying out late without permission, and truancy. The remaining three were associated with possible delinquent behavior associated with being on the street: telling lies, stealing, and hurting someone with a weapon. Table 15.2 indicates the cumulative decline as we remove each item from the diagnostic criteria for CD. Removing "running away" accounted for a 9.3% decrease in CD among the adolescents. Deleting "staying out late without permission" decreased the percentage of adolescents meeting criteria by only an additional 1%. Truancy contributed less than 1% additional decrease in prevalence.

The largest declines in rates of CD occurred when we eliminated delinquent behaviors that may be associated with surviving on the streets. Dropping "lying" from the criteria decreased the percentage of those meeting criteria for CD by nearly 5%, and eliminating "stealing" from the criteria further reduced the percentage of CD adolescents by almost 16%. Dropping "hurting someone with a weapon" from the criteria accounted for an additional decline of 3.5%.

Eliminating the three items that include or that depend on runaway episodes reduced the percentage of the adolescents who met criteria for CD by just 11.2%. Associating the remaining three behavioral items with

Table 15.2 Homeless-Specific Criteria for Conduct Disorder (*N* = 428)

	Total (%)
Conduct disorder	75.7
Without "runaway"	66.4
Without "out late without permission"	65.4
Without "truant"	64.5
Without "lies"	59.6
Without "stolen"	43.7
Without "hurt with weapon"	40.2

Note: Changes in percentages are cumulative.

runaway episodes is a bit more conjectural. Although many of the runaways may engage in consistent lying about their situations, whereabouts, and behaviors, fewer may actually steal things, and still fewer hurt someone with a weapon. For example, only 38.7% of the males and 9.6% of the females admitted to burglary or theft (see Chapter 12, this volume). Also, many of the adolescents had engaged in these behaviors prior to their first runaway episode. A conservative estimate, therefore, would take into account the degree to which items directly associated with runaway episodes. These three criteria would reduce the prevalence of CD a little more than 10 percentage points.

Antisocial personality disorder

By Wave 13, 67.5% of the now young adults met criteria for APD. Following North and colleagues (1993), we eliminated 10 diagnostic criteria that may be associated with homelessness one at a time to investigate the impact on rates of APD (Table 15.3). The total reduction in the percentage who met criteria for APD by eliminating all 10 of the related criteria was 11.3%. The criteria that accounted for the greatest reductions were behavioral items: fighting and getting money illegally. Situational criteria such as "no regular address" and "moving repeatedly" reduced the prevalence rates little more than a percentage point.

Our findings are congruent with those of North and colleagues (1993), and we draw the same conclusion. Although the social context of homelessness contributes to the APD diagnosis, the impact is not great. Even stretching the effects of homelessness to behaviors such as risky sex and getting money illegally only results in about a about a 10% reduction in prevalence.

Table 15.3 Homeless-Specific Criteria for Antisocial Personality (*N* = 194)

	Total (%)
Antisocial personality disorder	67.5
Without "no regular address"	66.0
Without "moved repeatedly"	65.5
Without "out of work"	65.5
Without "left jobs"	64.4
Without "not show work"	63.9
Without "borrow—not repay"	63.4
Without "get money illegally"	61.3
Without "fights"	58.2
Without "risky sex"	57.2
Without "multiple partners"	56.2

Note: *Changes in percentages are cumulative.*

Major depressive episode

We identified two MDE criteria that could be directly attributed to runaway episodes: trouble sleeping and trouble concentrating. Neither had dramatic effects on meeting criteria for the diagnosis. About one third (30.4%) of the adolescents met criteria at Wave 1 for MDE. Eliminating "trouble sleeping" reduced the percentage MDE only to 29.2%; eliminating "trouble concentrating further decreased the percentage meeting criteria for MDE to 27.1%, a total reduction in prevalence of only 3.3% (not shown in tables). Although experiences leading up to a runaway episode and encounters during the episode or extended periods of homelessness may certainly contribute to MDE (see Chapter 4, this volume), contextual factors such as not being able to sleep or lack of concentration due to lack of sleep or hypervigilance associated with novel and threatening environments do not account for much in terms of overall rates of depression.

Resilient runaways

As noted previously, *resilience* is defined as maintaining competence in fundamental areas of adjustment in the face of adversity (Luthar, Cicchetti, & Becker, 2000). This would certainly apply to runaway and homeless adolescents who did not meet criteria for any psychiatric disorder during the course of the 3-year study. When we matched the sample for Wave 1 and Wave 13 (*N* = 194), 32% (*N* = 62) of the adolescents did not meet criteria for any substance use or mental disorder at Wave 1, and 26.8% ($N = 52$) did not meet criteria for any disorder at Wave 13. Of those with no 12-month diagnosis at Wave 1, more than one half (54.8%) went on to meet criteria for a 12-month diagnosis by Wave 13.

To get a better picture of those who did not meet criteria across time, we regressed age, gender, sexual orientation, ever having spent time on the street; tangible and social street network affiliations at Waves 2–13, substance use at Waves 2–13, victimization at Waves 2–13, and having no diagnosis at Wave 1 or not meeting diagnostic criteria at Wave 13. With all the variables in the model, substance use was negatively associated with being diagnosis-free at Wave 13. That is, the higher the substance use, the more likely the young person would meet diagnostic criteria for a mental or substance use disorder at Wave 13. The only other statistically significant variable was not meeting criteria for a mental or substance use disorder at Wave 1. This increased the likelihood of being diagnosis-free at Wave 13 nearly four times ($Exp(b) = 3.96$). Clearly, those who were mentally healthy at Wave 1 were those who remained so throughout the 3 years of the study.

Summary and discussion

When we saw the extent of psychiatric disorders among the runaway and homeless adolescents our immediate concern was that we were overdiagnosing due to situational conditions. We were particularly concerned that induced antisocial behaviors within the context of coping and survival strategies in response to threatening conditions and exposure to and participation in deviant underground economies contributed to the onset of the Axis II antisocial personality disorder at young adulthood. The estimate that two thirds of the adolescents who remained in the study met criteria for APD was sobering and augured for difficult times ahead during early adulthood. We wanted first to know if the estimate was valid or an artifact of the measure within a homeless population. Our findings for both CD and APD indicate that running away as an adolescent and experiencing homelessness as a young adult accounts for only approximately 10% of the rates for the diagnoses. When we take antisocial behaviors into account the estimates of CD and APD further decrease, but it is difficult to determine the extent to which social context or psychopathology contribute to these behaviors. Although there was a significant trend across the 3 years of the study toward fewer young people meeting criteria for a single diagnosis, the rates of individual diagnoses, while not increasing, were very stable. Moreover, even though statistically significant, aging out had a relatively modest effect on meeting criteria for a single diagnosis at Wave 13. If the adolescents come to the streets already meeting criteria for mental and substance use disorders, the trend from adolescence into early adulthood is that rates of mental disorder will remain stable or even slightly decrease. These findings are congruent with many studies of mental disorder among homeless adults that indicate that onset of mental and substance use disorders precede homelessness (Castaneda et al., 1993; Koegel & Burnam, 1987; North et al., 1998; Sullivan et al., 2000).

The best predictor for being diagnosis-free at Wave 13 was the absence of diagnosis at Wave 1. It appears that there is strong continuity of mental health among the most conventionally resilient adolescents. Those who did not meet criteria for a mental or substance use disorder by age 16 years were four times more likely to remain diagnosis-free over the next 3 years than those who met diagnostic criteria. However, even among this group, more than one half met diagnostic criteria 3 years later. When we consider movement from no diagnosis to meeting 12-month criteria for a diagnosis at Wave 13, the adolescents were more likely to meet criteria across time than to remain diagnosis-free.

Theoretical implications

The psychopathology the adolescents bring to the streets is maintained by street experiences. Although there is minimal aging out of mental disorders and substance use disorders, the central finding is one of continuity of mental disorders across the 3 years. That among those who were diagnosis-free at Wave 1 the experiences of running away and homelessness resulted in more than one half meeting diagnostic criteria 3 years later provides support for our amplification model of the effects of early independence (Whitbeck & Hoyt, 1999; Whitbeck, Hoyt, & Yoder, 1999). Whatever psychological damage the adolescents brought to the street was either exacerbated or maintained across time.

These findings and those of North and colleagues (1993) respond to concerns that diagnostic schedules overdiagnose homeless people. There appears to be some effect, but it is minimal. The implications, particularly in regards to the persistence of antisocial behaviors from adolescence to emerging adulthood, are dismaying. Our assessment is that these are life course persistent antisocial adolescents (Moffitt, 1997). Whether this would have been the case had they not run away or become homeless is impossible to discern; however, it is certainly true that running away contributed to the momentum of self-reinforcing negative life events that served to perpetuate maladaptive behaviors. The effect of running away and homelessness may be to ensnare the young people in an antisocial trajectory by eliminating potential avenues of change and exposure to prosocial opportunities.

Policy implications

In our opinion these findings are evidence for reassessing our national response to runaway and homeless adolescents. We are failing on several levels. First, we are failing to prevent running away. Early evaluation and intervention is needed to protect adolescents from abusive caretakers, to prevent their families from decaying around them, and to address early behavioral and academic problems. There is general agreement that the current foster home, group home continuum does not work for everyone. It especially does not work for young people who no longer agree that they are "children." Here is how one young man (aged 20 years) who had been taking care of himself since he was 11 years of age and had raised his siblings until he finally left home around 18 years of age put it:

> I can tell you this—that when a kid is going through things like I was going through, the parents are abandoning them. Ain't nobody really want to do anything with them. The one thing a kid doesn't need is a staff member from a treatment center telling them how bad of a fuck up they are. They really don't need that, you know.

Yet there is little national motivation to rethink how we respond to runaways. Indeed, runaway and homeless adolescents after a period of media attention in the 1980s and 1990s appear to have slipped from national awareness.

Second, we are failing to intervene soon enough and thoroughly enough to protect the adolescents from the various risks they will encounter during runaway episodes such as engaging in street survival strategies and experiencing victimization. The evidence is very clear that first-time runaways and those new to the street are more malleable and that ties to home and school erode over time. Living on the streets is scary and uncomfortable. Interventions that respond to these feelings by creating safe places will likely be used. Also, our street interviewers evolved into outreach workers and significant sources of advice and support for the adolescents we were following—this with formal contacts only at 3-month intervals and maintaining a presence on the streets. This makes us wonder what the effects of more frequent contact and intensive case management would be. Increased funds for outreach workers coupled with safe houses may well interrupt the street socialization process and help stabilize a higher proportion of these young people.

Conclusions

Although the continuity of psychiatric diagnosis across time, particularly the movement from adolescent CD to young adult APD is not encouraging, there is evidence that there are windows of opportunity for interventions, especially among first-time runaways or those new to street life. It is not surprising that psychological damage incurred prior to running away is maintained by life on the street or that those who do not meet criteria are likely to do so across time. There is little on the streets that would promote prosocial adaptations and a great many people and experiences that reinforce antisocial trajectories. The societal question is whether we will write off these young people as too expensive and too difficult to respond to or whether we will attempt to develop appropriate interventions. One wonders what the national response would be if 500,000 adolescents were suddenly diagnosed with a life-threatening infectious disease, yet the same number of runaway and homeless adolescents at risk remain largely ignored.

chapter 16

"No one knows what happens to these kids"

From runaways to young adults

After 3 years the young people who remained in the study ranged in age from 19 to 22 years with an average age of 20.4 years. By now, their life experiences had taken what may be a permanent toll on their emotional and physical well-being. At our most conservative estimates, dropping diagnostic criteria that may be associated with experiencing homelessness, at least one half met 12-month criteria for antisocial personality disorder (APD) and at least one fourth met 12-month criteria for major depressive episode (MDE) (see Chapter 13, this volume). Using "raw" estimates, without accounting for potential contextual effects, the 12-month prevalence rates were higher: 67.5% APD, 30.4% MDE, 35.5% posttraumatic stress disorder (PTSD), and 49% substance use disorders (SUDs). These rates of mental and substance use disorders alone portend serious problems in meeting the challenges of successful adulthood. When we factor in their current education, employment, and living arrangements the challenges are even greater.

We have enough information from following the young people from late adolescence into early adulthood to begin to provide some answers to the question that initiated this study: "No one knows what happens to these kids." The adolescents arrived on the streets or in shelters already significantly emotionally damaged. The rates of Wave 1 mental and substance use disorders were several times that expected in general population studies. Unfortunately, the mental and substance use disorders they brought into early independence were remarkably stable across time. For example, among those who met criteria for conduct disorder (CD), nearly all who remained in the study (87.9%) met criteria for APD 3 years later. There were no significant changes at the .05 level for any of the individual diagnoses between Waves 1 and 13. Also, CD, APD, and MDE could not be accounted for by responses to running away or by street experiences. Eliminating diagnostic criteria associated with runaway episodes or homelessness reduced the percentages who met criteria for these diagnoses by only about 10 percentage points. This suggests that the diagnoses are not artifacts of stressful environmental conditions that will disappear when the stressors are eliminated. At least in the cases of these homeless young people, housing is not the simple answer to all that ails them.

Although there was a general trend showing a decline in prevalence of single diagnoses (with the exception of APD), the Wave 13 prevalence for any single diagnosis was still 50%, down from 63.9% at Wave 1. The continuity of CD to APD was about twice that expected among CD adolescents in the general population and higher than projections of APD from prison samples and clinical samples and for homeless adults. The high rate of APD (67.5%) among the young people in our sample was two to three times those reported among adult homeless people (21%, Koegel, Burnam, & Farr, 1988; 25%, North, Smith, & Spitznagel, 1993). This suggests that individuals with histories of runaway episodes and homelessness as adolescents may comprise a special subpopulation of more aggressive and antisocial homeless and marginally housed adults.

Life course persistent antisocial behaviors and runaway and homeless adolescents

As noted in Chapter 1 of this volume, Moffitt (1997) suggest two potential trajectories of antisocial behaviors from early childhood to adulthood: adolescence-limited and life course persistent. Unlike adolescence-limited problem behaviors that originate later in adolescence and are unlikely to persist into adulthood, life course persistent problem behaviors originate early and are more likely to continue into young adulthood. From this perspective the developmental process is one of interrelated, self-perpetuating chains of events. Early maladaptive behaviors, some of which are attributable to often subtle, neurological problems, are sustained and even amplified over time through social environments of ineffective parenting, nonconventional peers, academic failures, early substance use, and accruing criminal records. The early lives of chronic runaways and homeless adolescents we have depicted in this volume closely parallel Moffitt's life course persistent trajectory. The most compelling evidence of this is that two thirds of the Wave 13 young people met criteria for APD.

Life on their own

When we asked the young people at Waves 1 and 13 their feelings about being on their own, little changed during the 3 years of the study. At Wave 1, 80.4% of the adolescents told us that they "really want to get out of street life"; at Wave 13, it was 83%. Yet only 27.4% at Wave 1 and 24.6% at Wave 13 told us that they were "happier at home than they are now," and the number (43.6% both Waves) who reported that "no one would want to live in the home you came from" remained unchanged between Waves 1 and 13. Young women were more likely to agree with this statement than were young men (51% vs. 32.4% at Wave 13). Less than one half of the young people at both waves agreed that "life out here is better than you thought it would be" (40.2%, Wave 1; 45.3%, Wave 13), and almost all (84.6%, Wave 1; 87.8%, Wave 13) told us that they were "doing the things you need to do to get out of street life." Clearly their goal was independence, not family reunification. Many could go back home if they chose to. At Wave 1, 38.4% said that they "could go back home if you wanted to"; by Wave 13 this had increased to almost one half (47.1%).

"What's happened to these kids": 3 years later

After 3 years, how much progress had these young people made toward establishing themselves as independent adults? Based on their situations at their last interview, we evaluated their progress toward conventional adulthood using Arnett's (1998, p. 305) five most cited criteria for emerging adulthood: (1) accepting responsibility for oneself; (2) financial independence; (3) independent decision making; (4) general independence/self-sufficiency; and (5) establishing an independent household. As noted in Chapter 1 of this volume, two of the criteria—*accepting responsibility for oneself* and *independent decision making*—already had occurred early and off-time, setting the stage for much of what came after. By running away and staying away from adult caretakers, the adolescents had chosen or had been forced to assume responsibility for themselves at a period in their development where conventional adolescents benefit from adult supervision and mentoring. They had begun independent decision making when conventional adolescents were still responding to structured environments of family and school where there were behavioral boundaries and consequences for bad decisions. The safe late-adolescent environment that allows for experimentation with self-responsibility and independent decisions and a gradual transition toward full independence was supplanted by more abrupt and conflicted transitions to independence.

General independence/self-sufficiency is very difficult to assess. Many of the adolescents became self-sufficient within the street economy at least part of the time. They became acclimated to a fluid lifestyle made up of widely varying living situations that fluctuated from street life to doubling up to some form of shelter or institutional setting. This may be self-sufficiency in some sense, but not the manner in which it is typically thought of in terms of emerging adulthood. To achieve conventional self-sufficiency one needs to meet Arnett's (1998) final two criteria: financial independence and establishing an independent household.

These last two criteria take more time and cannot be achieved by simply asserting early independence. For example, their lifestyles thus far have held numerous barriers to *financial independence*. Education has been interrupted, delayed, or plagued with academic and behavioral problems for most of the adolescents. Also, there are the typical employment issues faced by all homeless people. It is difficult to get a job and maintain steady employment when you do not have a regular place to live, a phone, or a permanent address. Minimum wage jobs barely pay the rent, and any interruption in employment or reduction in work hours almost certainly will result in problems keeping up with rent. Engaging in the street economy to survive such as dealing drugs reduces one's motivation and attractiveness for employment. Resulting criminal records may be accruing; drug and alcohol issues may also reduce employability.

Although we can't be certain that current employment equates with financial independence, it is the best indicator we have. By Wave 13 of the study, just over one half (55%) of the young people who remained in the study told us that they were currently employed full or part time (Figure 16.1).

The second pivotal criterion for adulthood mentioned in the Arnett (1998) study is *establishing an independent household*. We chose to operationalize this in Wave 13 of the study by whether the young person told us that the place they stayed last night was in their own apartment where they were currently paying rent. A total of 45% of the young people met this somewhat stringent criterion for independent living. Most of the renters were employed (29.3%), but 15.7% were paying rent without employment. These could be young people who received some sort of social welfare assistance, who were living with someone who paid the rent or those who were doing well in the underground economy.

A related task of growing up not cited by Arnett (1998) but mentioned by Eccles and colleagues (1993) as a primary challenge of adolescent development is acquiring the skills to initiate and maintain stable adult intimate relationships. As noted in Chapter 13 of this volume, most of the adolescents aspired to and preferred stable love relationships. At the time of our last interview, 28.7% of the young people reported they were currently married or in a "marriage-like" relationship. Of those in stable, "marriage-like" relationships 12.6% were employed, and 16.2% were paying rent (Figure 16.1).

One way to think about a "successful" transition to adulthood would be having a job, having an independent place to live (i.e., paying rent), and being in a stable intimate (i.e., married or marriage-like) relationship. Less than 10% (8.9%) of the young people met all three of these criteria for adulthood when we last saw them. However, the age range of 19–22 years is well below the current median age for first marriage (27.1 for males;

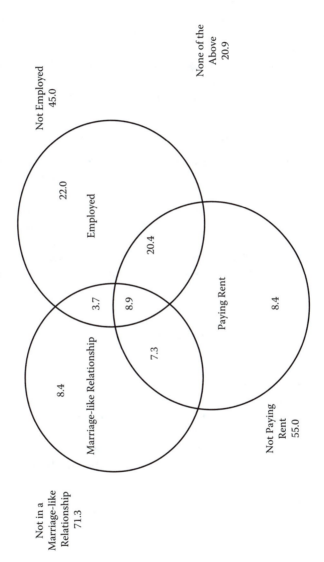

Figure 16.1 Summary of stable relationships, employment, and paying rent.

25.3 for females; U.S. Census Bureau, 2006), which makes this criterion for adulthood a bit stringent. Excluding those who were in a stable intimate relationship, 20.4% of the young people were paying rent and had a job at the time of their last interview. We should not omit the fact that 20.9% of the young people were not employed, not in stable relationship, and not paying rent at the end of the study. Admittedly, this last interview is a "snapshot" of a very fluid lifestyle. However, this finding suggests that after 3 years of the study, about the same number of the young people met none of our criteria for conventional adulthood as met Arnett's (1998) criteria of independent living and employment.

Summary and discussion: breaking the chain

Over the 3 years of the study, we came to fear that a significant proportion of runaway and homeless youth would remain on society's margins much of their lives. Their life experiences at home and on their own have resulted in missed opportunities for conventional developmental tasks with the subsequent cumulative negative consequences. The prevalence of APD at Wave 13 is probably the most discouraging indicator of future life chances in the study. It is very likely these personality-disordered young people will experience relationship troubles, will lack stable employment, and will be involved in the mental health or criminal justice system over their adult lives.

As noted in Chapter 1 of this volume, Kessler and colleagues (2005) estimate that one half of all lifetime mental disorders occur by age 14 years and three fourths occur by age 24 years (Kessler, Berglund, Demler, Jin, & Walters, 2005). Homeless and runaway young people likely have higher rates of early mental and substance use disorders than any other similarly aged group in the country and are also more likely to have co-occurring disorders, but because they are so difficult to access, they are totally unaccounted for in epidemiological studies.

Although our findings seem discouraging, if we understand the consequences of early independence and the mechanisms through which it interferes with conventional development, we can think more clearly about prevention. There are two key policy implications. First, we must be proactive to keep adolescents off the streets and from engaging in the street economies. This is where the harm done at the family level is compounded and perpetuated. However, to accomplish this means radically changing the ways we now provide services to runaway and homeless adolescents. To begin with, we need to reexamine family-based interventions. These may be effective if problems are caught at or before the first runaway episode and if the family problems are not yet severe. However, some families simply cannot be "fixed," and these are the families most of the young people in our studies are drifting out of or leaving. Services providers have been intimidated by strong institutional norms that focus on family reunification. However, family reunification for most of the young people in this study was not an option. These adolescents have moved on, and the intervention approach needs to take this into account. Regardless of social norms about reuniting families, most of these adolescents are not turning back to their families in spite of the risks they encounter on their own. It is almost certain that they will resist or manipulate situations in which they are required to relinquish independence. How long will we continue what is an obviously failed strategy? Interventions that reframe early independence as a strength and building on it need to be empirically developed and tested.

Second, these adolescents already have severe emotional and behavioral problems at the point they run away. We believe the evidence is compelling that street victimization perpetuates and exacerbates these problems. However, there is also evidence from a longitudinal study in Los Angeles that 70% of "newly homeless" returned home (Milburn et al., 2007). It appears that if we can engage runaways early enough in the process, further damage can be avoided. If we cannot prevent runaway episodes or drifting out, the primary effort should be to prevent further victimization. This means safe houses, drop-in centers, and shelters that are accessible, safe, and inviting. Too often, strict rules about alcohol and drug use create barriers to staying in shelters. Some shelters require school attendance. Others are viewed as unsafe. In our view, as long as the adolescent is not violent, he or she should be provided safe shelter. Shelters must be adequately staffed to provide for safety, but protected environments should be provided even if the adolescent is high or has been drinking if he or she is not violent. This is when they are most at risk, especially the young women. Special attention should be given to provide safe shelters that are known to be female and gay and lesbian friendly. The primary goal here is not treatment but simply to prevent further harm.

Moreover, there is promising evidence that brief interventions could be effective. For example, brief motivational interviewing (BMI) is a treatment approach that could be easily implemented in shelter or drop environments. Recent studies indicate that this approach is effective with substance abusers (Barnett, Monti, & Wood, 2001; D'Amico, Miles, Stern, & Meredith, 2007; Mitcheson, McCambridge, & Byrne, 2007; Vasilaki, Hosier, & Cox, 2006) and with treatment compliance among HIV patients (Adamian, Golin, Shain, & Devellis, 2004), and it is already being used with mixed results among homeless adolescents (Baer, Garrett, Beadnell, Wells, & Peterson, 2007; Peterson, Baer, Wells, Ginzler, & Garrett, 2006). Though not a controlled trial, there is initial evidence that the technique had positive effects in an intervention with homeless women sex workers

(Yahne, Miller, Irvin-Vitela, & Tonigan, 2002). More scientifically rigorous randomized controlled studies are needed to evaluate BMI techniques among runaway and homeless adolescents.

As noted in Chapter 1 of this volume, it is estimated that 1.6 million adolescents run away annually (Hammer, Finkelhor, & Sedlak, 2002) and that two thirds of these are 15–17 years of age. A total of 22% leave home for more than 1 week. In this study, 85.7% of the adolescents had run away on two or more occasions. A rough national estimate of "chronic" runaways such as those in this study would be in excess of 300,000 adolescents. Yet it is all too clear that homeless young people are not even on the national radar. However, if the situations we have documented exist in these small to moderately sized cities in the Midwest, you can be sure they are occurring in similarly sized cities across the country.

The media attention of the 1980s and 1990s has lapsed. Street kids are no longer an interesting story. Homeless adults have become part of the urban landscape in America, and there seems to be no sense of national shame for their conditions. We fear that we also are becoming insensitive to adolescent and young adult homelessness as well. Although our current strategies are not working, there is little pressure or national urgency for new initiatives. It is true that developing innovative new strategies to address adolescent homelessness will take expertise, time, and money. However, these data make it clear that as runaway and homeless adolescents move into adulthood they will be high-cost service users in the health, mental health, substance abuse, and criminal justice systems. The price will be paid either way.

References

Aarons, G., Brown, S., Hough, R., Garland, A., & Wood, P. (2001). Prevalence of adolescent substance abuse disorders across five sectors of care. *Journal of the Academy of Child and Adolescent Psychiatry, 40,* 419–426.

Achenbach, T., Conners, C., Quay, H., Verhulst, F., & Howell, C. (1989). Replication of empirically derived syndromes as a basis for taxonomy of child/adolescent psychopathology. *Journal of Abnormal Child Psychology, 17,* 299–323.

Adamian, M., Golin, C., Shain, L., & Devellis, B. (2004). Brief motivational interviewing to improve adherence to antiretroviral therapy: Development and qualitative pilot assessment of an intervention. *AIDS Patient Care, 18,* 229–238.

Aderibigbe, Y., Bloch, R., & Walker, W. (2001). Prevalence of depersonalization and derealization experiences in a rural population. *Social Psychiatry and Psychiatric Epidemiology, 36,* 63–69.

Adlaf, E., & Zdanowicz, Y. (1999). A cluster-analytic study of substance abuse problems and mental health among street youths. *American Journal of Drug and Alcohol Abuse, 25,* 639–660.

Ahrens, B., & Linden, M. (1996). Is there a suicidality syndrome independent of specific major psychiatric disorder? Results of a split half multiple regression analysis. *Acta Psychiatrica Scandinavica, 94,* 79–86.

Allison, P. (2000). Multiple imputation for missing data: A cautionary tale. *Sociological Methods and Research, 28,* 301–309.

Ambrosini, P., & Puig-Antich, J. (1985). Major depression in children and adolescents. In D. Schaffer, A. Ehrhardt, & L. Greenhill (Eds.), *The clinical guide to child psychiatry* (pp.182–191). New York: Free Press.

American Psychiatric Association. (1980). *Diagnostic and statistical manual of mental disorders,* 3rd ed. Washington, DC: Author.

American Psychiatric Association. (1987). *Diagnostic and statistical manual of mental disorders,* 3rd ed., rev. Washington, DC: Author.

American Psychiatric Association. (2000). *Diagnostic and statistical manual of mental disorders,* 4th ed., text rev. Washington, DC: Author.

Andover, M., Pepper, C., Ryabchenko, K., Orrico, E., & Gibb, B. (2005). Self-mutilation and symptoms of depression, anxiety, and borderline personality. *Suicide and Life-Threatening Behavior, 35,* 81–591.

Angold, A., & Costello, E. (1993). Depressive comorbidity in children and adolescents: Empirical, theoretical, and methodological issues. *American Journal of Psychiatry, 150,* 1779–1791.

Angold A., & Costello, E. (2001). The epidemiology of depression in children and adolescents. In I. Goodyer (Eds.), *The depressed child and adolescent* (pp.141–178). Cambridge, England: Cambridge University Press.

Antonaides, M., & Tarasuk, V. (1998). A survey of food problems experienced by Toronto street youth. *Canadian Journal of Public Health, 89,* 371–375.

Arnett, J. (1998). Learning to stand alone: The contemporary American transition to adulthood. *Human Development, 41,* 295–315.

Arnett, J. (2000). Emerging adulthood: A theory of development from the late teens through the twenties. *American Psychologist, 55,* 469–480.

Arnett, J. (2004). *Emerging adulthood: The winding road from the late teens through the twenties.* New York: Oxford University Press.

Baer, J., Garrett, S., Beadnell, B., Wells, E., & Peterson, P. (2007). Brief motivational intervention with homeless adolescents: evaluating effects on substance use and service utilization. *Psychology of Addictive Behaviors, 21,* 582–586.

Bao, W., Whitbeck, L., & Hoyt, D. (2000). Life stressors, social support networks, and depressive symptoms among homeless and runaway adolescents. *Journal of Health and Social Behavior, 41,* 408–420.

Barkin, S., Balkrishnan, R., Manuel, J., Anderson, R., & Gelberg, L. (2003). Health care utilization among homeless adolescents and young adults. *Journal of Adolescent Health, 32,* 253–256.

Barnes, P., el-Hajj, H., Preston-Martin, S., Cave, M., Jones, B., Otaya, M., et al. (1996). Transmission of tuberculosis among the urban homeless. *Journal of the American Medical Association, 275,* 305–307.

Barnett, N., Monti, P., & Wood, M. (2001). Motivational interviewing for alcohol involved adolescents in the emergency room. In E. F. Wagner & B. H. Waldron (Eds.), *Innovations in adolescent substance abuse intervention* (pp. 143–168). Oxford: Elsevier Science Ltd.

Bartusch, D., Lynam, D., Moffitt, T., & Silva, P. (1997). Is age important? Testing a general versus developmental theory of antisocial behavior. *Criminology, 35,* 13–48.

Beardslee, W., & Wheelock, I. (1994). Children of parents with affective disorders: Empirical findings and clinical implications. In W. Reynolds & H. Johnson (Eds.), *Handbook of depression in children and adolescents* (pp. 463–480). New York: Plenum Press.

Beautrais, A., Joyce, P., & Mulder, R. (1996). Risk factors for serious suicide attempts among youths aged 13 to 24. *Journal of the Academy of Child and Adolescent Psychiatry, 35,* 1174–1182.

Beitchman, J., Zucker, K., Hood, J., DaCosta, G., Akman, D., & Cassavia, E. (1992). A review of the long-term effects of child sexual abuse. *Child Abuse & Neglect, 16*, 101–118.

Bennum, M. (1983). Depression and hostility in self-mutilation. *Suicide and Life-Threatening Behaviors, 13*, 71–84.

Berdahl, T., Hoyt, D., & Whitbeck, L. (2005). Predictors of first mental health service utilization among homeless and runaway youth. *Journal of Adolescent Health, 37*, 145–154.

Berstein, E., & Putnam, F. (1986). Development, reliability, and validity of a dissociation scale. *Journal of Nervous and Mental Disease, 174*, 727–735.

Biederman, J., Faraone, S., Mick, E., & Lelon, E. (1991). Psychiatric comorbidity among referred juveniles with major depression: Fact or artifact? *Journal of the Academy of Child & Adolescent Psychiatry, 34*, 579–590.

Bierman, K. (2004). *Peer rejection: Developmental processes and intervention strategies.* New York: Guilford Press.

Blazer, D., Kessler, R., McConagle, K., & Swartz, M. (1994). The prevalence of major depression in a national community sample: The National Comorbidity Survey. *American Journal of Psychiatry, 151*, 979–986.

Booth, R., & Zhang, Y. (1996). Severe aggression and related conduct problems among runaway and homeless adolescents. *Psychiatric Services, 47*, 75–80.

Booth, R., & Zhang, Y. (1997). Conduct disorder and HIV risk behaviors among runaway and homeless adolescents. *Drug and Alcohol Dependence, 48*, 69–76.

Bremmer, J., & Brett, E. (1997). Trauma-related dissociative stress and long-term psychopathology in posttraumatic stress disorder. *Journal of Traumatic Stress, 10*, 37–49.

Brent, D. (1987). Correlates of medical lethality of suicide attempts in children and adolescents. *Journal of the American Academy of Child and Adolescent Psychiatry, 26*, 87–91.

Breslau, N., Davis, G., Andreski, P., & Peterson, E., (1991). Traumatic events and posttraumatic stress disorder in an urban population of young adults. *Archives of General Psychiatry, 48*, 216–222.

Briere, J. (2006). Dissociative symptoms and trauma exposure: Specificity, affect dysregulation, and posttraumatic stress. *Journal of Nervous and Mental Disease, 194*, 78–82.

Briere, J., & Gil, E. (1998). Self-mutilation in clinical and general population samples: Prevalence, correlates, and functions. *American Journal of Orthopsychiatry, 68*, 609–620.

Briere, J., & Runtz, M. (1988). Symptomatology associated with childhood sexual victimization in a nonclinical adult sample. *Child Abuse & Neglect, 12*, 51–59.

Briere, J., & Runtz, M. (1993). Child sexual abuse: Long-term sequelae and implications for psychological assessment. *Journal of Interpersonal Violence, 8*, 312–330.

Brosky, B., & Lally, S. (2004). Prevalence of trauma, PTSD, and dissociation in court-referred adolescents. *Journal of Interpersonal Violence, 19*, 801–814.

Browne, A., & Finkelhor, D. (1986). Impact of child sexual abuse: A review of the research. *Psychological Bulletin, 99*, 66–77.

Buckner, J., & Bassuk, E. (1997). Mental disorders and service utilization among youths from homeless and low-income housed families. *Journal of the American Academy of Child and Adolescent Psychiatry, 36*, 890–900.

Bukstein, O., Brent, D., & Kraminer, Y. (1989). Comorbidity of substance abuse and other psychiatric disorders in adolescents. *American Journal of Psychiatry, 46,* 225–230.

Burbach, D., & Borduin, C. (1986). Parent–child relations and the etiology of depression: A review of methods and findings. *Clinical Psychology Review, 6,* 133–153.

Burge, D., & Hammen, C. (1991). Maternal communication: Predictors of outcome at follow-up in a sample of children at high and low risk for depression. *Journal of Abnormal Psychology, 100,* 174–180.

Burnam, M., & Koegel, P. (1988). Methodology for obtaining a representative sample of homeless persons. *Evaluation Review, 12,* 117–152.

Burt, M. (1996). *Practical methods for counting homeless people: A manual for state and local jurisdictions* (2nd ed.). Washington, DC: Urban Institute.

Burt, M., Aron, L., Douglas, T., Valente, J., Lee, E., & Iwen, B. (1999). Homelessness: Programs and the people they serve. Summary Report Findings of the National Survey of Homeless Assistance Providers and Clients (Technical report prepared for Interagency Council on the Homeless). Washington, DC: Urban Institute.

Burt, M., & Taeuber, C. (1991). Overview of seven studies that counted or estimated homeless populations, In C.M. Taeuber (Ed.), *Conference proceedings for enumerating homeless persons: Methods and data needs.* Washington, DC: U.S. Department of Commerce, Economics and Statistics Administration, Bureau of the Census.

Cairns, R., Cairns, B., Neckerman, H., Gest, S., & Gariepy, J. (1988). Social networks and aggressive behavior: Peer support or peer rejection? *Developmental Psychology, 24,* 815–823.

Cairns, R., & Cairns, B. (1994). *Lifetimes and risks: Pathways of youth in our time.* Cambridge, England: Cambridge University Press.

Cairns, R., Neckerman, H., & Cairns, N. (1989). Social networks and the shadows of synchrony. In G. Adams, T. Gulotta, & R. Montemayor (Eds.), *Advances in adolescent development* (pp. 275–305). Beverly Hills, CA: Sage.

Carlson, E., & Putnam, F. (1993). An update on the dissociative experiences scale. *Dissociation, 6,* 16–27.

Carlson, E., & Putnam, F. (2000). Dissociative experiences scale. In A. John Rush Jr. (Ed.), *The handbook of psychiatric measures* (pp. 621–623). Washington, DC: American Psychiatric Association.

Carlson, J., Sugano, E., Millstein, S., Auerswald, C. (2006). Service utilization and the life cycle of youth homelessness. *Journal of Adolescent Health, 38,* 624–627.

Carrion, V., & Steiner, H. (2000). Trauma and dissociation in delinquent adolescents. *Journal of American Academy of Child and Adolescent Psychiatry, 39,* 353–359.

Carver, K., Joyner, K., & Udry, J. (2003). National estimates of adolescent romantic relationships. In P. Florsheim, (Ed.), *Adolescent romantic relations and sexual behavior: Theory, research, and practical implications.* Mahwah, NJ: Lawrence Erlbaum and Associates.

Caspi, A., & Bem, D. (1990). Personality continuity and change across the life course. In L. Pervin (Ed.), *Handbook of personality theory and research* (pp. 549–575). New York: Guilford.

Caspi, A., Bem, D., & Elder, G., Jr. (1989). Continuities and consequences of interactional styles across the life course. *Journal of Personality, 57,* 375–406.

Caspi, A., & Moffitt, T. (1995). The continuity of maladaptive behavior: From description to understanding in the study of antisocial behavior. In D. Cicchetti & D. Cohen (Eds.), *Developmental psychology* (pp. 472–511). New York: Wiley.

Castaneda, R., Lifshutz, H., Galanter, M., & Franco, H. (1993). Age at onset of alcoholism as a predictor of homelessness and drinking severity. *Journal of Addictive Disorders, 12*, 65–77.

Cauce, A., Paradise, M., Embry, L., Morgan, C., Lohr, Y., Theopolis, J., et al. (1998). Homeless youth in Seattle: Youth characteristics, mental health needs, and intensive case management. In M. Epstein, K. Kutash, & A. Duchnowski (Eds.), *Outcomes for children and youth with behavioral and emotional disorders and their families: Programs and evaluation best practices* (pp. 611–632). Austin, TX: Pro-ed, Inc.

Cauce, A., Paradise, M., Ginzler, J., Embry, L., Morgan, C., Lohr, Y., et al. (2000). The characteristics and mental health of homeless adolescents: Age and gender differences. *Journal of Emotional and Behavioral Disorders, 9*, 220–239.

Chen, X., Thrane, L., Whitbeck, L., & Johnson, K. (2006). Adolescent mental disorder, comorbidity, and post-runaway arrests. *Journal of Research on Adolescence, 16*, 379–402.

Chen, X., Tyler, K., Whitbeck, L., & Hoyt, D. (2004). Early sexual abuse, street adversity, and drug use among female runaway adolescents in the Midwest. *Journal of Drug Issues, 34*, 1–22.

Cheung, A., & Hwang, S. (2004). Risk of death among homeless women: A cohort study and review of the literature. *Canadian Medical Association Journal, 170*, 1243–1247.

Chilcoat, H., & Menard, C. (2003). Epidemiological investigations: Comorbidity of posttraumatic stress disorder and substance abuse disorder. In P. Ouimette & P. Brown, (Eds.), *Trauma and substance abuse* (pp. 9–28). Washington, DC: American Psychological Association.

Chu, J., & Dill, D. (1990). Dissociative symptoms in relation to childhood physical and sexual abuse. *American Journal of Psychiatry, 147*, 887–892.

Cillessen, A., van IJzendoorn, H., van Lieshout, C., & Hartup, W. (1992). Heterogeneity among peer-rejected boys: Subtypes and stabilities. *Child Development, 63*, 893–905.

Clausen, J. (1991). Adolescent competence and the shaping of the life course. *American Journal of Sociology, 96*, 805–842.

Clogg, C. (1995). Latent class models. In G. Arminger, C. Clogg, & M. Sobel (Eds.), *Handbook of statistical modeling for the social and behavioral sciences* (pp. 311–359). New York: Plenum Press.

Cochran, B., Stewart, A., Ginzler, J., & Cauce, A. (2002). Challenges faced by homeless GLBT: Comparison of gay, lesbian, bisexual, and transgender homeless adolescents with their heterosexual counterparts. *American Journal of Public Health, 92*, 53–61.

Cohen, J. (1990). Things I have learned (so far). *American Psychologist, 45*, 1304–1312.

Coie, J., & Dodge, K. (1998). Aggression and antisocial behavior. In N. Eisenberg (Eds.), *Handbook of child psychology: Social, emotional, and personality development* (5th ed., pp. 779–862). New York: John Wiley & Sons.

Collins, W. (1990). Parent–child relationships in the transition to adolescence: Continuity and change in interaction, affect, and cognition. In R. Montemayor, G. Adams, & T. Gullotta (Eds). *From childhood to adolescence: A transitional period?* (pp. 85–106). Newbury Park, CA: Sage.

Collins, L., Schafer, J., & Kam, C. (2001). A comparison of inclusive and restrictive strategies in modern missing data. *Psychological Methods, 6,* 330–351.

Collin-Vezina, D., & Hebert, M. (2005). Comparing dissociation and PTSD in sexually abused school-aged girls. *Journal of Nervous and Mental Disease, 193,* 47–52.

Compas, B., Howell, D., Phares, V., Williams, R., & Ledoux, N. (1989). Parent and child stress and symptoms: An integrative analysis. *Developmental Psychology, 25,* 550–559.

Conger, R., Conger, K., Elder, G., Lorenz, F., Simons, R., & Whitbeck, L. (1992). A family process model of economic hardship and adjustment of early adolescent boys. *Child Development, 63,* 526–541.

Conger, R., Conger, K., Elder, G., Lorenz, F., Simons, R., & Whitbeck, L. (1993). Family economic stress and adjustment of early adolescent girls. *Developmental Psychology, 29,* 206–219.

Connolly, J., Geller, S., Marton, P., & Kutcher, S. (1992). Peer responses to social interaction with depressed adolescents. *Journal of Child Clinical Psychology, 21,* 365–370.

Cooper, J., Kapur, N., Webb, R., Lawlor, M., Gutherie, E., Mackway-Jones, K., et al. (2005). Suicide after deliberate self-harm: A 4-year cohort study. *American Journal of Psychiatry, 162,* 297–303.

Cotterell, J. (1994). Analyzing the strength of supportive ties in adolescent social supports. In F. Nestman & K. Hurrelmann, (Eds.), *Social networks and social supports in childhood and adolescents* (pp. 257–267). New York: Walter de Gruyter.

Creamer, M., O'Donnell, M., & Pattison, P. (2003). The relationship between acute stress disorder and posttraumatic stress disorder in severely injured trauma survivors. *Behavior Research & Therapy, 42,* 315–328

Cytryn, L., & McKnew, D. (1972). Proposed classification of childhood depression: A reassessment. *American Journal of Psychiatry, 137,* 149–155.

Dachner, N., & Tarasuk, V. (2002). Homeless "squeegee kids": Food insecurity and daily survival. *Social Science & Medicine, 54,* 1039–1049.

Daddis, M., Braddock, D., Cuers, D., Elliott, A., & Kelly, A. (1993). Personal and family distress in homeless adolescents. *Community Mental Health Journal, 29,* 413–422.

D'Amico, E., Miles, J., Stern, S., & Meredith, L. (2007). Brief motivational interviewing for teens at risk of substance use consequences: A randomized pilot study in a primary care clinic. *Journal of Substance Abuse Treatment, 35,* 53–61.

Daniel, L. (1998). Statistical significance testing: A historical overview of misuse and misinterpretations with implications for the editorial policies of educational journals. *Research in the Schools, 5,* 23–32.

Daniels, D., & Moos, R. (1990). Assessing life stressors and social resources among adolescents; Applications to depressed youth. *Journal of Adolescent Research, 5,* 268–289.

Darbyshire, P., Muir-Cochrane, E., Fereday, J., Jureidini, J., & Drummond, A. (2006). Engagement with health and social care services: Perceptions of homeless young people with mental health problems. *Health and Social Care in the Community, 14,* 553–562.

Darche, M. (1990). Psychological factors differentiating self-mutilating and non-self-mutilating adolescent inpatient females. *Psychiatric Hospital, 21,* 31–35.

Dempster, A., Laird, N., & Rubin, D. (1977). Maximum likelihood from incomplete data via the EM algorithm. *Journal of the Royal Statistical Society, 39,* 1–38.

Dennis, M. (1991). Changing the conventional rules: Surveying homeless people in nonconventional locations. *Housing Policy Debate, 2,* 1–32.

Dennis, M., Iachan, R., Thornberry, J., & Bray, R. (1991). The RTI method: Sampling over time, In C.M. Taeuber (Ed.), *Enumerating homeless persons' Methods and Data Needs,* (pp.167–170).Washington, DC: Bureau of the Census, U.S. Department of Commerce.

DeRosa, C., Montgomery, S., Kipke, M., Iverson, E., Ma, J., & Unger, J. (1999). Service utilization among homeless and runaway youth in Los Angeles, California: Rates and reasons. *Journal of Adolescent Health, 24,* 449–458.

Devine, J., & Wright, J. (1992). Counting the homeless: S-Night in New Orleans. *Evaluation Review, 16,* 409–417.

Deykin, E., & Buka, S. (1997). Prevalence and risk factors for posttraumatic stress disorder among chemically dependent adolescents. *American Journal of Psychiatry, 154,* 752–757.

Deykin, E., Levy, J., & Wells, V. (1987). Adolescent depression, alcohol and drug abuse. *American Journal of Public Health, 77,* 178–182.

Diseth, T. (2005). Dissociation in children and adolescents as a reaction to trauma—An overview of conceptual and neurobiological factors. *Nordic Journal of Psychiatry, 59,* 79–91.

Dishion, T., Andrews, D., & Crosby, L. (1995). Antisocial boys and their friends in early adolescence: Relationship characteristics, quality and interactional process. *Child Development, 66,* 139–151.

Dodge, K. (1989). Problems in social relationships. In E. Mash & R. Barkley (Eds.), *Treatment of childhood disorders* (pp. 222–244). New York: Guilford Press.

Dodge, K., Lochman, J., Harnish, J., Bates, J., & Pettit, G. (1997). Reactive and pro-active aggression in school children and psychiatrically impaired chronically assaultive youths. *Journal of Abnormal Psychology, 106,* 37–51.

Downey, G., & Coyne, J. (1990). Children of depressed parents: An integrated review. *Psychological Bulletin, 108,* 50–76.

Downey, G., & Walker, E. (1992). Distinguishing family-level and child-level influences on the development of depression and aggression in children at risk. *Development and Psychopathology, 4,* 81–95.

Dubner, A., & Motta, R. (1999). Sexually and physically abused foster care children and posttraumatic stress disorder. *Journal of Consulting and Clinical Psychology, 67,* 367–373.

Eccles, J., Midgley, C., Wigfield, A., Buchanan, C., Reuman, D., Flanagan, C., et al. (1993). Development during adolescence: The impact of stage/environment for on young adolescents' experiences in schools and families. *American Psychologist, 48,* 90–101.

Egeland, B., & Sussman-Stillman, A. (1996). Dissociation as a mediator of child abuse across generations. *Child Abuse & Neglect, 20,* 1123–1132.

Elklit, A., & Brink, O. (2004). Acute stress disorder as a predictor of posttraumatic stress disorder in physical assault victims. *Journal of Interpersonal Violence, 19,* 709–726.

Ennett, S., Bailey, S., & Federman, E. (1999). Social network characteristics associated with risky behaviors among runaway and homeless youth. *Journal of Health & Social Behavior, 40,* 63–78.

Ensign, J. (1998). Health issues of homeless youth. *Journal of Social Distress and the Homeless, 7,* 159–174.

Ensign, J. (2000). Reproductive health of homeless adolescent women in Seattle, Washington, USA. *Women & Health, 31,* 133–150.

Ensign, J. (2004). Quality of health care: The views of homeless youth. *Health Services Research, 39,* 695–707.

Ensign, J., & Bell, M. (2004). Illness experiences of homeless youth. *Qualitative Health Research, 14,* 1239–1254.

Ensign, J., & Panke, A. (2002). Barriers and bridges to care: voices of homeless female adolescent youth in Seattle, Washington, USA. *Journal of Advanced Nursing, 37,* 166–172.

Espelage, D., Holt, M., & Henkel, R. (2003). Examination of peer group contextual effects on aggression during early adolescence. *Child Development, 74,* 205–220.

Evans, E., Hawton, K., Rodham, K., & Deeks, J. (2005). The prevalence of suicidal phenomena in adolescents: A systematic review of population-based studies. *Suicide & Life-Threatening Behavior, 35,* 239–250.

Farber, E., Kinast, C., McCoard, W., and Falkner, D. (1984). Violence in families of adolescent runaways. *Child Abuse and Neglect, 8,* 295–299.

Farrington, D., & Coid, J. (2003). *Early prevention of adult antisocial behavior.* Cambridge, England: Cambridge University Press.

Farrow, J., Deisher, R., Brown, R., Kulig, J., & Kipke, M. (1992). Health and health needs of homeless and runaway youth: A position paper of the society for adolescent medicine. *Journal of Adolescent Health, 13,* 717–726.

Favazza, A. (1998). The coming of age of self-mutilation. *Journal of Nervous and Mental Disease, 186,* 259–268.

Favazza, A., DeRosear, L., & Conterio, K. (1989). Self-mutilation and eating disorders. *Suicide and Life Threatening Behaviors, 19,* 352–361.

Feeny, N., Zoellner, L., Fitzgibbons, L., & Foa, E. (2000). Exploring the roles of emotional numbing, depression, and dissociation in PTSD. *Journal of Traumatic Stress, 13,* 489–498.

Feeny, N., Zoellner, L., & Foa, E. (2000). Anger, dissociation, and posttraumatic stress disorder among female assault victims. *Journal of Traumatic Stress, 13,* 89–100.

Feitel, B., Margetson, N., Chamas, J., & Lipman, C. (1992). Psychosocial background and behavioral and emotional disorders of homeless and runaway youth. *Hospital and Community Psychiatry, 43,* 155–159.

Feldman, M. (1988). The challenge of self-mutilation: A review. *Comprehensive Psychiatry, 29,* 252–269.

Feldman, S., Rubinstein, J., & Rubin, C. (1988). Depressive affect and restraint in early adolescents: Relationships with family structure, family process, and friendship. *Journal of Early Adolescence, 8,* 279–296.

Fergusson, D., & Lynskey, M. (1995). Suicide attempts and suicide ideation in a birth cohort of 16-year old New Zealanders. *Journal of the Academy of Child and Adolescent Psychiatry, 34,* 1308–1317.

Fergusson, D., Lynskey, M., & Horwood, L. (1996). Factors associated with continuity and change in disruptive behavior patterns between childhood and adolescence. *Journal of Abnormal Child Psychology, 24,* 533–553.

Finkelhor, D. (1984). *Child sexual abuse: New research and theory.* New York: Free Press.

Finkelhor, D. (1990). Early and long-term effects of child sexual abuse: An update. *Professional Psychology: Research and Practice, 21,* 325–330.

Finkelhor, D., & Browne, A. (1986). Impact of child sexual abuse: A review of the research. *Psychological Bulletin, 99,* 66–77.

Finkelhor, D., Hotaling, G., & Sedlak, A. (1990). *Missing, abducted, runaway, and thrownaway children in America (1st report): Numbers and characteristics.* National Incidence Studies. Washington, DC: U.S. Department of Justice, Office of Justice Programs, Office of Juvenile Justice and Delinquency Prevention.

Follette, V., Polusny, M., Bechtle, A., & Naugle, A. (1996). Cumulative trauma: The impact of child sexual abuse, adult sexual assault, and spouse abuse. *Journal of Traumatic Stress, 9,* 25–35.

Forehand, R., McCombs, A., Long, N., Brody, G., & Fauber, R. (1988). Early adolescent adjustment to recent parental divorce: the role of interparental conflict and adolescent sex as mediating variables. *Journal of Consulting and Clinical Psychology, 56,* 624–627.

Furman, W., & Shaffer, L. (2003). The role of romantic relationships in adolescent development. In P. Florsheim (Ed.), *Adolescent romantic relationships and sexual behavior* (pp. 3–22). Mahwah, NJ: Lawrence Erlbaum Associates.

Garrison, C., Addy, C., McKeown, R., Cuffe, S., Jackson, A., & Waller, J. (1993). Nonsuicidal physically self-damaging acts in adolescents. *Journal of Child and Family Studies, 2,* 339–352.

Garrison, C., Schlucter, M., Schoenbach, V., & Kaplan, B. (1989). Epidemiology of depressive symptoms in young adolescents. *Journal of the American Academy of Child and Adolescent Psychiatry, 28,* 343–351.

Gelberg, L., Gallagher, T., Andersen, R., & Koegel, P. (1997). Computing priorities as a barrier to medical care among homeless adults in Los Angeles. *American Journal of Public Health, 87,* 217–220.

Gershuny, B., & Thayer, J. (1999). Relations among psychological trauma, dissociative phenomena, and trauma related distress: A review and integration. *Clinical Psychology Review, 19,* 631–657.

Glazer, K. (1967). Masked depression in children and adolescents. *American Journal of Psychotherapy, 21,* 565–574.

Goldscheider, F., & DaVanzo, J. (1985). Living arrangements and the transition to adulthood. *Demography, 22,* 545–563.

Goldston, D. (2003). *Measuring suicidal behavior and risk in children and adolescents.* Washington, DC: American Psychological Association.

Goldston, D., Daniel, S., & Mayfield, E. (2006). Suicidal and nonsuicidal self-harm behaviors. In D. Wolfe & E. Mash (Eds.), *Behavioral and emotional disorders in adolescents* (pp. 343–382). New York: Guilford Press.

Goodman, L., Saxe, L., & Harvey, M. (1991). Homelessness as psychological trauma. *American Psychologist, 46,* 1219–1225.

Goodyer, I. (2001). Life events: Their nature and effects. In I. M. Goodyer (Ed.), *The depressed child and adolescent* (pp. 204–232). Cambridge, England: Cambridge University Press.

Gould, M., King, R., Greenwald, S., Fisher, P., & Schwab-Stone, M. (1998). Psychopathology associated with suicidal ideation and attempts among children and adolescents. *Journal of the American Academy of Child and Adolescent Psychiatry, 37,* 915–923.

Greene, J., & Ringwalt, C. (1996). Youth and familial substance abuse's association with suicide attempts among runaway homeless youth. *Substance Use & Misuse, 31,* 277–298.

Grotevant, H. (1998). Adolescent development in family contexts. In N. Eisenberg (Vol. Ed.) & W. Damon (Series Ed.), *Handbook of child psychology: Social, emotional, and personality development* (5th ed., pp. 1097–1149). New York: Wiley.

Grunbaum, J., Kann, L., Kinchen, S., Ross, J., Hawkins, J., Lowry, R., et al. (2004). Youth risk behavior surveillance: United States, 2003. *Morbidity and Mortality Weekly Report Surveillance Summary, 53,* 1–96.

Guertin, T., Lloyd-Richardson, E., Spirito, A., Donaldson, D., & Boergers, J. (2001). Self-mutilative behavior in adolescents who attempt suicide by overdose. *Journal of the Academy of Child and Adolescent Psychiatry, 40,* 1062–1069.

Guttmacher Institute. (2006). *U.S. teenage pregnancy statistics: National and state trends and trends by race and ethnicity.* New York: Author.

Hagen, J., & McCarthy, B. (1997). *Mean streets: Youth crime and homelessness.* New York: Cambridge University Press.

Hammer, H., Finkelhor, D., & Sedlak, A. (2002). *Runaway/thrownaway children: National estimates and characteristics.* Report of Estimates from the National Incidence Studies, NISMART. Washington, DC: U.S. Department of Justice, Office of Justice Programs, Office of Juvenile Justice and Delinquency Prevention.

Harrington, R., Rutter, M., Weissman, M., Fudge, H., Groothues, C., Bredenkamp, D., et al. (1997). Psychiatric disorders in the relatives of depressed probands. I. Comparison of prepubertal adolescent and early adult onset cases. *Journal of Affective Disorders, 42,* 9–22.

Hartup, W. (1989). Social relationships and their developmental significance. *American Psychologist, 44,* 120–126.

Haugaard, J. (2004). Recognizing and treating uncommon behavioral and emotional disorders in children and adolescent who have been severely maltreated: Dissociative disorders. *Child Maltreatment, 9,* 146–153.

Hill, J. (2002). Biological, psychological, and social processes in the conduct disorders. *Journal of Child Psychology and Psychiatry, 43,* 133–164.

Hill, J., & Maughan, B. (2001). *Conduct disorders in childhood and adolescence.* Cambridge, England: Cambridge University Press.

Hinshaw, S., & Lee, S. (2003). Conduct and oppositional defiant disorders. In R. Barkley & J. Mash (Eds.), *Child psychopathology* (pp. 144–198). New York: Guilford Press.

Holzer, L., & Schwarz, F. (2004). The missing psychotic disorders. *Journal of Adolescent Health, 35,* 432–433.

House Committee on Education and Labor, Subcommittee on Human Resources. Juvenile Justice, Runaway Youth, and Missing Children's Act, Amendments, 98th Congress, 2nd Session, March 7, 1984.

Hoyt, D., Ryan, K., & Cauce, A. (1999). Personal victimization in high risk environment: Homeless and runaway adolescents. *Journal of Research in Crime and Delinquency, 36*, 371–392.

Huband, N., & Tantum, D. (2004). Repeated self-wounding: Women's recollection of pathways to cutting and of the value of different interventions. *Psychology and Psychotherapy: Theory, Research, and Practice, 77*, 413–428.

Huesmann L., Eron, L., Lefkowitz, M., & Walder, L. (1984). Stability of aggression overtime and generations. *Developmental Psychology, 20*, 722–136.

Hughes, J., Cavell, T., & Grossman, P. (1997). A positive view of self: Risk or protection for aggressive children? *Development & Psychopathology, 9*, 75–94.

Hurry, J. (2000). Deliberate self-harm in children and adolescents. *International Review of Psychiatry, 12*, 31–36.

Hwang, S. (2000). Mortality among men using homeless shelters in Toronto, Ontario. *Journal of the American Medical Association, 283*, 2152–2157.

Hwang, S., Orav, J., O'Connell, J., Lebow, J., & Brennan, T. (1997). Causes of death in homeless adults in Boston. *Annals of Internal Medicine, 126*, 625–628.

Iachan, R. (1989). Sampling in time and space. Proceedings of the survey research methods section, *American Statistical Associations*, 636–640. Retrieved February 11, 2008, from: http://www.amastat.org/sections/srms/Proceedings/papers/1989_116.pdf

Iachan, R., & Dennis, M. (1991). The design of homeless surveys. *Proceedings of the section on survey research methods of the American Statistical Association* (pp. 181–185). Alexandria, VA: American Statistical Association.

Irwin, H. (1994). Proneness to dissociation and traumatic childhood events. *Journal of Nervous and Mental Disease, 182*, 456–461.

Jacobsen, L., Southwick, S., & Kosten, T. (2001). Substance use disorders in patients with Posttraumatic stress disorder: A review of the literature. *American Journal of Psychiatry, 158*, 1184–1190.

Janus, M., Archambault, F., Brown, S., & Welsh, L. (1995). Physical abuse in Canadian runaway adolescents. *Child Abuse & Neglect, 19*, 433–447.

Janus, M., Burgess, A., & McCormack, A. (1987). Histories of sexual abuse in adolescent male runaways. *Adolescence, 22*, 405–417.

Jensen, P., Roper, M., Fisher, P., Piacentini, J., Canino, G., Richters, J., et al. (1995). Test–retest reliability of the Diagnostic Interview Schedule for Children (DISC.2.1). *Archives of General Psychiatry, 52*, 67–71.

Johnston, L., O'Malley, P., Bachman, J., & Schulenberg, J. (2005). *Teen drug use down but progress halts among youngest teens.* University of Michigan New and Information Services: Ann Arbor, MI. Retrieved June 7, 2006, from: http://www.monitoringthefuture.org

Johnson, K., Whitbeck, L., & Hoyt, D. (2005a). Predictors of social network composition among homeless and runaway adolescents. *Journal of Adolescence, 28*, 231–248.

Johnson, K., Whitbeck, L., & Hoyt, D. (2005b). Substance abuse disorders among homeless and runaway adolescents. *Journal of Drug Issues, 35*, 799–816.

Joyce, R., McKenzie, J., Mulder, R., Luty, S., Sullivan, P., Miller, A., et al. (2006). Genetic, developmental and personality correlates of self-mutilation in depressed patients. *Australian and New Zealand Journal of Psychiatry, 40*, 225–229.

Kaplan, E., & Meier, P. (1958). Nonparametric estimation from incomplete observations. *Journal of the American Statistical Association, 53*, 457–481.

Kashani, J., Carlson, G., Beck, N., Hoeper, E., Corcoran, C., McAllister, J., et al. (1987). Depression, depressive symptoms, and depressed mood among a community sample of adolescents. *American Journal of Psychiatry, 144,* 931–934.

Kaufman, J. (1991). Depressive disorders in maltreated children. *Journal of the American Academy of Child and Adolescent Psychiatry, 30,* 257–265.

Kaufman, J., & Widom, C. (1999). Childhood victimization, running away, and delinquency. *Journal of Research in Crime and Delinquency, 36,* 347–370.

Kendall-Tackett, K., Williams, L., & Finkelhor, D. (1993). Impact of sexual abuse on children: A review and synthesis of recent empirical studies. *Psychological Bulletin, 113,* 164–180.

Kennedy, M. (1991). Homeless and runaway youth mental health issues: No access to the system. *Journal of Adolescent Health, 12,* 576–579.

Kessler, R. (1994a). The National Comorbidity Survey of the United States. *International Review of Psychiatry, 6,* 365–376.

Kessler, R. (1994b). Building on the ECA: The National Comorbidity Survey and the children's ECA. *International Journal of Methods in Psychiatric Research, 4,* 81–94.

Kessler, R. (2000). Posttraumatic stress disorder: The burden to the individual and to society. *Journal of Clinical Psychiatry, 61,* 4–12.

Kessler, R., Berglund, P., Demler, O., Jin, R., & Walters, E. (2005). Lifetime prevalence and age-of-onset distributions of *DSM-IV* disorders in the National Comorbidity Survey replication. *Archives of General Psychiatry, 62,* 593–602.

Kessler, R., McGonagle, K., Zhao, S., Nelson, C., Hughes, M., Eshleman, S., et al. (1994). Lifetime and 12-month prevalence of DSM-III-R psychiatric diagnoses in the United States: Results from the National Comorbidity Survey. *Archives of General Psychiatry, 51,* 8–19.

Kessler, R., Nelson, C., McGonagle, K., Edlund, M., Frank, R., & Leaf, P. (1996). The epidemiology of co-occurring addictive and mental disorders: Implications for prevention and service utilization. *American Journal of Orthopsychiatry, 66,* 17–31.

Kessler, R., Sonnega, A., Bromet, E., Hughes, M., & Nelson, C. (1995). Posttraumatic stress disorder in the National Comorbidity Survey. *Archives of General Psychiatry, 52,* 1048–1060.

Kessler, R., Sonnega, A., Bromet, E., Hughes, M., Nelson, C., & Breslau, N. (2005). Epidemiological risk factors for trauma and PTSD. In R. Yehuda, (Ed.), *Risk factors for posttraumatic stress disorder* (pp. 23–60). Washington DC: American Psychiatric Press.

Kidd, S. (2004). The walls are closing in, and we were trapped: A qualitative analysis of street youth suicide. *Youth & Society, 36,* 30–55.

Kidd, S., & Kral, M. (2002). Suicide and prostitution among street youth: A qualitative analysis. *Adolescence, 37,* 411–430.

Kilpatrick, D., Acierno, R., Resnick, H., Saunders, B., & Best, C. (1997). A 2-year longitudinal analysis of the relationships between violent assault and substance use in women. *Journal of Consulting and Clinical Psychology, 65,* 834–847.

Kilpatrick, D., Ruggerio, K., Acierno, R., Saunders, B., Resnick, H., & Best, C. (2003). Violence and risk of PTSD, major depression, substance abuse/dependence, and comorbidity: Results from a National Survey of Adolescents. *Journal of Consulting and Clinical Psychology, 71,* 692–700.

Kingree, J., Braithwaite, R., & Woodring, T. (2001). Psychosocial and behavioral problems in relation to recent experience as a runaway among adolescent detainees. *Criminal Justice and Behavior, 28*, 190–205.

Kipke, M., Montgomery, D., & MacKenzie, R. (1997). Substance abuse among youth seen at a community-based clinic. *Journal of Adolescent Health, 14*, 289–294.

Kipke, M., Montgomery, S., Simon, T., & Iverson, E. (1997). Substance abuse disorders among runaway and homeless youth. *Substance Use & Misuse, 32*, 969–986.

Kipke, M., Montgomery, S., Simon, T., Unger, J., & Johnson, C. (1997). Homeless youth: Drug use patterns and HIV risk profiles according to peer group affiliation. *AIDS and Behavior, 1*, 247–259.

Kipke, M., O'Conner, S., Palmer, R., & MacKenzie, R. (1995). Street youth in Los Angeles: Profile of a group at high risk for human immunodeficiency virus infection. *Archives of Pediatric Adolescent Medicine, 149*, 513–519.

Kipke, M., Simon, T., Montgomery, D., Unger, J., & Iverson, E. (1997). Homeless youth and their exposure to violence while living on the streets. *Journal of Adolescent Health, 20*, 360–367.

Kipke, M., Unger, J., O'Conner, S., Palmer, R., & LaFrance, S. (1997). Street youth, their peer group affiliation and differences according to residential status, subsistence patterns, and use of services. *Adolescence, 32*, 655–669.

Kirby, J., Chu, J., & Dill, D. (1993). Correlates of dissociative symptomatology in patients with physical and sexual abuse histories. *Comprehensive Psychiatry, 34*, 258–263.

Kisiel, C., & Lyons, J. (2001). Dissociation as a mediator psychopathology among sexually abused children and adolescents. *American Journal of Psychiatry, 158*, 1034–1039.

Klein, J., & Moeschberger, M. (1997). *Survival analysis: Techniques for censored and truncated data. Statistics for biology and health.* New York: Springer-Verlag.

Klein, J., Woods, A., Wilson, K., Prospero, M., Greene, J., & Ringwalt, C. (2000). Homeless and runaway youths' access to health care. *Journal of Adolescent Health, 27*, 331–339.

Klerman, G. (1988). The current age of youthful melancholia: Evidence for increase in depression among adolescents and young adults. *British Journal of Psychiatry, 152*, 4–14.

Klerman, G., & Weissman, M. (1989). Increasing rates of depression. *Journal of the American Medical Association, 261*, 2229–2235.

Klonsky, E., Oltmanns, T., & Turkheimer, E. (2003). Deliberate self-harm in a nonclinical population: Prevalence and psychological correlates. *American Journal of Psychiatry, 160*, 1501–1508.

Koegel, P., & Burnam, M. (1987). *The epidemiology of alcohol abuse and dependence among the homeless: Findings from the inner city of Los Angeles.* Rockville, MD: National Institute on Alcohol Abuse and Alcoholism.

Koegel, P., Burnam, A., & Farr, R. (1988). The prevalence of specific psychiatric disorders among homeless individuals in the inner city of Los Angeles. *Archives of General Psychiatry, 45*, 1085–1092.

Koegel, P., Burnam, M., & Morton, J. (1996). Enumerating homeless people: Alternative strategies and their consequences. *Evaluation Review, 20*, 378–403.

Koegel, P., Melamid, E., & Burnam, A. (1995). Childhood risk factors for homelessness among homeless adults. *American Journal of Public Health, 85,* 1642–1649.

Koegel, P., Sullivan, G., Burnam, A., Morton, S., & Wenzel, S. (1999). Utilization of mental health and substance abuse among homeless adults in Los Angeles. *Medical Care, 37,* 306–317.

Koenig, L., Doll, L., O'Leary, A., & Pequegnat, W. (2004). *From child sexual abuse to adult sexual risk: Trauma, revictimization, and intervention.* Washington, DC: American Psychological Association.

Koopman, C., Rosario, M., & Rotheram-Borus, M. (1994). Alcohol and drug use and sexual behaviors placing runaways at risk for HIV infection. *Addictive Behaviors, 19,* 95–103.

Koss, M., & Dinero, T. (1999). Discriminant analysis of risk factors for sexual victimization among a national sample of college women. *Journal of Clinical and Consulting Psychology, 57,* 242–250.

Kosterman, R., Graham, J., Hawkins J., Catalano, R., & Herrenkohl, T. (2001). Childhood risk factors for persistence of violence in the transition to adulthood: A social development perspective. *Violence and Victims, 16,* 355–370.

Kovacs, M. (1981). Rating scales to assess depression in school-aged children. *Acta Paedopsychiatica: International Journal of Child and Adolescent Psychiatry, 46,* 305–315.

Kozaric-Kovacic, D., & Borovecki, A. (2005). Prevalence of psychotic comorbidity in combat-related posttraumatic stress disorder. *Military Medicine, 170,* 223–226.

Kress, V. (2003). Self-injurious behaviors: Assessment and diagnosis. *Journal of Counseling and Development, 81,* 490–498.

Krueger, R. (1999). The structure of common mental disorders. *Archives of General Psychiatry, 56,* 921–926.

Krueger, R., & Markon, K. (2006). Reinterpreting comorbidity: A model-based approach to understanding and classifying psychopathology. *Annual Review of Clinical Psychology, 2,* 111–133.

Kufeldt, K., & Nimmo, M. (1987). Youth on the street: Abuse and neglect in the eighties. *Child Abuse and Neglect, 11,* 531–543.

Kupersmidt, J., Burchinal, M., & Patters, C. (1995). Developmental patterns of childhood peer relations as predictors of externalizing problem behaviors. *Development & Psychology, 7,* 825–843.

Kurtz, P., Kurtz, G., & Jarvis, S. (1991). Problems of maltreated runaway youth. *Adolescence, 26,* 544–555.

La Greca, A., Silverman, W., & Wasserstein, S. (1998). Children's predisaster functioning as a predictor of posttraumatic stress following Hurricane Andrew. *Journal of Consulting and Clinical Psychology, 66,* 883–892.

Lahey, B., Applegate, B., Waldman, I., Loft, J., Hankin, B., & Rick, J. (2004). The structure of child and adolescent psychopathology: Generating new hypotheses. *Journal of Abnormal Psychology, 113,* 358–385.

Lahey, B., Goodman, S., Waldman, I., Bird, H., Canino, G., Jensen, P., et al. (1998). Relation of age of onset to the type and severity of child and adolescent conduct problems. *Journal of Abnormal Child Psychology, 27,* 247–260.

Lahey, B., Waldman, I., & McBurnett, K. (1999). Annotation: The development of antisocial behavior: An integrative causal model. *Journal of Child Psychiatry, 5,* 669–682.

Laye-Gindhu, A., & Schonert-Reichl, K. (2005). Nonsuicidal self-harm among community adolescents: Understanding the "whats" and "whys" of self-harm. *Journal of Youth and Adolescence, 34,* 447–457.

Leboyer, M., Slama, F., Siever, L., & Bellivier, F. (2005). Suicidal disorders: A nosological entity per se? *American Journal of Medicine & Genetics: Seminars in Medical Genetics, 133,* 3–7.

Lee, J., Gaetz, S., & Goettler, F. (1994). The oral health of Toronto's street youth. *Journal of Canadian Dental Association, 60,* 545–548.

Lefkowitz, M., & Burton, N. (1978). Childhood depression: A critique of the concept. *Psychological Bulletin, 85,* 716–726.

Leslie, M., Stein, J., & Rotheram-Borus, M. (2002). Sex-specific predictors of suicidality among runaway youth. *Journal of Clinical and Adolescent Psychology, 31,* 27–40.

Levitt, J., Sansone, R., & Cohn, M. (2004). *Self-harm behavior and eating disorders.* New York: Brunner Routledge.

Lewinsohn, P., Rohde, P., & Seeley, J. (1995). Adolescent suicidal ideation and attempts: Prevalence, risk factors, and clinical implications. *Clinical Psychology: Science and Practice, 3,* 25–46.

Lewinsohn, P., Rohde, P., Seeley, J., & Hops, H. (1991). Comorbidity of unipolar depression: Major depression with dysthymia. *Journal of Abnormal Psychology, 100,* 205–213.

Lipsey, M., & Derzon, J. (1998). Predictors of violent or serious delinquency in adolescence and early childhood. In R. Loeber & D. P. Farrington (Eds.), *Serious and violent juvenile offenders: Risk factors and successful interventions* (pp. 86–105). Thousand Oaks, CA: Sage Publications.

Little, R., & Rubin, D. (1987). *Statistical analysis with missing data.* New York: John Wiley & Sons.

Loeber, R. (1982). The stability of antisocial and delinquent child behavior: A review. *Child Development, 53,* 1431–1446.

Loeber, R. (1988a). Natural histories of conduct problems, delinquency, and associated substance use: Evidence for developmental progressions. In B. Lahey & A. Kazdin (Eds.), *Advances in clinical child psychology* (pp. 73–124). New York: Plenum Press.

Loeber, R. (1988b). Behavioral precursors and accelerators of delinquency. In W. Buikhuisen & S. Mednick (Eds.), *Explaining criminal behavior* (pp. 51–67). Leiden: Brill.

Loeber, R. (1991). Antisocial behavior: More enduring than changeable? *Journal of the American Academy of Child and Adolescent Psychiatry, 30,* 393–397.

Loeber, R., Burke, J., & Lahey, B. (2002). What are the adolescent antecedents to antisocial personality disorder? *Criminal Behaviour and Mental Health, 12,* 24–36.

Loeber, R., & Coie, J. (2001). Continuities and discontinuities of development, with particular emphasis on emotional and cognitive components of disruptive behavior. In J. Hill & B. Maughan (Eds.), *Conduct disorders in childhood and adolescence* (pp. 379–407). Cambridge, England: Cambridge University Press.

Loeber, R., Green, S., & Lahey, B. (2003). Risk factors for adult antisocial personality. In D. Farrington & J. Coid (Eds.), *Early prevention of adult antisocial behavior* (pp. 79–108). Cambridge, England: Cambridge University Press.

Loeber, R., & Hay, D. (1997). Key issues in the development of aggression and violence from childhood to early adulthood. *Annual Review of Psychology, 48,* 371–410.

Loewenstein, R., & Bennett, G. (1996). Patterns of dissociation in clinical and non-clinical samples. *Journal of Nervous and Mental Disease, 184,* 673–679.

Loranger, A., Susman, V., Oldham, J., & Russakoff, L. (1987). The personality disorder examination: A preliminary report. *Journal of Personality Disorders, 1,* 1–13.

Low, G., Jones, D., MacLeod, A., Power, M., & Duggan, C. (2000). Childhood trauma and self-harming behavior: A pilot study. *British Journal of Medical Psychology, 73,* 269–278.

Luthar, S., Cicchetti, D., & Becker, B. (2000a). The construct of resilience: A critical evaluation and guidelines for future work. *Child Development, 71,* 543–562.

Luthar, S., Cicchetti, D., & Becker, B. (2000b). Research on resilience: Response to commentaries. *Child Development, 71,* 573–575.

Lynam, D. (1996). Early identification of chronic offenders: Who is the fledgling psychopath? *Psychological Bulletin, 20,* 209–234.

Maaranen, P., Tanskanen, A., Honkalampi, K., Haatainen, K., Hintikka, J., & Viiamaki, H. (2005). Factors associated with pathological dissociation in the general population. *Australian and New Zealand Journal of Psychiatry, 39,* 387–394.

MacAniff, L., & Kiselica, M. (2001). Understanding and counseling self-mutilation in female adolescents and young adults. *Journal of Counseling & Development, 79,* 46–52.

MacLean, M., Embry, L., & Cauce, A. (1999). Homeless adolescents' paths to separation from family: Comparison of family characteristics, psychological adjustment, and victimization. *Journal of Community Psychology, 27,* 179–187.

MacMillan, H., Fleming, J., Streiner, B., Lin, E., Boyle, M., Jamieson, E., et al. (2001). Childhood abuse and lifetime psychopathology in a community sample. *American Journal of Psychiatry, 158,* 1878–1883.

Mann, B., & Sanders, S. (1994). Child dissociation and the family context. *Journal of Abnormal Child Psychology, 22,* 373–388.

March, J. (1993). What constitutes a stressor? The "Criterion A" issue. In J. Davidson & E. Foa (Eds.), *Posttraumatic stress disorder, DSM IV, and beyond* (pp. 37–54). Washington, DC: American Psychiatric Press.

Masten, A., & Powell, J. (2003). A resiliency framework for research, policy and practice. In S. Luthar (Ed.), *Resiliency and vulnerability: Adaptation in the context of childhood adversity.* (pp. 1–29). Cambridge, England: Cambridge University Press.

Maughan, B. (2001). Conduct disorder in context. In J. Hill & B. Maughan (Eds.), *Conduct disorders in childhood and adolescence* (pp. 169–201). Cambridge, England: Cambridge University Press.

McAnally, G. (1989). I was homeless: A look beneath the safety net. *Humanist, 49,* 12.

McCarthy, B., & Hagen, J. (1992). Surviving on the street: The experiences of homeless youth. *Journal of Adolescent Research, 7,* 412–430.

McCaskill, P., Toro, P., & Wolfe, S. (1998). Homeless and matched housed adolescents: A comparative study of psychopathology. *Journal of Clinical Child Psychology, 27*, 306–319.

McCutcheon, A. (1987). *Latent class analysis*. Beverly Hills, CA: Sage Publications.

McDaniel, J., Purcell, D., & D'Augelli, A. (2001). The relationship between sexual orientation and risk for suicide: Research findings and future directions for research and prevention. *Suicide and Life-Threatening Behavior, 31*, 84–105.

McMorris, B., Tyler, K., Whitbeck, L., & Hoyt, D. (2002). Familial and on-the-street risk factors associated with alcohol use among homeless and runaway adolescents. *Journal of Alcohol Studies, 63*, 34–43.

Messman, T., & Long, P. (1996). Child sexual abuse and its relationship to revictimization in adult women: A review. *Clinical Psychology Review, 16*, 397–420.

Messman-Moore, T., & Long, P. (2003). The role of childhood sexual abuse sequelae in the sexual revictimization of women: An empirical review and theoretical reformulation. *Clinical Psychology Review, 23*, 537–571.

Messman-Moore, T., Long, P., & Siegfried, N. (2000). The revictimization of child sexual abuse survivors: An examination of the adjustment of college women with child sexual abuse, adult sexual assault, and adult physical abuse. *Child Maltreatment, 5*, 18–27.

Milburn, N., Rosenthal, D., Rotheram-Borus, M., Mallett, S., Batterham, P., Rice, E., et al. (2007). Newly homeless youth typically return home. *Journal of Adolescent Health, 40*, 574–576.

Milburn, N., Rotheram-Borus, M., Batterham, P., Brumback, B., Rosenthal, D., & Mallett, S. (2005). Predictors of close family relationships among homeless young people. *Journal of Adolescence, 28*, 263–275.

Milburn, N., Rotheram-Borus, M., Rice, E., Mallet, S., & Rosenthal, D. (2006). Cross-national variations in behavioral profiles among homeless youth. *American Journal of Community Psychology, 37*, 63–76.

Mitcheson, L., McCambridge, J., & Byrne, S. (2007). Pilot cluster-randomized trial of adjunctive motivational interviewing to reduce crack cocaine use in clients on methadone maintenance. *European Addiction Research, 13*, 6–10.

Moffitt, T. (1997). Adolescent-limited and life-course persistent offending: A complementary pair of developmental theories. In T. P. Thornberry (Ed.), *Developmental theories of crime and delinquency* (pp. 11–55). New Brunswick, NJ: Transaction Publishers.

Moffitt, T., Caspi, A., Dickson, N., Silva, P., & Stanton, W. (1996). Childhood-onset versus adolescent-onset antisocial conduct problems in males: Naturally history from ages 3 to 18 years. *Development and Psychopathology, 8*, 399–424.

Molnar, B., Buka, S., & Kessler, R. (2001). Child sexual abuse and subsequent psychopathology: Results from the National Comorbidity Survey. *American Journal of Public Health, 91*, 753–760.

Molnar, B., Shade, S., Kral, A., Booth, R., & Watters, J. (1998). Suicidal behavior and sexual/physical abuse among street youth. *Child Abuse & Neglect, 22*, 213–222.

Moran, P. (1999). The epidemiology of antisocial personality disorder. *Social Psychiatry and Psychiatric Epidemiology, 34*, 231–242.

Mounier, C., & Andujo, E. (2003). Defensive functioning of homeless youth in relation to experiences of child maltreatment and cumulative victimization. *Child Abuse and Neglect, 27*, 1187–1204

Muehlekamp, J., & Gutierrez, P. (2004). An investigation of differences between self-injurious behavior and suicide attempts in a sample of homeless adolescents. *Suicide and Life Threatening Behavior, 34,* 12–23.

Mulder, R., Beautrais, A., Joyce, P., & Fergusson, D. (1998). Relationship between dissociation, childhood sexual abuse, childhood physical abuse, and mental illness in a general population sample. *American Journal of Psychiatry, 155,* 806–811.

Mundy, P., Robertson, M., Robertson, J., & Greenblatt, M. (1990). The prevalence of psychotic symptoms in homeless adolescents. *Journal of the American Academy of Child and Adolescent Psychiatry, 29,* 724–731.

Myers, M., Stewart, D., & Brown, S. (1998). Progression from conduct disorder to antisocial personality disorder following treatment for adolescent substance abuse. *American Journal of Psychiatry, 155,* 470–485.

National Institutes of Health. (2005). *Code of Federal Regulations Title 45, Public Welfare. Part 46—Protection of Human Subjects (45 CFR 46.117).* Department of Health & Human Services: Office for the Protection from Research Risks. Retrieved July 22, 2008, from: http://www.hhs.gov/ohrp/humansubjects/guidance/45cfr46.htm

Newman, D., Moffitt, T., Caspi, A., Magdom, L., Silva, P., & Stanton, W. (1996). Psychiatric disorder in a birth cohort of young adults: Prevalence, comorbidity, clinical significance, and new case incidence from ages 11 to 21. *Journal of Counseling and Clinical Psychology, 64,* 552–562.

Noell, J., Rohde, P., Seeley, J., & Ochs, L. (2001). Childhood sexual abuse, adolescent sexual coercion and sexually transmitted infection acquisition among homeless female adolescents. *Child Abuse & Neglect, 25,* 344–353.

Noll, J., Horowitz, L., Bonnano, G., Trickett, P., & Putnam, F. (2003). Revictimization and self-harm in females who experienced childhood sexual abuse. *Journal of Interpersonal Violence, 18,* 1452–1471.

Noll, J., Trickett, P., & Putnam, F. (2003). A prospective investigation of the impact of childhood sexual abuse on the development of sexuality. *Journal of Consulting and Clinical Psychology, 71,* 575–586.

North, C., Pollio, D., Smith, E., & Spitznagel, E. (1998). Correlates of early onset and chronicity of homelessness in a large urban homeless population. *Journal of Nervous and Mental Disease, 186,* 393–400.

North, C., Pollio, D., Thompson, S., Spitznagel, E., & Smith, E. (1998). The associations of psychiatric diagnosis with weather conditions in a large urban homeless sample. *Social Psychiatry and Psychiatric Epidemiology, 33,* 206–210.

North, C., Smith, E., & Spitznagel, E. (1993). Is antisocial personality a valid diagnosis among the homeless? *American Journal of Psychiatry, 150,* 578–583.

O'Carrol, P., Berman, A., Maris, R., Moscicki, E., Tanney, B., & Silverman, M. (1996). Beyond the tower of Babel: A nomenclature for suicidology. *Suicide and Life-Threatening Behavior, 26,* 237–252.

O'Connell, J. (2004). Dying in the shadows: The challenge of providing health care for homeless people. *Canadian Medical Association Journal, 170,* 1251–1252.

Oldham, J., Skodol, A., Kellman, H., Hyler, S., Rosnick, L., & Daves, M. (1995). Diagnosis of *DSM III-R* personality disorders by two structured interviews: Pattern of comorbidity. *American Journal of Psychiatry, 149,* 213–220.

Olfson, M., Gameroff, M., Marcus, S., Greenburg, T., & Shaffer, D. (2005). National trends in hospitalization of youth with intentional self-inflicted injuries. *American Journal of Psychiatry, 162,* 1328–1335.

O'Toole, T., Gibbon, J., Hanusa, B., & Fine, M. (1999). Utilization of health care services among subgroups of urban homeless and housed poor. *Journal of Health Politics, Policy, and Law, 24,* 91–114.

Padgett, D., Struening, E., & Andrews, H. (1990). Factors affecting the use of medical, mental health, alcohol, and drug treatment services by homeless adults. *Medical Care, 28,* 805–821.

Paolucci, E., Genuis, M., & Violato, C. (2001). A meta-analysis of the published research on the effects of child sexual abuse. *Journal of Psychology, 135,* 17–36.

Paris, J. (2005). Understanding self-mutilation in borderline personality disorder. *Harvard Review of Psychiatry, 13,* 179–185.

Parker, J., & Asher, S. (1993). Friendship and friendship quality in middle childhood: Links with peer group acceptance and feelings of loneliness and social dissatisfaction. *Developmental Psychology, 29,* 611–621.

Patterson, G. (1982). *Coercive family process.* Eugene, OR: Castalia.

Patterson, G. (1986). Performance models for antisocial boys. *American Psychologist, 41,* 432–444.

Patterson, G., Dishion, T., & Bank, L. (1984). Family interaction: A process model of deviancy training. *Aggressive Behavior, 10,* 253–267.

Pawlby, S., Mills, A., & Quinton, D. (1997). Vulnerable adolescent girls: Opposite-sex relationships. *Journal of Child Psychology and Psychiatry, 38,* 909–920.

Pennbridge, J., Yates, G., David, T., & MacKenzie, R. (1990). Runaway and homeless youth in Los Angeles County, California. *Journal of Adolescent Health Care, 11,* 159–165.

Peterson, P., Baer, J., Wells, E., Ginzler, J., &.Garrett, S. (2006). Short-term effects of a brief motivational intervention to reduce alcohol and drug risk among homeless adolescents. *Psychology of Addictive Behaviors, 20,* 254–264.

Pfohl, B., Coryell, W., Zimmerman, M., & Stangl, D. (1986). *DSM-III* personality disorders: Diagnostic overlap and internal consistency of individual *DSM-III* criteria. *Comprehensive Psychiatry, 27,* 21–34.

Phelan, J., & Link, B. (1999). Who are "the homeless"? Reconsidering the stability and composition of the homeless population. *American Journal of Public Health, 89,* 1334–1338.

Pizem, P., Massicotte, P., Vincent, J., & Barolet, R. (1994). The state of oral and dental health of the homeless and vagrant population of Montreal. *Journal of the Canadian Dental Association, 60,* 1061–1065.

Plattner, B., Silvermann, M., Redlich, A., Carrion, V., Feucht, M., Friedrich, M., et al. (2003). Pathways to dissociation: Intrafamilial versus extrafamilial trauma in juvenile delinquents. *Journal of Nervous and Mental Disease, 191,* 781–788.

Poythress, N., Skeem, J., & Lilienfeld, S. (2006). Associations among early abuse, dissociation, and psychopathy in an offender sample. *Journal of Abnormal Psychology, 115,* 288–297.

Puig-Antich, J., Goetz, D., Davies, M., Kaplan, T., Davies, S., Ostrow, L., et al. (1989). A controlled family history of prepubertal major depressive disorder. *Archives of General Psychiatry, 46,* 406–418.

Puig-Antich, J., Kaufman, J., Ryan, N., Williamson, D., Dahl, R., Lukens, E., et al. (1993). The psychosocial functioning and family environment of depressed adolescents. *Journal of the American Academy of Child and Adolescent Psychiatry, 32*, 244–253.

Puig-Antich, J., Lukens, E., Davies, M., Goetz, D., Brennen-Quattrock, J., & Todak, G. (1985). Psychosocial function in prepubertal children with major depressive disorders. Interpersonal relationships during the depressive episode. *Archives of General Psychiatry, 42*, 500–507.

Putnam, F. (1991). Dissociative phenomena. In. A. Tasman (Ed.), *Annual review of psychiatry* (pp. 159–174).Washington, DC: American Psychiatric Press.

Putnam, F. (1993). Dissociative disorders in children: Behavioral profiles and problems. *Child Abuse & Neglect, 17*, 39–45.

Putnam, F., Carlson, E., Ross, C., Anderson, G., Clark, P., Torem, M., et al. (1996). Patterns of dissociation in clinical and nonclinical samples. *Journal of Nervous and Mental Disease, 184*, 673–679.

Putnam, F., Hornstein, N., & Peterson, G. (1996). Clinical phenomenology of child and adolescent dissociative disorders. *Child and Adolescent Psychiatric Clinics of North America, 5*, 351–360.

Pynoos, R., Frederick, C., Nader, K., & Arroyo, W. (1987). Life threat and post-traumatic stress in school-age children. *Archives of General Psychiatry, 44*, 1057–1063.

Quay, H. (1986). Conduct disorders. In H. Quay & J. Werry (Eds.), *Psychopathological disorders of childhood* (pp. 35–72). New York: John Wiley & Sons.

Radloff, L. (1991). The use of the center for epidemiologic studies depression scale in adolescents and young adults. *Journal of Youth and Adolescence, 20*, 149–166.

Rafferty, A. (1996). Bayesian model selection in social research. In P. Marsden (Ed.), *Sociological Methodology* (pp. 111–163). Oxford: Basil Blackwell.

Raine, W. (1982). Self-mutilation. *Journal of Adolescence, 5*, 1–13.

Raj, A., Silverman, J., & Amaro, H. (2000). The relationship between sexual abuse and sexual risk among high school students: Findings from the 1997 Massachusetts youth risk behavior survey. *Maternal and Child Health Journal, 4*, 125–134.

Reid, J., Patterson, G., & Snyder, J. (2002). *Antisocial behavior in children and adolescents*. Washington, DC: American Psychological Association.

Reinherz, H., Giaconia, R., Silverman, A., Friedman, A., & Pakiz, B. (1995). Early psychosocial risks for adolescent suicidal ideation and attempts. *Journal of the American Academy of Child and Adolescent Psychiatry, 34*, 599–611.

Resnick, H., Kilpatrick, D., Dansky, B., & Saunders, B. (1993). Prevalence of civilian trauma and posttraumatic stress disorder in a representative national sample of women. *Journal of Consulting and Clinical Psychology, 61*, 984–991.

Rew, L., Taylor-Seehafer, M., & Fitzgerald, M. (2001). Sexual abuse, alcohol, and other drug use and suicidal behaviors in homeless adolescents. *Issues in Comprehensive Pediatric Nursing, 24*, 225–240.

Reynolds, W. (1992). Depression in children and adolescents. In W. Reynolds (Ed.), *Internalizing disorders in children and adolescents* (pp. 149–135). Amsterdam: Elsevier.

Reynolds, W. (1994). Depression in adolescents: Contemporary issues and perspectives. In T. Ollendick & R. Prinz (Eds.), *Advances in clinical child psychology* (pp. 261–316). New York: Plenum Press.

Rice, E., Milburn, N., & Rotheram-Borus, M. (2007). Pro-social and problematic social network influences on HIV/AIDS risk behaviors among newly homeless youth in Los Angeles. *AIDS Care, 19,* 697–704.

Rice, E., Milburn, N., Rotheram-Borus, M., Mallett, S., & Rosenthal, D. (2005). The effects of peer group network properties on drug use among homeless youth. *American Behavioral Scientist, 48,* 1102–1123.

Rich, C., Combs-Lane, A., Resnick, H., & Kilpatrick, D. (2002). Child sexual abuse and adult sexual revictimization. In L. Koenig, L. Doll, A. O'Leary, & W. Pequegnat (Eds.), *From child sexual abuse to adult sexual risk: Trauma, revictimization, and intervention* (pp. 49–68). Washington, DC: American Psychological Association.

Rie, H. (1966). Depression in childhood: A survey of some pertinent contributions. *Journal of the American Academy of Child Psychiatry, 5,* 553–583.

Rind, B., & Tromovitch, P. (1997). A meta-analytic review of findings from national samples on psychological correlates of child sexual abuse. *Journal of Sex Research, 34,* 237–255.

Ringwalt, C., Greene, J., & Robertson, M. (1998). Familial backgrounds and risk behaviors of youth with thrown away experiences. *Journal of Adolescence, 21,* 241–252.

Roberts, R., & Bengtson, V. (1996). Affective ties to parents in early adulthood and self-esteem across 20 years. *Social Psychology Quarterly, 59,* 96–106.

Robins, L. (1991). Conduct disorder. *Journal of Child Psychology and Psychiatry, 32,* 193–212.

Robins, L., Tipp, J., & Przybeck, T. (1991). Antisocial personality. In L. Robins & D. Regier (Eds.), *Psychiatric disorders in America* (pp. 224–271). New York: Free Press.

Robertson, M., Westerfelt, A., & Irving, P. (1991). Research note: The impact of sampling strategy on estimated prevalence of major mental disorder among homeless adults in Alameda County, CA. *Abstracts of the American Public Health Association meeting,* Atlanta, GA.

Rodgers, J. (1996). Sexual transitions in adolescence. In J. Graber, J. Brooks-Gunn, & A. Peterson (Eds.), *Transitions through adolescence: Interpersonal domains and context* (pp. 85–110). Mahwah, NJ: Lawrence Erlbaum Associates.

Rohde, P., Lewinsohn, P., & Seeley, J. (1991). Comorbidity of unipolar depression: Comorbidity with other mental disorders in adolescents and adults. *Journal of Abnormal Psychology, 100,* 214–222.

Rohde, J., Mace, D., & Seeley, J. (1997). The association of psychiatric disorders with suicide attempts in a juvenile delinquent sample. *Criminal Behaviour and Mental Health, 7,* 187–200.

Rohde, P., Noell, J., Ochs, L., & Seeley, J. (2001). Depression, suicidal ideation, and STD-related risk in homeless older adolescents. *Journal of Adolescence, 24,* 447–460.

Rosenthal, R., Rinzler, C., Wallsh, R., & Klausner, R. (1972). Wrist-cutting syndrome: The meaning of a gesture. *American Journal of Psychiatry, 128,* 47–52.

Ross, S., & Heath, N. (2002). A study of the frequency of self-mutilation in a community sample of adolescents. *Journal of Youth and Adolescence, 31,* 67–77.

Ross, S., & Heath, N. (2003). Two models of adolescent self-mutilation. *Suicide and Life-Threatening Behavior, 33,* 277–287.

Ross, C., Joshi, S., & Currie, R. (1990). Dissociative experiences in the general population. *American Journal of Psychiatry, 147,* 1547–1552.

Ross, C., Norton, G., & Anderson, G. (1988). The Dissociative Experiences Scale: A replication study. *Dissociation, 1,* 21–22.

Ross, R., & McKay, H. (1979). *Self-mutilation.* Lexington, MA: Lexington Books.

Rossi, P., Wright, J., Fisher, G., & Willis, G. (1987). The urban homeless: Estimating composition and size. *Science, 235,* 1336–1341.

Rotheram-Borus, M. (1993). Suicidal behavior and risk factors among runaway youth. *American Journal of Psychiatry, 150,* 103–107.

Rotheram-Borus, M., Koopman, C., & Ehrhardt, A. (1991). Homeless youths and HIV infection. *American Psychologist, 46,* 88–97.

Rotheram-Borus, M., Luna, G., Marotta, T., & Kelly, H. (1994). Going nowhere fast: Methamphetamine use and HIV infection. In R. Battjes, Z. Sloboda, & W. Grace (Eds.), *The contexts of HIV risk among drug users and their sexual partners. National Institute on Drug Abuse Monograph No. 143* (pp. 155–183). Rockville, MD: US Department of Health & Human Services.

Rotheram-Borus, M., Mahler, K., Koopman, C., & Langabeer, K. (1996). Sexual abuse history and associated multiple risk behavior in adolescent runaways. *American Journal of Orthopsychiatry, 66,* 390–400.

Rotheram-Borus, M., Meyer-Bahlburg, H., Koopman, C., Rosario, M., Exner, T., Henderson, R., et al. (1992). Lifetime sexual behaviors among runaway males and females. *Journal of Sex Research, 29,* 15–29.

Rotheram-Borus, M., Rosario, M., & Koopman, C. (1991). Minority youth at risk: Gay males and runaways. In S. Gore & M. Colton (Eds.), *Adolescent stress: Courses and consequences* (pp. 181–200). New York: Aldine de Gruyter.

Roy, E., Haley, N., Leclerc, P., Leclerc, P., Boudreau, J., & Boivin, J. (2004). Morality in a cohort of street youth in Montreal. *Journal of the American Medical Association, 292,* 569–574.

Rubin, D. (1987). *Multiple imputation for nonresponse in surveys.* New York: John Wiley & Sons.

Rutter, M., Quinton, D., & Hill, J. (1990). Adult outcome of institution-reared children: Males and females compared. In L. Robbins & M. Rutter (Eds.), *Straight and deviant pathways from childhood to adulthood* (pp. 135–157). Cambridge, England: Cambridge University Press.

Ryan, K., Kilmer, R., Cauce, A., Watanabe, H., & Hoyt, D. (2000) Psychological consequences of child maltreatment in homeless adolescents: Untangling the unique effects of maltreatment and family environment. *Child Abuse & Neglect, 24,* 333–352.

Sachsse, U., Von Der Heyde, S., & Huether, G. (2002). Stress regulation and self-mutilation. *American Journal of Psychiatry, 159,* 672.

Sakai, J., Stallings, M., Mikulich-Gilbertson, S., Corley, R., Young, S., Hopfer, C., et al. (2004). Mate similarity for substance dependence and antisocial personality disorder symptoms among parents of patients and controls. *Drug and Alcohol Dependence, 16,* 165–175.

Saltonstall, M. (1984). *Street youth and runaways on the streets of Boston: One agency's response.* Boston: The Bridge.

Sampson, R., Laub, J., & Wimer, C. (2006). Does marriage reduce crime? A counterfactual approach to within individual causal effects. *Criminology, 44,* 465–507.

Sandberg, D., & Lynn, S. (1992). Dissociative experiences, psychopathology and adjustment, and child and adolescent maltreatment in female college students. *Journal of Abnormal Psychology, 101,* 717–723.

Sansone, R., Songer, D., & Gaither, G. (2001). Diagnostic approaches to borderline personality and their relationship to self-harm behavior. *International Journal of Psychiatry in Clinical Practice, 5,* 273–277.

SAS Institute. (2004). *SAS 9.1 User's Guide.* Cary, NC: Author.

Saxe, G., Chawla, N., & Van der Kolk, B. (2002). Self-destructive behavior in patients with dissociative disorders. *Suicide and Life-Threatening Behaviors, 32,* 313–320.

Schachar, R., Rutter, M., & Smith, A. (1981). The characteristics of situationally and pervasively hyperactive children; Implications for syndrome definition. *Journal of Child Psychology and Psychiatry, 22,* 372–392.

Schafer, J. (1997). *Analysis of incomplete multivariate data.* London: Chapman & Hall.

Schafer, J., & Graham, J. (2002). Missing data: Our view of the state of the art. *Psychological Methods, 7,* 147–177.

Schnazer, B., Dominguez, B., Shrout, P., & Caton, C. (2007). Homelessness, health status, and health care use. *American Journal of Public Health, 97,* 464–469.

Schultheiss, D., & Blustein, D. (1994). Role of adolescent-parent relationships in college student development and adjustment. *Journal of Counseling Psychology, 41,* 248–255.

Schwartz, R., Cohen, P., Hoffmann, N., & Meeks, J. (1989). Self-harm behaviors (carving) in female adolescent drug abusers. *Clinical Pediatrics, 28,* 340–346.

Schweitzer, R., Hier, T., & Terry, D. (1994). Parental bonding, family systems, and environmental predictors of adolescent homelessness. *Journal of Emotional and Behavioral Disorders, 2,* 39–45.

Shaffer, D., Schwab-Stone, M., Fisher, P., Cohen, P., Piacentini, J., Davies, M., et al. (1993). The Diagnostic Interview Schedule for Children—revised version (DISC-R). Preparation, field testing, interrater reliability and acceptability. *Journal of the American Academy of Child and Adolescent Psychiatry, 32,* 643–650.

Shiner, M. (1995). Adding insult to injury: Homelessness and health service use. *Sociology of Health & Illness, 17,* 525–549.

Shirar, L. (1996). *Dissociative children.* New York: Norton.

Silberg, J. (2000). Fifteen years of dissociation in maltreated children: Where do we go from here? *Child Maltreatment, 5,* 119–136.

Silbert, M., & Pines, A. (1981). Sexual child abuse as an antecedent to prostitution. *Child Abuse & Neglect, 13,* 407–411.

Silver, L. (1988). The scope of the problem in children and adolescents. In J. Looney (Ed.), *Chronic mental illness in children and adolescents* (pp. 39–51). Washington, DC: American Psychiatric Press.

Silverman, A., Reinherz, H., & Giaconia, R. (1996). The long-term sequelae of child and adolescent abuse: A longitudinal community study. *Child Abuse & Neglect, 20,* 709–723.

Silverman, W., & Treffers, P. (2001). *Anxiety disorders in children and adolescents.* Cambridge, England: Cambridge University Press.

Simeon, D., Guralnik, O., Schmeidler, J., Sirof, B., & Knutelska, M. (2001). The role of childhood interpersonal trauma in depersonalization disorder. *American Journal of Psychiatry, 158,* 1027–1033.

Simonoff, E., Pickles, A., Meyer, J., Silberg, J., Maes, H., Loeber, R., et al. (1997). The Virginia twin study of adolescent behavioral development. *Archives of General Psychiatry, 54,* 801–808.

Simons, R., & Whitbeck, L. (1991). Sexual abuse as a precursor to prostitution and victimization among adolescent and adult homeless women. *Journal of Family Issues, 12,* 361–379.

Skegg, K. (2005). Self-harm. *Lancet, 366,* 1471–1483.

Skegg, K., Nada-Raja, S., Dickson, N., Paul, C., & Williams, S. (2003). Sexual orientation and self harm in men and women. *American Journal of Psychiatry, 160,* 541–546.

Skegg, K., Nada-Raja, S., & Moffitt, T. (2004). Minor self-harm and psychiatric disorder: A population-based study. *Suicide and Life-Threatening Behavior, 34,* 187–196.

Smith, K., Conroy, R., & Ehler, B. (1984). Lethality of suicide attempt rating scale. *Suicide and Life-Threatening Behavior, 14,* 215–242.

Solorio, M., Milburn, N., Andersen, R., Trifskin, S., & Rodriguez, M. (2006). Emotional distress and mental health service use among urban homeless adolescents. *Journal of Behavioral Health Services & Research, 33,* 381–393.

Spirito, A., & Esposito-Smythers, C. (2006). Attempted and completed suicide in adolescence. *Annual Review of Clinical Psychology, 2,* 2237–2266.

Spitzer, C., Klauser, T., Grabe, H., Lucht, M., Stieglitz, R., Schneider, W., et al. (2003). Gender differences in dissociation. *Psychopathology, 36,* 65–70.

Stanley, B., Gameroff, M., Michalsen, V., & Mann, J. (2001). Are suicide attempters who self-mutilate a unique population? *American Journal of Psychiatry, 158,* 427–432.

Stewart, A., Steiman, M., Cauce, A., Cochran, B., Whitbeck, L., & Hoyt, D. (2004). Victimization and posttraumatic stress disorder among homeless adolescents. *Journal of the Academy of Child and Adolescent Psychiatry, 43,* 325–331.

Stiffman, A. (1989). Suicide attempts among runaway youths. *Suicide and Life-Threatening Behavior, 19,* 147–159.

Sullivan, G., Burnam, A., & Koegel, P. (2000). Pathways to homelessness among the mentally ill. *Social Psychiatry and Psychiatric Epidemiology, 35,* 444–450.

Sullivan, P., & Knutson, J. (2000). The prevalence of disabilities and maltreatment among runaway children. *Child Abuse & Neglect, 24,* 1275–1288.

Sumner, G., Andersen, R., Wenzel, S., & Gelberg, L. (2001). Weighting for period perspective in samples of the homeless. *American Behavioral Scientist, 45,* 80–104.

Sutton, J. (2004). Understanding dissociation and its relationship to self-injury and childhood trauma. *Counseling and Psychotherapy Journal, 15,* 24–27.

Suyemoto, K. (1998). The functions of self-mutilation. *Clinical Psychology Review, 18,* 531–554.

Suyemoto, K., & MacDonald, M. (1995). Self-cutting female adolescents. *Psychotherapy, 32,* 162–171.

Swanson, M., Bland, R., & Newman, S. (1994). Antisocial personality disorders. *Acta Psychiatrica Scandanavia, 89,* 63–70.

Swanston, H., Plunkett, A., O'Toole, B., Shrimpton, S., Parkinson, P., & Oates, R. (2003). Nine years after sexual abuse. *Child Abuse & Neglect, 27,* 967–984.

Terr, L. (1979). The children of Chowchilla. *Psychoanalytic Study of the Child, 34,* 547–623.

Terr, L. (1991). Childhood traumas: An outline and overview. *American Journal of Psychiatry, 148,* 10–20.

Thompson, S. (1994). Changing lives, changing genres: Teenage girls' narratives about sex and romance, 1978–1986. In A. Rossi (Ed.), *Sexuality across the life course* (pp. 209–232). Chicago: University of Chicago Press.

Thornton, A. (1990). The courtship process and adolescent sexuality. *Journal of Family Issues, 11,* 239–273.

Tjaden, P., & Thoennes, N. (2000). Full report of the prevalence, incidence, and consequences of violence against women: Findings from the national violence against women survey. *Centers for Disease Control and Prevention.* Retrieved August 3, 2008, from: http://www.cdc.gov/ncipc/factsheets/svfacts.htm

Tremblay, R., Boulerice, R., Harden, P., McDuff, P., Perusse, D., Pihl, R., et al. (1996). Do children in Canada become more aggressive as they approach adolescence? In M. Cappe & L. Fellegi (Eds.), *Growing up in Canada* (pp. 127–137). Ottawa: Statistics Canada.

Tyler, K., Cauce, A., & Whitbeck, L. (2004). Family risk factors and prevalence of dissociative symptoms among homeless and runaway youth. *Child Abuse & Neglect, 28,* 355–366.

Tyler, K., Hoyt, D., & Whitbeck, L. (2000). The effects of early sexual abuse on later sexual victimization among female homeless and runaway adolescents. *Journal of Interpersonal Violence, 15,* 235–250.

Tyler, K., Hoyt, D., Whitbeck, L., & Cauce, A. (2001a). The effects of a high-risk environment on the sexual victimization of homeless and runaway youth. *Violence & Victims, 16,* 441–455.

Tyler, K., Hoyt, D., Whitbeck, L., & Cauce, A. (2001b). The impact of childhood sexual abuse on later sexual victimization among runaway youth. *Journal of Research on Adolescence, 11,* 151–176.

Tyler, K., & Johnson, K. (2006). Trading sex: Voluntary or coerced? The experiences of homeless youth. *Journal of Sex Research, 43,* 1–9.

Tyler, K., Whitbeck, L., Hoyt, D., & Cauce, A. (2004). Risk factors for sexual victimization among male and female homeless and runaway youth. *Journal of Interpersonal Violence, 19,* 503–520.

Tyler, K., Whitbeck, L., Hoyt, D., & Johnson, K. (2003). Self-mutilation and homeless youth: The role of family abuse, street experiences and mental disorders. *Journal of Research on Adolescence, 13,* 457–474.

Tyler, K., Whitbeck, L., Hoyt, D., & Yoder, K. (2000). Predictors of self-reported sexually transmitted diseases among homeless and runaway adolescents. *Journal of Sex Research, 37,* 369–377.

U.S. General Accounting Office. (1989). *Homelessness: Homeless and runaway youth receiving services at federally funded shelters* (GAO/HRD 90-45). Washington, DC: Author.

U.S. Census Bureau. (2006). *Current population survey: March and annual social and economic supplements (2005 and earlier).* Retrieved November 22, 2007, from: http://www.census.gov/population/socdemo/hh-fam/ms2.pdf

Unger, J., Simon, T., Newman, T., Montgomery, S., Kipke, M., & Albornoz, M. (1998). Early adolescent street youth: An overlooked population with unique problems and services needs. *Journal of Early Adolescence, 18,* 325–348.

Van Den Bosch, L., Verheul, R., Langeland, W., & Van Den Brink, W. (2003). Trauma, dissociation, and posttraumatic stress disorder in female borderline patients with and without substance abuse problems. *Australian and New Zealand Journal of Psychiatry, 37,* 549–555.

Van der Hart, O., Nijenuis, E., & Steele, K. (2005). Dissociation: An insufficiently recognized major feature of complex posttraumatic stress disorder. *Journal of Traumatic Stress, 18,* 413–423.

Van der Kolk, B., Perry, C., & Herman, J. (1991). Childhood origins of self-destructive behavior. *American Journal of Psychiatry, 148,* 1665–1671.

Van IJzendoorn, M., & Schuengel, C. (1996). The measurement of dissociation in normal and clinical populations: Meta-analytic validation of the Dissociative Experiences Scale (DES). *Clinical Psychology Review, 16,* 365–382.

Van Leeuwen, J., Boyle, S., Salomonsen-Sautel, S., Baker, D., Garcia, J., Hoffman, A., et al. (2006). Lesbian, gay, and bisexual homeless youth: An eight-city public health perspective. *Child Welfare League of America, 2,* 151–170.

Vasilaki, E., Hosier, S., & Cox, W. (2006). The efficacy of motivational interviewing as a brief intervention for excessive drinking: a meta-analytic review. *Alcohol and Alcoholism, 41,* 328–335.

Vernberg, E., La Greca, A., Silverman, W., & Prinstein, M. (1996). Prediction of post traumatic stress symptoms in children after a hurricane. *Journal of Abnormal Psychology, 105,* 237–248.

Vitaro, F., Tremblay, R., & Bukowski, W. (2001). Friends, friendships, and conduct disorders. In J. Hill & B. Maughan (Eds.), *Conduct disorders in childhood and adolescence* (pp. 346–378). Cambridge, England: Cambridge University Press.

Votta, E., & Manion, I. (2003). Factors in the psychological adjustment of homeless adolescent males: The role of coping style. *Journal of the American Academy of Child Adolescent Psychiatry, 42,* 778–785.

Wagner, B., Compas, B., & Howell, D. (1988). Daily and major life events: A test of an integrative model of psychosocial stress. *American Journal of Community Psychology, 16,* 465–490.

Wallach, H., & Dollinger, S. (1999). Dissociative disorders in childhood and adolescence. In S. Netherton, D. Holmes, & C. Walker (Eds.), *Child and adolescent psychological disorders* (pp. 344–366). New York: Oxford University Press.

Wallerstein, J., & Corbin, S. (1991). The child and the vicissitudes of divorce. In M. Lewis (Ed.), *Child and adolescent psychiatry: A comprehensive textbook,* (pp. 1108–1117). Baltimore, MD: Williams & Watkins.

Waschbusch, D. (2002). A meta-analytic examination of comorbid hyperactive-impulsive-attention problems and conduct problems. *Psychological Bulletin, 128,* 118–150.

Whitbeck, L., Chen, X., Hoyt, D., Tyler, K., & Johnson, K. (2004). Mental disorder, subsistence strategies, and victimization among gay, lesbian, and bisexual homeless and runaway adolescents. *Journal of Sex Research, 41,* 329–342.

Whitbeck, L., Chen, X., & Johnson, K. (2006). Food insecurity among runaway and homeless adolescents. *Public Health Nutrition, 9,* 47–52.

Whitbeck, L., Conger, R., & Kao, M. (1993). The influence of parental support, depressed affect, and peers on the sexual behaviors of adolescent girls. *Journal of Family Issues, 14,* 261–278.

Whitbeck, L., & Hoyt, D. (1999). *Nowhere to grow: Homeless and runaway adolescents and their families.* New York: Aldine de Gruyter.

Whitbeck, L., Hoyt, D., & Ackley, K. (1997a). Abusive family backgrounds and later victimization among runaway and homeless adolescents. *Journal of Research on Adolescence, 7,* 375–392.

Whitbeck, L., Hoyt, D., & Ackley, K. (1997b). Families of homeless and runaway adolescents: A comparison of parent/caretaker and adolescent perspectives on parenting, family violence, and adolescent conduct. *Child Abuse and Neglect, 2,* 517–528.

Whitbeck, L., Hoyt, D., & Bao, W. (2000). Depressive symptoms and co-occurring depressive symptoms, substance abuse, and conduct problems among runaway and homeless adolescents. *Child Development, 71,* 721–732.

Whitbeck, L., Hoyt, D., Miller, M., & Kao, M. (1992). Parental support, depressed affect, and sexual experience among adolescents. *Youth and Society, 24,* 166–177.

Whitbeck, L., Hoyt, D., & Yoder, K. (1999). A risk-amplification model of victimization and depressive symptoms among runaway and homeless adolescents. *American Journal of Community Psychology, 2,* 292–296.

Whitbeck, L., Hoyt, D., Yoder, K., Cauce, A., & Paradise, M. (2001). Deviant behavior and victimization among homeless and runaway adolescents. *Journal of Interpersonal Violence, 16,* 1175–1204.

Whitbeck, L., Johnson, K., Hoyt, D., & Cauce, A. (2004a). Mental disorder and comorbidity among runaway and homeless adolescents. *Journal of Adolescent Health, 35,* 132–140.

Whitbeck, L., Johnson, K., Hoyt, D., & Cauce, A. (2004b). Response. *Journal of Adolescent Health, 35,* 433.

Whitbeck, L., & Simons, R. (1993). A comparison of adaptive strategies and patterns of victimization among homeless adolescents and adults. *Violence and Victims, 8,* 191–204.

Whitlock, J., Eckenrode, J., & Silverman, D. (2006). Self-injurious behaviors in a college population. *Pediatrics, 117,* 1939–1947.

Wilson, A., Calhoun, K., & Bernat, J. (1999). Risk recognition and trauma-related symptoms among sexually revictimized women. *Journal of Consulting and Clinical Psychology, 67,* 705–710.

Windle, M. (1989). Substance use and abuse among adolescent runaways: A four-year follow-up study. *Journal of Youth & Adolescence, 18,* 331–334.

Witkin, A., Milburn, N., Rotheram-Borus, M., Batterham, P., May, S., & Brooks, R. (2005). Finding homeless youth. *Youth & Society, 1,* 62–84.

Wittchen, H. (1994). Reliability and validity studies of the Who-Composite International Diagnostic Interview (CIDI): A critical review. *Journal of Psychiatric Research, 28,* 57–84.

Wittchen, H., & Kessler, R. (1994). *Modifications of the CIDI in the National Comorbidity Study: The development of the UM-CIDI.* (NCS Working Paper #2). Ann Arbor: The University of Michigan.

World Health Organization. (1990). *Composite International Diagnostic Interview (CIDI). Version 1.0.* Geneva: Author.

Wright, J., Rubin, B., & Devine, J. (1998). *Beside the golden door: Policy, politics, and the homeless.* New York: Aldine de Gruyter.

Wright, J., & Devine, J. (1992). Counting the homeless: The Census bureau's "S-Night" in five U.S. Cities. *Evaluation Review, 16,* 355–364.

Wyatt, G., Guthrie, D., & Notgrass, C. (1992). Differential effects of women's child sexual abuse and subsequent sexual revictimization. *Journal of Consulting and Clinical Psychology, 60,* 167–173.

Yahne, C., Miller, W., Irvin-Vitela, L., & Tonigan, J. (2002). Magdalena pilot project: Motivational outreach to substance abusing women street sex workers. *Journal of Substance Abuse Treatment, 23,* 49–53.

Yamaguchi, K. (1991). *Event history analysis.* Newbury Park, CA: Sage.

Yates, G., MacKenzie, R., Pennbridge, J., & Cohen, E. (1988). A risk profile comparison of runaway and nonrunaway youth. *American Journal of Public Health, 78,* 820–821.

Yoder, K. (1999). Comparing suicide attempters, suicide ideators, and nonsuicidal homeless and runaway adolescents. *Suicide and Life-Threatening Behavior, 29,* 25–36.

Yoder, K., Hoyt, D., & Whitbeck, L. (1998). Suicidal behavior among homeless and runaway adolescents. *Journal of Youth and Adolescence, 27,* 753–771.

Yoder, K., Longley, S., Whitbeck, L., & Hoyt, D. (2008). A dimensional model of psychopathology among homeless adolescents: Suicidality, internalizing, and externalizing disorders. *Journal of Abnormal Child Psychology, 36,* 95–104.

Yoder, K., Whitbeck, L., & Hoyt, D. (2003). Gang involvement and membership among homeless and runaway youth. *Youth & Society, 34,* 441–467.

Yoder, K., Whitbeck, L., & Hoyt, D. (2008). Dimensionality of thoughts of death and suicide: Evidence from a study of homeless adolescents. *Social Indicators Research, 86,* 83–100.

Zhao, S., Kessler, R., & Wittchen, H. (1994). *Diagnostic algorithms for NCS/DSM-III-R.* (NCS Working Paper #7). Ann Arbor: University of Michigan.

Ziliak, S., & McCloskey, D. (2007). *The cult of statistical significance: How the standard error costs us jobs, justice, and lives.* Ann Arbor: University of Michigan Press.

Zlotnick, M., Shea, R., Pearlstein, T., Simpson, E., Costello, E., & Begin, A. (1996). The relationship between dissociative symptoms, alexithymia, impulsivity, sexual abuse, and self-mutilation. *Comprehensive Psychiatry, 37,* 12–16.

Subject Index

Author Index